The M
the Ards

Harry Allen

BALLYHAY BOOKS

Published by Ballyhay Books,
an imprint of Laurel Cottage Ltd.
Donaghadee, N. Ireland 2004.
Copyrights Reserved.
© Text by Harry Allen 2004.
ISBN 1 900935 42 2

… for Valerie

CONTENTS

❧

Biography

Harry Allen was educated at Sullivan Upper School, Holywood and Stranmillis College. He taught History and other subjects, mostly at Donaghadee High School. An awakening interest in local history led to him completing a B.A. degree, principally in Historical Research Methods at the Open University. This in turn gave rise to secondments at the Public Record Office of Northern Ireland and the Belfast Teachers' Centre. He then served on a number of teams, supported by the Department of Education of Northern Ireland and other educational bodies, helping to stimulate the teaching of history by encouraging local fieldwork, history trails and the use of original documents.

He has contributed to a number of radio and television programmes about aspects of local history, and has written many articles and booklets on a number of historical subjects. After leaving full-time teaching he served for most of the 1990s as an Action for Community Employment manager, but is recently retired and living in Donaghadee. He is married with two sons and is still an enthusiastic student of local history, especially of the Ards Peninsula and north Down areas. He is currently the Chairman of Donaghadee Historical Society.

Background and Acknowledgements

The initiative for this work came from Northern Ireland's part of the European Union Special Support Programme for Peace and Reconciliation. In November 1997 the regional Ards Partnership, in conjunction with Donaghadee Community Workforce, appointed me to research and write a book about the 1798 Rebellion. Their proposal was for a book to focus on the involvement of the people of the Ards and the north part of Down in that rebellion, on the influence they had on it and that it had on them.

All those concerned in the project agreed from the beginning that much of the story of the principal events during the summer of 1798 is well-enough known and has mostly been accessible to any student of the rebellion for two hundred years. What appeared to be called for was an account of the specifically regional aspects of the Rebellion story that may hitherto have been omitted from the many published works.

When this book was first discussed it did not set out to be controversial; on the contrary. Because of the nature of the contract I had the luxury of extended time for research not always afforded to the amateur historian. This meant that a number of primary sources were discovered that prompted a different and more challenging approach. Located documents, sometimes standing alone and sometimes when studied alongside other evidence, occasionally appeared to challenge some of the traditional accounts. Sometimes the archive evidence even contradicted parts of published works. Some of this 'new' evidence was so compelling that it could not be explained away nor ignored. What began as a local story gradually grew to become more than this. It gradually became apparent that what had transpired in the Ards and marching baronies, during the crucial years of 1796 and 1797, had been pivotal in the turning of the wheel of potential revolution in Ireland. It demanded a hearing.

Many of the less familiar letters and reports of the period are so instructive that it is a matter of some gratification for me to be able to call attention to them. These writings shed light on events, activities, people and beliefs in County Down during those turbulent 1790s. I hope readers of this book will enjoy the story of the men of the Ards, and that it will encourage debate about some of the issues.

I am indebted to a number of people who were most helpful in the compilation and production of the book draft. My background is in education, but more in the forestry plantations of secondary schools than in the sheltered groves of académe. I am neither a professional historian nor a full-time scholar. If I am a competent enough person to discover and tell this story I owe my greatest debt to Dr. W.H.Crawford. When I first met Bill at a local history course in 1975 I was a physical education/history teacher desperately looking for help in making the study of history more interesting to post-Primary School pupils. Bill gave me that help and a great deal more besides.

He convinced me that local history is more accessible than is generally thought, and that its study is both fascinating and academically valid. He also taught me that as much evidence as possible should be considered and different opinions questioned before a story was accepted. Perhaps most usefully he encouraged me to learn more about examining sources and advised me to study for a degree in historical research methods.

I am most indebted to the staffs, past and present, of the various libraries and archives who showed great courtesy when helping me find useful references and documents. I am grateful for permission to quote from material in their care. A full list of the repositories visited can be found in the bibliography of this book. All were most useful and informative sources and I am grateful for permission to use pieces from them. The greater bulk of the archive material was found in the vaults of the National Archives of Ireland and in the Public Record Office of Northern Ireland. My special thanks go to Aideen Ireland from the National Archives and Dr. Gerry Slater and his staff from

PRONI who also facilitated the cover photograph which was kindly taken by Norwood Steele.

I must express my most sincere thanks to the Ards Partnership and the management of the Donaghadee Workforce for their forbearance and assistance during 1997 and 1998. I would particularly like to mention John Caldwell, Jack McNally, Neil Gordon, Patricia Lemon, John McIlroy, Vivien McMaster, all of Donaghadee Workforce and Tom Rowley of the Ards Partnership for their help, advice and support at that time. Trevor McCavery, Peter Carr and Vivian McIver read the early drafts and gave much-needed encouragement and assistance. I thank them for that.

Finally I am most grateful to Jane Crosbie for her careful reading of the completed manuscript and for her helpful suggestions, although it should be stressed that any remaining misconceptions or errors in the text are entirely mine.

INTRODUCTION

The actual rebellion in Ireland in 1798 lasted barely a month. Yet it has had a library of books devoted to it. A great many of these concentrate their attentions on the events in County Wexford, sometimes to the detriment of the story of the north and sometimes to its almost complete exclusion. Those books which do have a northern focus often give the bulk of the work to the United Irishmen in Belfast and/or the happenings in County Antrim, with varying degrees of a lesser emphasis on 1797/98 affairs in County Down. A long list of the best of all of these is included in the bibliography of this book. A perusal of this list will show just how little attention has been paid to the crucial contributions made by County Down folk to the momentous events in Ireland at the end of the Eighteenth Century. Some of these people were for the development of republicanism or anti-establishmentarianism and some against.

The Act of Union following so closely after the Rebellion, and the changes in the polarization of Irish society since then, have prevented many from taking an objective view of the people of Down at that time and their actions. But these actions cannot be ignored if one is trying to come to an understanding of the 1798 Rebellion as a whole. When it comes to tackling the subject of the insurrection in Down the huge diversity of the views, opinions and reports available to the historian inevitably makes a synthesis of the story a little complicated. When the subject matter of such a work comprises such highly emotive issues as Irish Republicanism, Reform of Parliament, class differences, sectarian hatreds and bloody military campaigns, then the difficulties are compounded.

Modern-day readers can be struck by the odd familiarity of terms and expressions, attitudes and occurrences, but we must not make the mistake of viewing too rigidly, from the perspective of the present day, the comments and actions demonstrated by people who were writing in the late Eighteenth Century. The places may have been the same, but the times were different. Two centuries later the notion of Presbyterians striving militantly for an Irish Republic, and many Anglican and even Catholic loyalists despising them for it and doing all they could to stop them, does not always chime comfortably with modern perceptions.

Contrary to some popular opinion there is no shortage of County Down sources about the United Irishmen and their attempt at insurrection. Indeed the magnitude of the archive of contemporary correspondence is surprisingly large. Everyone involved appears to have taken exceptional care that all their papers, letters, reports and even artifacts were preserved for posterity. It seems that in the rebellion's immediate aftermath a great number of contemporary chroniclers realized just how significant the years of the 1790s were in Ireland. The people who preserved their papers realised that those few hot days in June 1798 might have changed not only Ireland's, but also Britain's, history.

Sadly it also seems that for a clear understanding of what really was happening in those parlous times it is not sufficient just to read all the published books on the subject. It is necessary to seek out the pertinent original material that has heretofore been left unused, or even unread, possibly because these sources are conserved in a number of widely spread archives. Not all of the available sources are equally reliable. Often the contemporary chroniclers had something of an ulterior motive in writing what they did, or they may have held passionate beliefs that could have affected their objectivity. A general is often tempted to show his own and his enemy's losses in numbers as favourable to his side as he can honourably, or even dishonourably, present them; a correspondent might desire to appear more knowledgeable, courageous or influential than he really was; or an informer might commit to paper almost anything, if he thought it was what was wanted by his masters.

It is only very rarely that an eyewitness can have a complete grasp of everything that was happening, even within his purview. He can only rarely be able to see events from a different point of view from his own. Of necessity there must be gaps to be filled. But such is the great treasure trove of personal correspondence, diaries, first-hand accounts and government papers which can still be studied that the story almost builds itself from the words of the men and women who lived through these testing times.

Some previously unpublished documents have been able to shed a new light on the known story to illuminate the enormous significance of what happened in North Down during the decade that culminated at Ballynahinch. This northern half-county was not the only hotbed of dissension, but it was certainly a crucible for thoughts and actions. Much of the story in this book is told by the people who lived through the events in Down. Their words, where possible, have been transcribed as they first committed them to paper.

For readers with a desire to find out more about the affairs of the time in other parts of Ireland, or who wish to read in one book a definitive history of the rebellion as it affected the whole island of Ireland, this may not be the publication for them. Although it will try to set their actions in the proper historical context, this book will focus almost entirely on people, places and events in County Down. Most of the emphasis will be on those people who lived in the parishes of the Ards peninsula and in the neighbouring barony of Lower Castlereagh.

A student of the Rebellion who has a desire to retrace the steps of the rebels during the years leading up to June 1798 will be pleased to find that this book attempts to indicate all the places they went and the paths they trod. Their ghosts may be seen where they occupied Portaferry, Donaghadee and Newtownards, made camps at Inishargie, Movilla, Scrabo and Creevy Rocks, or died at Saintfield or Ballynahinch. Some of the central characters were female, but given the structure of society and the nature of the events at the time the great majority of these people will inevitably be male. Their peregrinations may have taken them away from hearth and home but this book will try to follow them, for they were the men of the Ards.

THE PEOPLE OF THE ARDS

In ancient shadows and twilights
Where childhood had strayed,
The world's great sorrows were born
And its heroes were made.

George William Russell, (AE), 1867 – 1935. Germinal

The two north-eastern counties of Ireland, Antrim and Down, have always been a bit different - different from the rest of Ireland and different from each other. Physically and geologically they have been close to south-west Scotland for millions of years. Antrim is largely layers of white chalk and black basalt often overlaid with peat flatlands and cleft by many deep glens. The countryside of Down varies from the Palaeozoic greywackes in the north of the county to the granite mountains of Mourne in the south. The southern parts of Antrim and the northern parts of Down share the fertile egg-basket topography of drumlin country with the valley of the River Lagan dividing the two counties. For centuries these two counties presented a harsh but rewarding environment for determined farmers.

On the one hand this type of landscape presented new settlers over the centuries with solid ground for their houses and some good well-sheltered land for their crops and livestock, but on the other it demanded constant labour to win the badly drained bog land for productive use. These were always lands that repaid hard work. Numerous industrious families made happy homes here over many centuries.

Anyone who worked this land recognised its worth and knew that, if necessary, the land of east Ulster was worth fighting for.

In 1177 John de Courcy marched north from Dublin with 23 Anglo-Norman knights. He had been advised about the worth of these counties east of the River Bann and was determined enough to occupy and settle them. Right up to the sixteenth century there was continual conflict between the Anglo-Norman settlers and the native Ulster chiefs for the control of the two eastern counties.

Gallowglasses came ('came back' some would argue) from the western isles and highlands of Scotland as mercenaries. Many of these and other Scottish Gaels stayed and settled in east Ulster and of course they brought much of their culture and identity with them. The people of Strathclyde and south-west Scotland would always have been very familiar with Antrim and Down and vice-versa. Any person gazing from Galloway in Scotland could easily have seen the hills of the Antrim Coast and the heights of the Ards Peninsula across the water on most days of the year. The sea was not seen at that time as a barrier to travel, but more as a reliable thoroughfare. On a good sailing day a party could make the twenty-mile boat journey between Galloway and the Ards for trade, a visit or migration, in roughly the same time it would have taken them to travel five miles on the poor, unpaved and often muddy roads of the day.

Henry VIII declared himself 'King' rather than 'Lord' of Ireland and made a half-hearted effort to assert his sovereignty. Both of his daughters, Mary I and her half-sister Elizabeth I, were worried that what they were assured was an unstable Ulster would prove troublesome to England if the French, or their allies, the Scots, decided to subvert it. Elizabeth had a technical title to the Clandeboye lands of south Antrim and north Down. Unfortunately the O'Neills had been in actual possession of the lands for three centuries and Brian McPhelim O'Neill regarded himself as the lord of that soil. The Queen's principal Secretary of State, Sir Thomas Smith, *"procured a colony ... called the Ardes. It was a rich and pleasant country on the eastern coast of Ulster."* He and his son, also Thomas, were keen to settle these Clandeboye lands, *"that those half-barbarous people might be taught some civility."*[1]

Naturally, like all such colonists, they wished also to gain profit for themselves. They realised that they would first of all have to win the land, probably in bloody conflict. Sometimes supported by the Savages of the Lower Ards, the Smiths and O'Neill rampaged around the Ards, talking about negotiation but mostly looking for an opportunity to wrong-foot their rivals. However, Thomas Smith, the son, died suddenly in Comber in 1573 and the following year the whole undertaking collapsed, leaving the Ards in a very poor state.

The 1590s saw the Nine Years War of the O'Neills and O'Donnells against the English. By the time this ended in 1603 the land of Ulster was devastated and its population seriously depleted. By the time of the Flight of the Earls the lands of the Upper Clandeboye, especially in the Ards, were being described as a wasteland. The fertile fields of east Ulster were hardly more productive than a desert.

This, or more accurately the year 1606, brings to our story of the Ards two men from Ayrshire, who between them arguably changed this land more than any others. The men were Hugh Montgomery of Braidstane and James Hamilton of Dunlop. In essence they cleverly got title to much of Con O'Neill's Clandeboye lands between them. Sir William Smith, nephew and heir to Sir Thomas Smith, claimed that he was, *"tricked out of it by the Knavery of a Scot, one Hamilton (who was a schoolmaster, though afterwards made a person of honour)."*[2]

Soon after they secured title to their lands Hamilton and Montgomery were bringing, from the little harbour of Portpatrick in Galloway, kinsfolk and neighbours from their home counties to north Down. In the words of their chronicler, the settlers who came with Hugh Montgomery found the parishes of Donaghadee and Newtownards, *"more wasted than America when the Spaniards landed there,"* and that on their first survey of those parishes:

30 cabins could not be found, nor any stone walls, but ruined roofless churches, and a few vaults at Gray Abbey, and a stump of an old castle in Newton, in each of which some Gentlemen sheltered themselves at their firstcoming over.[3]

The colonisation of 'the Great Ardes' by the men from southern Scotland succeeded beyond everyone's wildest dreams. There is some reason to believe that James VI and I, the new king of the by-now united England and Scotland, was greatly impressed by the reports he was reading of developments in Down and Antrim. The successes in these two counties undoubtedly helped persuade James to agree to the proposals for an official Ulster Plantation and indeed may well have inspired them. Certainly the continuing growth of trade, wealth and new settlers in those counties was such that Antrim and Down were excluded from the legislation for the new scheme.

Montgomery and Hamilton had little trouble attracting potential tenants to their estates. Regular reports were carried back to the Borders and Lowlands by successful immigrants to north Down and by traders and pedlars. By 1611 Montgomery had a prosperous little town at Newtownards and a seaport of his own at Donaghadee. Hamilton had a similar town and small port at Bangor and a village at Holywood, all populated with Scots. The development of the other small towns of the Ards and north Down soon followed.

Although Montgomery and Hamilton had been inclined to bring in some English settlers, these were few in number and most definitely not the beginning of a trend.[4] All through the Seventeenth Century the Ards and north Down, like south Antrim, gradually filled with Scots. Some continued to arrive from the north of England, but the great majority came from Scotland's Southern Uplands and the Lowlands -- the Laaland Scots who were most determinedly not like their Catholic, Gaelic-speaking, kilt-wearing fellow-countrymen in the Highlands. These migrants were dour, hard-working and very predominantly Presbyterian farmers, who spoke their own broad-dialect form of English. Naturally they brought their character and their culture with them.[5] The Rev. Andrew Stewart, minister in Donaghadee, wrote a famous and often-quoted reproof of these people:

> From Scotland came many and from England not a few, yet all of them generally the scum of both nations, who, for debt, or breaking and fleeing from justice, or seeking shelter, came hither, hoping to be without fear of man's justice in a land where there was nothing or but little, as yet, of the fear of God. And in a few years there flocked such a multitude of people from Scotland that these northern counties ... were in a good measure planted which had been waste before. Going for Ireland was looked upon as the miserable mark of a deplorable person, yea, it was turned to a proverb and one of the worst expressions of disdain that could be invented was to tell a man that Ireland would be his hinder end.[6]

However, the Ulster-Scots brought with them their strong Presbyterianism, with its crucial inclination to dissent and their Protestant ethic of hard work. These people feared and obeyed God, but were reluctant to accept any other authority. They had a love of learning, a desire to improve the land the Lord had placed them in and a resolute determination not to allow anyone with only temporal power to tell them what they could or could not do, think or believe. They kept themselves fairly well to themselves. They tended to group together for mutual support and, in the early days, for safety. For over a century they proudly described themselves first and foremost as Scottish. Like their fellow-settlers from the British Isles who were going to the New World, the colonists largely carried their own life-styles with them. They learned from the Irish natives' local knowledge, but they farmed, worked, worshipped and celebrated in their own age-old ways.

Some intermarried with the Irish and the other settlers and many of the native Irish anglicized (or caledonicized) their names, religion and speech, so there was a degree of assimilation. However, because of the strongly perceived differences in religion, given emphasis by the language and culture, this assimilation could only ever be partial. The renewal of the National Covenant in Scotland in 1638, followed the very next year by the imposition of Thomas Wentworth's 'Black Oath' forcing all Ulster people to renounce the Covenant, two more years later by the 1641 rebellion and then Owen Roe O'Neill's crushing defeat of General Monro had gradually demonstrated to all Ulster's Presbyterians that they were between the rock of being threatened by the Catholics in Ulster and the hard place of being persecuted by the Stuart kings and the Anglican Church. With their ministers already forbidden to perform marriages, baptisms or funerals according to their church's procedures, the grumbles of discontent became louder and louder. It was not difficult for them to assume a siege mentality. A few years later when the apprentice boys of Derry closed their city gates in 1689 to keep McDonnell's Catholic army out, it immediately became a potent symbol for this cast of mind and one that for many survives right up to today.

Something that possibly emphasised the process was the Test Act in

1704. Its passing told the Presbyterians that even though they might distrust their Catholic neighbours as much as the Anglicans did, the establishment still regarded both communities with the same contempt. With the passing of the Act, Ulster Presbyterians discovered that they were now prohibited from any influence in the government of their country. For anyone to serve in a military or civil office under the Crown he must partake of the sacrament of communion according to the rites of the Anglican Church, something which was anathema to any devout Presbyterian or Roman Catholic.[7]

Where the Ulster-Scots immigrants predominated there inevitably came more during the following decades. One hundred and fifty years after the arrival of these settlers, the populations of seven parishes in north Down were recorded as follows:

1764 Population Figures for the Parishes in the
Barony of the Ards in north County Down[8]

Parish	Total Pop.	Pres.	% Pres	C of I	Papists	Quakers
Newtownards	4880	4750	97	60	50	20
Dundonald	926	889	96	21	16	---
Holywood	1771	1750	99	14	7	---
Bangor	3437	3025	88	400	12	---
Donaghadee	1948	1848	95	100	---	---
Ballywalter	1525	1475	97	50	---	---
Greyabbey	1550	1500	97	50	---	---
TOTALS	16037	15237	95	695	85	20

This population count was taken at a time not long after Ulster's population had been badly affected by the terrible, but now almost forgotten, famine of the 1740s. For twenty years before that famine and for fifty years after it, many of the Ulster Presbyterians chose to leave the land their grandparents had settled. Most of these young people chose to follow their example by trying their luck in a new country. But instead of their ancestors' twenty-mile jaunt across the North Channel, they tackled the three thousand mile voyage to the New World – there to become the renowned Scotch-Irish of the Thirteen Colonies.

The majority of the Ulster-Scots did not leave Ireland. Some were too old or infirm; some were content with what they had; some were cautious about the unknown. But the fact remains that from the landing of the *Friend's Goodwill* of Larne in 1717 until the War of American Independence, between a quarter and a half million Presbyterians left their families in Ulster and settled in Virginia and the Carolinas. Of course they were not all Presbyterians, but the overwhelming majority were, just as were the populations of the Ulster counties of Antrim, Down and Londonderry from where they mostly came. We know much about the temperament and character of these colonists. Because they clung together in their new land and because of the noted strength of their will, not to mention what were sometimes called the flaws in their nature, they were often seen as being a little different from other settlers. The descriptions, tributes and complaints written about the Scotch-Irish in America are very illuminating about the people who went across the Atlantic, but the qualities ascribed to them can usually be applied just as accurately to their cousins who stayed behind in the old homestead, running a family business or looking after the farm.

The United States President, Theodore Roosevelt, could have been talking about an Ardsman when he praised the character of the Ulstermen who helped to build his nation:

> They were a truculent and obstinate people and gloried in the warlike renown of their forefathers, the men who had followed Cromwell and who had shared in the defence of Derry and in the victories of the Boyne and Aughrim.[9]

These Ulster families had left their native land and their loved ones in a desire to be free; free from what they saw as the oppression of an undeservedly privileged minority who could run the country for their own benefit with the taxes, tithes and services of the downtrodden majority. When they realised that in the New World they were threatened with the same sort of oppression, they joined forces in their thousands with the other dissidents. Men of Ulster backgrounds were very much to the fore in the American struggle to achieve independence from Britain. A good proportion of the thinkers and leaders were of Ulster descent and in fact so many had actually been born in Ulster that they forced a change in the wording of the first American

Constitution to allow for patriots born outside the Thirteen Colonies to serve in the first Continental Congress.[10]

The men of Ulster, many of them sons of Down, fought as Minutemen, Rangers and auxiliary troops in George Washington's struggles against the British. At some point during the war the First U.S. President paid these redoubtable fighters a famous tribute:

> If defeated everywhere else, I will make my last stand for liberty among the Scotch-Irish of my native Virginia.[11]

If Ulster-Scots could so naturally take the awesome step of resisting their lawful government in America, it was never going to be too daunting for their cousins to consider similar steps in the Ulster counties where they had been established for almost two centuries. During those years, often in the face of great difficulty, these Presbyterians had turned the wilderness they had found into productive farmland. The land had been almost stripped of its trees and had become a veritable wilderness when Montgomery and Hamilton's settlers first saw it. These hard workers were soon able to manage new woodlands of useful timber where it suited. They had bent their backs to drain many of the huge expanses of moss, or bog land. They had introduced much more efficient technology to tilling the fields, harvesting the grain and then winnowing, threshing and milling it. As early as 1619 Captain William Pynnar was writing both of the difficulties faced by the early planters and how the Scots were leading the way in making the countryside of Ulster productive:

> Many English do not yet plough nor use husbandry, being fearful to stock themselves with cattle or servants for those labours. Neither do the Irish use tillage, for they are also uncertain of their stay ... Were it not for the Scottish, who plough in many places, the rest of the country might starve.[12]

By the time their American cousins were sending back letters about their lives and struggles in their new world, the old country had become a green and well-kept land. Cottages, villages and towns spattered the countryside and fields were producing regular crops of food and flax. Enormous numbers of cattle and horses were being shipped to England and the economy was making people happy. Many a crossroads echoed on a summer evening to the sounds of a fiddle and a flute as the country people met for some self-made entertainment. Many a hearthside gathering on a winter's evening heard stories of brave deeds and humorous occasions in the past. For many, life was good. On the other hand rents were often cripplingly high, thanks to the pyramid of rent-farmers and rack-renters. The hardship and despair this caused led many to seek the comfort that could be found on the inside of a whis-key jar. Cheap duty-free spirits caused much drunkenness and apathy – when it did not provoke anger and head-breaking faction fighting.

Whiteboys, Oakboys, Peep o' Day Boys, Orange Boys and Defenders kept the pot of distrust bubbling between the Catholics, Dissenters and Protestants. If the pot were ever to boil over, all of Ireland could easily be embroiled in a sectarian bloodbath. But, if the pot could only be persuaded to simmer gently for years without boiling over, it would suit the Protestant Ascendancy tolerably well. These well-placed men, almost exclusively Anglican in their beliefs and practices, had realised for a long time that it was essential for them to prevent any combining together of Catholic and Dissenter against those who owned and ran the country. They were convinced that God had divided mankind into a hierarchy of classes and that He had bestowed on the ruling class the right to govern the country and its people. That was the way it was; and that was how it must continue. They were not secretive about this. In fact, in 1792, in response to some letters and squibs about equal-ity, they put together an outline, uncompromisingly stating what the Protestant Ascendancy stood for and, bearing in mind the Test Act, emphasizing that it did not include Dissenters. Because many often use the term too loosely, it is worth quoting this original in full:

And that no doubt may remain of what we understand by the words, 'Protestant Ascendancy', we have further resolved, that we consider the Protestant Ascendancy to consist in,

A Protestant King of Ireland
A Protestant Parliament
A Protestant Hierarchy
Protestant Electors and Government
The Benches of Justice,
The Army and the Revenue,

Through all their branches and details,
Protestant!

And this system supported by a connection with the protestant realm of Britain.

Resolved that the foregoing letter be published in the Dublin Journal.[13]

By coincidence, at almost the same time as this manifesto was being loudly published in Dublin, an obscure tenant farmer called Andrew Cooper from Milecross, Craigantlet, near Newtownards, was writing a letter to his county governor, the Marquis of Downshire. He complained about the way he was being treated by Lord Londonderry, his landlord. He had received a notice a few days earlier from Londonderry's land agent, the Newtownards Church of Ireland Rector, the Reverend John Cleland. The part of the letter that had incensed him was where Cleland had written:

> I do hereby give you notice not to put in your grain of any sort or hay on your farm in Craigogantlet [sic] without giving me, the agent and manager of the Right Honourable Lord Londonderry, Rector of this Parish of Newtown, first due and legal notice at my house in Newtownards to come and receive his tithe of said grain and hay on said farm. Otherwise you will be sued for subtraction of tithe.[14]

Cooper explained to Lord Downshire that he and his family had lived on the same farm for over one hundred years and had never paid tithes. In fact no one had been paying tithes in the parishes of Newtownards and Comber for a very long time. The farmers in the neighbouring parishes of Holywood, Dundonald, Bangor and Donaghadee had been paying one tenth of their produce to their tithe rector, but this was the first time Cooper, or anyone else in Newtownards Parish, had been told to pay tithes since the dissolution of the monasteries in Henry VIII's time. No Presbyterian was happy to pay tithes. This was not just because it meant giving up one tenth of their farm's worth. It offended their very faith that they should be under any obligation, financial or otherwise, to any man, especially a representative of what they regarded as an erroneous and alien faith. Those who were well used to the compulsion of paying these tithes were resentful enough, but those who had historically been exempt were unshakable in their commitment to resist even the mere suggestion of their paying such a levy.

Their obduracy naturally served as a clarion call to their neighbours in the adjacent tithe-paying parishes who had just had it demonstrated to them that such payments were contrary to their beliefs.

This letter is the only one on the subject to survive, but it can hardly have been a unique demand to Cooper only. All of Londonderry's tenants well knew that before he had been ennobled, he had been a devout and ramrod-stiff Presbyterian, who bowed to no man. The improvement in his fortune and the changes in his behaviour, with the betrayal of principle this betokened, had caused great consternation, not only to his tenants but also to all who knew him. The people of the Ards saw that the man who had been an austere but reasonable Presbyterian had become an Anglican and that it now appeared he was becoming a petty tyrant.

Londonderry's tenants were no different from Dissenters throughout Antrim and Down in that they all abhorred the paying of tithes to the Anglican church – except of course that those in the Parish of Newtownards had never even been required to pay them. His Lordship's demand through his agent is so crassly arrogant and provocative at such a sensitive time that it is quite astonishing to read. If such a policy were now to be pursued on his estates and then spread to those of neighbouring landlords, then he and Cleland would have engineered the very circumstances that the ascendancy most dreaded – the cottiers, small farmers and artisans united in their distrust and hatred of the landlord class.

Because they will appear frequently in this history of the Ards, it is worth closing this chapter by describing these very influential characters from the Ards. Alexander Stewart was a moderately wealthy commoner from Ballylawn in the Inishowen peninsula of Donegal and near the city of Londonderry. He had bought lands in the Ards from Robert Colville in 1744 and then had made some judicious family marriages. In 1766 his son, Robert Stewart, had married the eighteen-year-old Lady Sarah Seymour-Conway, daughter of Lord Hertford of Lisburn. She lost their first child in infancy, had a young son and then contracted a fatal illness while carrying her third child.

Her only son, born in 1769, was named Robert after his father and eventually he became known to history as Lord Castlereagh.

Robert Stewart Sen. made a second marriage in 1775, this time to the Honorable Frances Pratt, daughter of Earl Camden and the elder sister of John Jeffreys Pratt, later to receive the title of the First Marquis of Camden and a man who was to become the Lord Lieutenant of Ireland. Robert Stewart Sen. had entered politics in 1771 when he was elected to represent County Down in the Irish Parliament and then had strived very hard to gain a title. He was raised to the peerage as Baron Londonderry in 1789. The name he chose for his title was in commemoration of the city near which the family's first Ulster lands lay. The baronetcy was later to provoke the backhanded compliment that he was, *almost the only Irishman who received His Majesty's favour without rendering service.*[15]

Stewart's title was raised to Viscount Castlereagh in 1795, Earl Londonderry on August the 9th 1796 and, after his son's triumphs at Paris and Vienna, Marquis of Londonderry. The use of the name Castlereagh for the viscountcy was from Castle Reagh, a ruin that stood in Con O'Neill's Clandeboye lands, some of which were in Stewart's estate. The castle itself is now totally gone. About 1808 Lord Downshire, who actually owned the castle, was so concerned for its preservation that he directed his steward to construct a protective wall round the site. It could only happen in Ireland that this wall was built with the remaining stones of the old castle.

The Reverend John Cleland first comes to history's attention when he arrives back from Glasgow University with a Master's degree in divinity. It would seem that he was already known to the Stewart family at Mount Stewart and was so well liked, especially by eight-year-old Robert Stewart Jnr. that he was appointed to tutor the boy. Cleland was both ambitious and diligent and by all accounts an excellent tutor. As young Robert grew to manhood, Cleland kept a close watch on the boy he had already identified as his ticket to fame and fortune.

One summer's day in 1787, young Robert, now eighteen, went out for a sail on Strangford Lough in a small boat with his friend, Henry Sturrock, son of the Rev. William Sturrock, Chancellor of Portaferry and later Archdeacon of Armagh. Suddenly a storm arose and the boys got into difficulties and their boat capsized. Luckily for them, a short time later Sturrock's father and John Cleland were sheltering in the Grecian Temple that still dominates the high ground in Mount Stewart estate just above the eastern shore of the Lough. One of the men spied the upturned boat and Cleland immediately rushed down to the water's edge. There he hailed two men with a yawl. The men quickly reached the upturned boat and rescued the two semi-conscious boys. The men were amazed to discover that the young Robert Stewart had kept himself and his friend afloat for an hour alongside the boat. Safely restored to the warmth of the Stewart home, the boys quickly recovered. The fine octagon on the hilltop was given the name of The Temple of the Winds to commemorate this almost-tragic occasion.

Cleland had by now been appointed the land steward of Mount Stewart and his security of tenure was henceforth totally assured by his prompt action and successful rescue of darling Robert. According to the Ulster antiquarian, Francis Joseph Bigger, much of Cleland's fortune and that of his assistant, Billy Strean of Newtownards, resulted from their simple insistence that all rents be paid in gold pieces. The discount was as usurious as 25 per cent, a satisfying enough profit, but supplemented even further by 'sweating' the gold coins by rubbing them vigorously in a canvas bag and then saving the resulting dust.[16]

1. *The Life of the Learned Sir Thomas Smith, Knight, Doctor of the Civil Law, Principal Secretary of State to King Edward the Sixth and Queen Elizabeth*, London, 1698.

2. *Ibid.*

3. G. Hill, ed. *The Montgomery Manuscripts*, Belfast, 1869, P. 58.

4. *Report of the Plantation Commissioners*, quoted in J. Braidwood, *Ulster and Elizabethan English in Ulster Dialects*, Belfast, 1964, pp. 17-18.

5. Philip Robinson, *The Plantation of Ulster*, Dublin and Belfast, 1984. Most of the information about the coming of the Scots to Ulster has come from this work.

6. The Rev. Andrew Stewart, Minister of Donaghadee, *His History*, as published with Adair's Narrative, pp. 313-314, quoted in G. Hill, ed., *The Montgomery Manuscripts*, Belfast, 1869, p. 61, Footnote No. 48.

7. A.T.Q. Stewart, *The Narrow Ground*, London, 1977.

8. Newtown Walk by Thomas Merry and Donaghadee Walk by James Hunter, 4th September 1764, (Groves MSS, PRONI, T/808/15261). This was a form of census before the first official government census of 1801. Both compilers quoted above separately added notes, not only that there were "No Papists" in Donaghadee, Ballywalter and Greyabbey, but that they had encountered no convents, chapels or places of Popish worship anywhere in the Barony.

9. Theodore Roosevelt, *Stories of the Great West*, New York, 1888, pp. 16-17.

10. Henry Jones Ford, *The Scotch-Irish in America*, Princeton, 1915, p. 518, quoted in Ronnie Hanna, *Land of the Free, Ulster and the American Revolution*. Lurgan, 1992.

11. W.F. Marshall, *Ulster Sails West*, N.P. 1943, p. 30.

12. William Pynnar, *Calendar of the Carew MSS*, preserved in the Archiepiscopal Library at Lambeth, London, 1867-73, quoted in Philip Robinson, *The Plantation of Ulster*, Belfast, 1984, p. 178.

13. Sir Richard Musgrave, *Memoirs of the Different Rebellions in Ireland*, Dublin, 1801, Appendix No. III, quoting an article that appeared on 11th September 1792.

14. Andrew Cooper, Milecross, Newtownards, 23rd September 1792, enclosing a notice from the Rev. John Cleland, (Downshire Papers, PRONI, D/607/433).

15. 10th Earl of Westmoreland, Lord Lieutenant of Ireland, 1798-1794, February 9th 1792, (Dropmore Papers, ii, 28), quoted in H. Montgomery Hyde, *The Rise of Castlereagh*, London, 1933.

16. Francis Joseph Bigger, *Four Shots from Down*, republished Ballynahinch, 1982, pp. 51-58.

Union and Truth

> *Oft in the stilly night,*
> *Ere slumber's chain has bound me*
> *Fond Memory brings the light*
> *Of other days around me;*
> *The smiles, the tears,*
> *Of boyhood years,*
> *The words of love then spoken;*
> *The eyes that shone,*
> *Now dimmed and gone,*
> *The cheerful heart now broken.*

Thomas Moore, (1779 - 1852)
Oft in the stilly night.[1]

During the American War in the 1770s, so many British troops had been shipped across the Atlantic that Ireland might have found itself in danger if attacked by a foreign power. This had provoked the formation of the Volunteers as a home defence force. For a decade this body provided both a grounding in military tactics for a number of young Ulstermen and an education in how to structure a militant hierarchy and organisation of authority. In the early 1790s a group of radically minded former Volunteers began to consider the formation of a similar but different organisation within the country, but not necessarily within the establishment. This new organisation would try to unite the people, not against an enemy from without, but against what they regarded as the enemy within. In 1791 this was constituted as the Irish Brotherhood. Soon after that, at the suggestion of Theobald Wolfe Tone, the name of their organisation was changed to the Society of United Irishmen.

Wolfe Tone's personal credo, taken from his Autobiography, was:

> To subvert the tyranny of our execrable government, to break the connection
> with England, the never-failing source of all our political evils, and to assert the

independence of my country – these were my objects. To unite the whole people of Ireland, to abolish the memory of all past dissensions, and to substitute
the common name of Irishman in place of the denominations of Protestant,
Catholic and Dissenter – these were my means.[2]

These modest words were, of course, written not long before Tone's
death and they have the benefit of hindsight. They and the selective
way history is remembered have ensured that the Society of United
Irishmen is regarded as having been first formed in Dublin in October
1791 and, to this day, Wolfe Tone is regarded by many as its "onlie
begetter." Tone himself only ever claimed to have been at the first
Belfast meeting of the United Irishmen by chance and to have ceased
to have any influence on the proceedings of the Dublin Society shortly
after its founding.

The real origins of the United Irishmen are shrouded in confusion.
Early publications and letters, misleading accounts published over the
past two centuries and eclectic reading of the original sources have
combined to make it a difficult task to apportion responsibilities with
any confidence. Tone recorded in his diary for 12th October 1791:

Introduced to McTier and Sinclair. A meeting between Russell, McTier, McCabe
and me. Mode of doing business by a Secret Committee, who … direct the
movements of Belfast … settled to dine with the Secret Committee at Drew's on
Saturday, when all the resolutions, &c … of the United Irish will be submitted.

In this diary Tone identifies everyone present at this first formal
meeting of the United Irishmen. Apart from him, all were Presbyterian.
He names Samuel Neilson, William Sinclair, Samuel McTier, William
McCleery, the brothers William and Robert Simms, Thomas McCabe,
Henry Haslett, William Tennent, John Campbell and Gilbert
McIlveen. This seems very straightforward, but there are other individuals with serious claims of the authorship of the Society's principles,
men who were not present at the historic meeting in Drew's. The first
actual meeting of the Secret Committee may have been on 1st April
1791 at the Dr. [Benjamin] Franklin Tavern run by Peggy Barclay in
Sugarhouse Entry off High Street in Belfast. It was there:

Resolved: - That we the undersigned do solemnly declare ourselves in favour of the proposal of Samuel Neilson, a merchant of this town whose name is firstly subscribed thereto, to form ourselves into an association to unite all Irishmen to pledge ourselves to our country, and by that cordial union maintain that balance of patriotism so essential for the restoration and preservation of our liberty, and the revival of our trade - Signed: Samuel Neilson, John Robb, Alexander Lowry, Thomas McCabe and Henry Joy McCracken.[3]

The name conspicuously missing both from these signatories and from Tone's list quoted above is that of William Drennan. This radically minded Presbyterian doctor, the son of a New Light minister, had realised that the time was right to revive his plans from seven years earlier. This was for a concerted and national effort to achieve constitutional reform. He wrote a letter to his brother-in-law, Samuel McTier, dated 21st May 1791. In it he described an organisation of people who loved Ireland and wished to make improvements to it. Possibly for the first time on paper, he gave this organisation the name of the Irish Brotherhood. He described it as:

A benevolent conspiracy - a plot for the people - no Whig Club - no party title - the Brotherhood its name - the Rights of Man and the Greatest happiness of the Greatest Number its end - its general end Real Independence to Ireland, and Republicanism its particular purpose.[4]

Thomas Paine had published the first part of The Rights of Man in March 1791 (the second part was not published until February 1792) and we can only imagine it was being devoured by all educated people who could find a copy.

In July 1791, McTier wrote two letters to Drennan, who at that time was in Dublin, stating that in Belfast they were intent on celebrating Bastille Day and the arrest of the King of France. The first asked for some assistance and the second spelt out how well Drennan had answered him:

… great preparations for celebrating the 14th. At the meeting of the different Volunteer corps they named me as one of a committee to prepare some declaration or resolutions to be published from the Meeting. … I will be most obliged to you if you'll do something for us.[5]

Last night we had a meeting of the Committee for preparing matters for the 14th, when I laid your paper before them, which was received with unanimous reprobation.[6]

There was great sectarian unease in many parts of the north of Ireland in that July of 1791. It had largely been fomented after some bloody clashes between the gangs of Protestant Peep O'Day Boys and Catholic Defenders in County Armagh. Indeed, in those heady days leading towards the formation of the first societies of the United Irishmen, both Drennan and Tone at first deemed it wise to leave out references to Catholic Emancipation in their resolutions. Tone quickly produced a thirty-two-page pamphlet entitled *An Argument on Behalf of the Catholics of Ireland*. It is plain that he had a sympathy with Roman Catholics, although he does not seem to have been particularly knowledgeable about their Church. He believed Irish Catholics were at a stage where they would be willing to join hands with their Dissenter neighbours in the cause of a better Ireland. But he drew a distinction between his sympathies with the Church and its members and with the Church's clergy. At one time he even described Irish Catholic priests as, *"men of low birth, low feelings, low habits, and no education"*. [7]

In fear that Catholics and Protestants might negotiate some separate accommodations that would later be found ineffective, Drennan told McTier that he regretted that he had, *"found no room to express the need for conciliating the Catholics."* McTier agreed and replied that he had arranged for the toasts on the 14th of July to include, *"May the Catholics and Protestants of Ireland be of one mind in ascertaining their rights as Men, and establishing the independence of their country,"* and *"May honest Catholic and Protestant be ever united."* [8] Writing again to McTier in early 1792, Drennan confirmed that he believed his efforts the previous summer had been the beginnings of an important movement:

Perhaps my little paper was the first seed of the coalition, I mean that of the Brotherhood, and, if so, I shall ever deem myself very happy – it appeared in June, and the address to the French, 14 July, the amendment to which was, I think, the first motion to Union on our part, answered by the Catholics ... and promoted by the establishment of the United Irishmen at Belfast and Dublin.[9]

An extract from Tone's diary alludes to the importance of Thomas Russell in the discussions during these auspicious months. Russell had become friendly with Wolfe Tone and his wife in their "little box at Irishtown" and had been a contributor to Tone's formulation of his own theories:

> Russell, who was by this time entirely in their confidence, wrote to me to draw up and transmit to him such a declaration as I thought proper, which I accordingly did. A meeting of the [Volunteer] corps was held in consequence ... and the declarations then passed unanimously.[10]

Tone wrote a letter to Russell in July 1791 enclosing a draft of his resolutions, where he makes it clear that he considers that the Irish Brotherhood is not the best name for this new organisation, *"I have left, as you see, a blank for the name, which, I am clearly of opinion, should be 'the Society of United Irishmen'."*[11]

In early November 1791, in Doyle's public house in Dublin, Napper Tandy, William Drennan and a small gathering of nearly twenty Protestant and Catholic gentlemen formed the Dublin Society of United Irishmen. To supplement their numbers and, no doubt, to bolster their confidence, they also elected a number of absent friends. These included Wolfe Tone and Thomas Russell.

These years of 1791-1792 were a time of great discontent with government in Ireland and debate about it was continual. Many Irish Presbyterians had warmly supported the people of America and France in their revolutionary struggles of the two previous decades and were now embracing the ideas of Tom Paine. These Presbyterians had a kinship with a great many of the American colonists and were kept well apprised of their discontent with government from London. A great many Ulster Presbyterians were not only highly literate, but regularly in correspondence with friends and family. These correspondents were passing news of events and progress in the New World to their kinfolk in the eastern counties of Ulster. Indeed the port of Donaghadee would have brought emigrants' letters and newspapers from Boston and Philadelphia to the people of north Down before some of the news contained in them was known in London.

Those Dissenters who had chosen to stay in Ireland while their brothers and sisters had sought religious and political freedom in far-off America knew all about that struggle and how their kinfolk had been forced into it by the intransigence of British (essentially English-Establishment) rule. They knew that these thousands had emigrated in order to escape what they saw as injustice, but had found that the system in the new world was as oppressive as it had been in the old one. Those who had remained in the old country knew well how their Ulster compatriots and other like-minded settlers had fought during the years of the late 1770s and the early 1780s and how they had finally won their freedom from unwelcome rule. They had all been receiving their letters from America, or reading those sent to their neighbours.

Presbyterians had always been a literate people. Their ministers may not have been recognised by the establishment, but they were obliged to have a university degree before they even commenced their clerical training. The members of the church congregations were very far from being ignorant peasants with thoughts only of survival and the yearly round. Most Sundays the farmers, labourers, tradesmen and fishermen would have taken leave of their travails of the week and spent the Sabbath in communion with their Lord and with their neighbours. They would have been able to comprehend anything they heard in their pastors' sermons and outside the kirk afterwards they would have been even better able to chew over and digest all those ideas that their discussions would have deemed worthy.

Many of Ulster's Dissenters would have regarded themselves as the inheritors of the Covenanters' difficulty with the concept of obedience to an earthly authority. Their own dissatisfaction with oligarchy had put them very much in harmony with their cousins in the Thirteen Colonies who had overthrown the yoke of King George III and English rule. A decade later they were just as inclined to sympathise with those who would overthrow what they saw as a similarly inequitable system in France.

There is no doubt that most educated opinion among Ireland's Dissenters was for some form of parliamentary reform and emancipation for their Catholic neighbours. The Rev. Dr. William Steel Dickson, the Presbyterian minister in Portaferry, was indignant that some apologists, in the long-established practice of reactionary governments, dissembled their arguments towards a *"gradual and progressive"* movement to full emancipation rather than a *"total and immediate"* concession. After all, ran their line of reasoning, *"the profound ignorance of the Catholics and consequent incapacity, not only of enjoying, but bearing liberty,"* must be kept in mind.

Doctor Dickson was not a recalcitrant country parson of little or no importance. At that time he was the Moderator of the General Assembly of the Presbyterian Synod of Ulster. He was prominent at the Dungannon Convention of February 15th 1793, there representing County Down. The key resolution of this Convention of delegates from the province of Ulster was that:

> By free and general communication, the provincial will, regulated by the will of the province, may be concentrated in a point, from which it may be directed to the other provinces of the kingdom, and flow, with clearness, harmony, and strength, into the houses of parliament, and presence of Majesty, in order that a complete and radical reform may be speedily effectuated.

Dickson was not reticent about his own efforts to sway any waverers at the Convention:

> I used every exertion, of which I was capable, both in public and private, to convince all, with whom I was conversant, of its necessity to restore our paralyzed constitution, conciliate the public mind, and establish his Majesty's throne in the affections of the people.[12]

These are hardly the words and actions of a treacherous republican. But the lucidity of Dickson's arguments, his spellbinding oratory and the forcefulness of his delivery marked him forever in the eyes of the establishment as a dangerous man.

There were other anti-establishment figures there too, but not everyone present was there to be critical of government. In a letter to William Drennan two days later, Samuel Neilson called attention to one determined opponent to reform, James Dawson. In a letter remarkable, not only for its sincere tribute to Dickson, but as an example of Neilson's grasp and recall of the business of the Convention, Neilson wrote:

Just returned from [Dungannon] ...14 Resolutions were adopted,
1st, attachment to form of government; 2nd, loyalty; 3rd, objection to republican
principles applied to Ireland; 4th, Catholic Emancipation; 5th, approbation of the
Reform being taken up by Parliament, and warning to proceed as they regard
the peace and constitution of the country; 6th, necessity of Reform; 7th, aboli-
tion of Boroughs and extension of franchise to districts in proportion to population and wealth; 7th[sic], pledging never to give up the idea of Reform; 8th,
reprobating militia; 9th, thanking volunteers; 10th, not to dissolve; 11th, a committee to consult the other Provinces on the propriety of a National Convention
and to call a future meeting. I forget the others...
Dickson of Portaferry attracted the applause of all parties and gave a sort of
tone to the Convention. He cut Jas. Dawson up most severely as a spy of government and was warmly applauded. I never heard any man express himself to
more purpose.[13]

The Dungannon Convention pushed government and its critics even
further apart. Government wanted to show all dissidents who was in
charge. But gradually those who had desired only a change of policy in
government now began to yearn for a complete change of its personnel
and for some even a change in its form.

In spite of all this fervour, the numbers joining the Society of
United Irishmen did not increase greatly after this. Templepatrick,
Doagh, Randalstown, Killead and Muckamore in County Antrim and
Saintfield in County Down did follow with small societies, but, apart
from three more new societies in Belfast, growth was slow. In those
parts of Ireland where the population was less militant, or perhaps
more motivated by sectarian feelings, support for the United Irishmen
would have to wait for other prompts before it became widespread.
Sympathy with their ideals was one thing, but identifiable oath-swear-
ing membership was another.

Towards the end of 1794 the humanitarian Whig, Lord Fitzwilliam,
had been re-appointed the Lord Lieutenant of Ireland. Fitzwilliam was
a very popular Viceroy, with all but the ultra-conservatives. When he
removed a number of these from office, including Under-Secretary
Edward Cooke, confidence was raised that many of the grievances
highlighted by the United Irishmen would soon receive serious attention. There were great hopes that Fitzwilliam and his senior diplomats
would soon ensure some agreeable measures being taken. This change

at the top persuaded many reasonable men who had previously been reluctant to join the United Irishmen.[14]

Suddenly in March 1795 Lord Fitzwilliam was recalled and the much more conservative Lord Camden appointed in his place. Lord Castlereagh must have recognised the opportunities that might arise from the appointment of his uncle to such an influential position, but for the liberally minded people of Ireland the news was greeted with dismay. The reactionaries celebrated being back in power -- but the great majority of the people did not share their jubilation:

> March 28th: – This day was observed as a day of national mourning by the inhabitants of this town [Belfast], on account of Lord Fitzwilliam's departure. There was not a shop or counting-house open during the whole day; all was one scene of sullen indignation.[15]

A few days before Fitzwilliam was recalled, Henry Grattan, in an address to the Catholics of Dublin, stated his admiration for the Viceroy and enumerated his fears for the future if he were to be replaced, as was certain, by a man and administration without sympathies for the Irish people:

> In supporting you, I support the Protestant: we have but one interest and one honour; and whoever gives privileges to you gives vigour to all… I tremble at the return to power of your old task-masters; that combination which galled the country with its tyranny, insulted her by its manners, exhausted her by its rapacity, and slandered her by its malice. Should such a combination … return to power, I have no hesitation to say, that they will extinguish Ireland, or Ireland must remove them; it is not your cause only, but that of the nation.[16]

This address caused a sensation at the time. Grattan's references to the inevitability of disobedience, soon followed by the quickly recognised severity of the Camden administration and then the cruel persecutions of many thousands of Catholics in County Armagh, all combined to drive thousands of Presbyterians and hundreds of members of other faiths into the multiplying ranks of the United Irishmen – particularly in Ireland's north-eastern counties.

One day in the month of June 1795 Henry Joy McCracken, Thomas Russell, Samuel Neilson, Robert Simms, William McCabe, Wolfe Tone and a few others, encouraged by this movement and the intensity of the feelings underpinning it, walked up the slopes of Belfast's Cave Hill. Their destination was McArt's Fort, an old Irish earthwork on a stark promontory poking out of the hill's basaltic hulk. Every person who has stood in any part of the lower Lagan valley has seen this angular outcrop. Long before the prominence on the recumbent face on the skyline was referred to as Napoleon's Nose, it was as familiar a landmark to everyone in north Down and south Antrim as it is today. The founders of the United Irishmen chose the spot for this meeting because of its remoteness from prying eyes and for its historic symbolism. When they reached their destination these young men made a pledge to bring about the complete separation of Ireland from Britain, or die in the attempt.

They did not succeed in their aim; some kept their pledge, others did not.[17] Two years after the rebellion was over, the Act of Union joined the United Kingdom of Great Britain and Ireland closer than ever. It would be left to succeeding generations of reformers to strive for an egalitarian society. Irish Nationalists would continue to work for the separation of the two islands. It would be left to later Irish Republicans to seek their all-Ireland republic.

In County Armagh the killing and banishing of Catholics continued through these years. General William Dalrymple, in a survey of north Armagh, found many Catholics, *"preparing for flight the moment their little harvests are brought in, some are gone to America, others to Connaught – their houses are placarded and their fears excessive."* Dalrymple and others reported many instances of 'placarding' in Armagh, where many families were being threatened that their houses would be burned to the ground, or they themselves were being advised that they, *"Shall be Blowed To the Blue flames of Hell."*[18]

On the 21st of September 1795, two months after the United Irish pledge at McArt's Fort, there was yet another armed clash in north Armagh. This one was less spontaneous than many of the usual faction fights and ultimately it was to become the most famous. A crowd of Defenders from County Tyrone were known to have crossed the River Blackwater and were hoping to meet up with some Peep o' Day Boys with whom they had crossed cudgels a little earlier. Being on their home turf, the County Armagh Peep o' Day Boys took position on a hill overlooking a crossroads called the Diamond and waited.

William Blacker, a wealthy landowner and a founder member of the Orange Order, later wrote that as soon as the Defenders reached the Diamond, the men on the hill opened fire with their flintlocks:

> With cool and steady aim at the swarm of Defenders, who were cooped up in the valley and presented an excellent mark for their shots. The affair was of brief duration ... from the bodies found afterwards by the reapers in the corn-fields, I am inclined to think that not less than thirty lost their lives... Unhappily a determination was expressed of driving from this quarter of the county the entire of its Roman Catholic population ... A written notice was thrown into or posted upon the door of a house warning the inmates, in the words of Oliver Cromwell, to betake themselves, 'to Hell or Connaught.'[19]

After this 'Battle of the Diamond' some of the Peep o' Day Boys then withdrew to the house of James Sloan in Loughgall where they formed the first Orange Lodge. Gradually at first, but soon quite quickly, the ripples spread from County Armagh and membership of the Orange Order grew. The members of the order eschewed all United Irish prop-ositions, whether reform, republicanism or Catholic emancipation and rejected all criticism of government.

After Lord Fitzwilliam was recalled, the Government, the Castle and the military had to strike a very delicate balance. Although they were fearful of the Order's potential en masse, they were keen enough to use the Orangemen's staunch loyalties in small doses. They needed them to support their actions against the disaffected, especially and most noticeably the Catholics of County Armagh. The government was also anxious that neither the United Irishmen nor the Orangemen would infect the militia, the only effective protection in the country against anarchy, Jacobinism and revolution.

For three years the Marquis of Downshire had been the Colonel of the Royal Downshire Regiment. Major George Matthews was his second-in-command and he shared his Lordship's opinions about the dangers of over-extreme views. In 1796 he warned Downshire that:

> The system of Orange Clubs have really taken place in the regiment, ... it is insinuated through the regiment that your Lordship approves of the Orangemen.

Your Lordship may rest assured that I will take every means in my power to put a stop to this business.

He followed it up with news both of his success within the Regiment and a wise comment about the inevitable outcome of extremism breeding more extremism:

I am in hopes I have put a stop for the present to the Orange Clubs, ... But there is nothing surer than that Orangeism, if it goes on, will be the means of making United men.[20]

This was a very astute reading of a situation that soon became a matter of some concern to the establishment. The harsh treatment the Defenders had been receiving did have the effect of swelling, rather than reducing, their numbers. Magistrates and courts with loyalist sympathies executed many Defenders and transported hundreds more to far-off colonies. The Catholic Archbishop of Dublin, John Troy, even excommunicated them, but still their ranks grew. The United Irishmen could see this as a way of expanding their own ranks from the, *"bourgeois radicals in Belfast, Lisburn and Dublin and Presbyterian farmers in Antrim and Down,"*[21] into mid-Ulster. The United Irishmen made overtures to the Defenders that they might join them. If the United Irishmen were on the 'up', meaning becoming organised in a more military fashion than heretofore, then, with the mutual support of the Defenders, they could be on the 'up and up.' The leaders of the Defenders either encouraged their members to join the United Irishmen, or else keep their separate identity and work with local United Irishmen Societies when their aims were sufficiently in accord and their combined strength was greater. It was an open secret by this time that Wolfe Tone and others had been lobbying in France for the support of the French Directory in Ireland. This was a great encouragement to all of the disaffected population and a source of fear for almost everyone else.

The continuing depredations of the Orange Boys among his tenants incensed Lord Gosford, the county governor of Armagh. At a meeting of the county's magistrates he railed against what he called the ferocious cruelty used against a group of people whose only crime was a profession of the Roman Catholic faith. In case his sympathies might be misconstrued, Gosford emphasised:

> I am as true a Protestant as any gentleman in this room. I inherit a property which my family derived under a Protestant title, and with the blessing of God I will maintain that title to the utmost of my power. I will never consent to make a sacrifice of Protestant ascendancy to Catholic claims ... but
> ... I know my own heart, and I should despise myself if, under any *intimidation*, I could close my eyes ... or my ears against the complaints of a *persecuted people*.[22]

The trouble was not confined to Armagh. Through 1796 north Down too saw many instances of sectarian unease. It seemed that every action designed to bolster the confidence of one side produced fear in the other. Swaggering or taunting engendered even stronger emotions. Early in the year Thomas Lane, Lord Downshire's land agent, was writing to him deploring, *"The Limericks [Militia] behave decently now; but drum and fife to Mass I don't like."*[23] A fortnight later he wrote:

> One Defender sentenced to be imprisoned for one year and fine security for seven. ...The parishes of Seapatrick, Tullylish and Donaghacloney were fined for outrages committed by Orange Boys and Peep o' Day Men (who are said to have been rather encouraged by some of the magistrates in Armagh), they have not confined their bloody pursuits to that county, but continually make inroads into this, and treat in the most inhuman manner every Catholic property they get to, and I am sorry to say so little kindness attaches itself to our Protestant tenants, that they even exult at the alarming situation of their neighbours.

In the same letter he shows that even those in the know were becoming alarmed by the realisation that a new movement had been growing in Belfast and north Down:

> Another bunch of miscreants are starting up to the north-east of us under the denomination of United Irishmen, who mean, as we are told, neither to pay tithes, cess or rent.[24]

As had been demonstrated at Loughgall, true Ulster style faction fighting was not always spontaneous. Lane described what was clearly an organised, if well-contained contest:

I had yesterday to attend at Blaris [the military Camp near Lisburn] to disperse a body of at least 150 men assembled to see a Protestant and Papist chieftain fight. The latter had prevailed on about 50 of the City of Limerick Militia to come to the ground to see *fair play*.[25]

Jacques Louis de Bougrenet, the Chevalier de la Tocnaye, traveled the length and breadth of Ireland through 1796 and 1797. This young Frenchman was a shrewd observer. His impressions as an interested outsider give modern readers a useful perspective on the everyday domestic practices and social habits that he saw in Ireland. He was astonished by the rigour of the military regime he witnessed and the apparent acceptance of it by the majority of the population. He was amazed how the curfew cleared the streets and doused the lights, both outdoors and indoors, at nine o'clock in the evening and that soldiers could so easily force men, women and children to remove anything green, even a small piece of ribbon, from their persons. To save any possible harassment he removed the green cord from the sword-cane umbrella he habitually carried.

And yet, he noted, in spite of all these restrictions the integrity of the quarrel of the more violent men persisted. With an uncanny resonance of more modern times De Latocnaye declared his incomprehension of this behaviour:

The country is a little paradise; it is impossible to conceive anything better cultivated or more romantic. What a pity then, that the spirit of discord and fury has laid hold of the inhabitants to a point that might well make one fear to live among them. Every morning there is news of crimes committed during the night. Not a day passes without murders or the burning of houses.

He also makes it very clear where he thought the spirit of discord resided in Ulster society, or perhaps more interestingly, where he considered that it did not:

In politics it must be said that the people are fairly reasonable in Ireland, and little division from this cause is found in the middle classes of society, among whom everyone is supposed to be of the same opinion. There is not much talk about the troubles, certainly there is less than in Great Britain.

De Bougrenet makes it clear that he did have some understanding of the make-up of the principal protagonists. He knew about Protestant Orangemen, with their orange cockades and ties, the more secretive Catholic Defenders and the United Irishmen, the last of whom, he said, professed that all religions were equal. He had some sympathy with the grievances all parties brought to the situation. He could distinguish between what he termed the "religious war" in County Armagh and the more reasoned political conflict in Counties Antrim and Down. What puzzled him most about what he saw was the determination on the part of the government to deal harshly with the symptoms of the discontent in the country, but with no sign of any understanding or caring about its causes. Only in 1797, he says, did this realisation come to them.[26]

1. *Union and Truth*, "The motto, or countersign, of the United Irish Societies." Charles Teeling, *History of the Irish Rebellion of 1798, a Personal Narrative*, Glasgow & London, 1876, written 1828, p. 10.

2. Wolfe Tone, quoted in A.T.Q. Stewart, *A Deeper Silence, The Hidden Roots of the United Irish Movement*, London, 1993.

3. Samuel Neilson, quoted by both Stewart in A Deeper Silence and Barkley in *A Short History of the Presbyterian Church in Ireland*, Belfast, 1959.

4. William Drennan to Samuel McTier, 21st May 1791, (Drennan Papers, PRONI, D/591/300).

5. Samuel McTier to William Drennan, 2nd July 1791, (Drennan Papers, PRONI, D/591/302).

6. McTier to Drennan, 9th July 1791, (Drennan Papers, PRONI, D/591/304).

7. Wolfe Tone, *An Argument on Behalf of the Catholics of Ireland*, Belfast, 1791.

8. McTier to Drennan, July 1791, (Drennan Papers, PRONI, D/591/303).

9. Drennan to McTier, early 1792, (Drennan Papers, PRONI, D/591).

10. Theobald Wolfe Tone, *The Autobiography*, 1763 - 1798, ed. R. Barry O'Brien, London, 1893.

11. Wolfe Tone to Thomas Russell, quoted in Rosamund Jacob, *The Rise of the United Irishmen*, 1791-94. London, 1937.

12 The Rev. Dr. William Steel Dickson, *A Narrative of the Confinement and Exile of William Steel Dickson, D.D.*, Dublin, 1812, pp. 94-97.

13. Samuel Neilson at Belfast to Dr Wm Drennan in Dublin, 17th Feb 1793, Belfast, (Drennan Papers, PRONI, D/591/390).

14. Charles Teeling, pp. 5-6.

15. *Northern Whig*, 28th March 1796.

16. Henry Grattan, responding to an address to him from the Catholics of Dublin, 14th March 1795, quoted in Teeling, pp. 6-8.

17. A.T.Q. Stewart, *The Summer Soldiers*, Belfast, 1995, p. 72.

18. General William Dalrymple, quoted in *Peep o' Day Boys and Defenders: Selected Documents on the County Armagh Disturbances* (Ed.) David W. Miller, Belfast, 1990, p. 129.

19. William Blacker, quoted in David W. Miller, p.121 and 125.

20. Major Geo. Matthews, Drogheda to Downshire, 3rd and 5th December 1796, (Downshire Papers, PRONI, D/607/D/366 and 373).

21. Jonathan Bardon, *A History of Ulster*, Belfast, 1992, p. 227.

22. Lord Gosford of Markethill, Armagh, speech to a meeting of magistrates in Armagh, 28th December 1795, quoted in Teeling, pp. 9-10.

23. Thomas Lane, to Marquis of Downshire, 3rd March 1796, (Downshire Papers, PRONI, D/607/D/039).

24. Lane, to Downshire in Dublin, 24th March 1796, (Downshire Papers, PRONI, D/607/D/043).

25. Lane, from Hillsborough to Downshire in Dublin, 24th May 1796, (Downshire Papers, PRONI, D/607/D/062).

26. Jacques Louis de Bougrenet, the Chevalier de la Tocnaye, *A Frenchman's Walk through Ireland*, 1796-1797, pp. 258-268.

TENSIONS MOUNT

They come, they come, see myriads come
Of Frenchmen to relieve us;
Seize, seize the pike, beat, beat the drum,
They come my friend to save us.

Plant, Plant the Tree,
Traditional Irish Ballad of the period

In the month of May 1796 Major George Matthews of the Hillsborough Yeomanry was no longer in any doubt about what was the overwhelming cause of the uncivilised behaviour all over Ulster. He informed his Colonel about a bad incident which had occurred on the Hillsborough - Dromore turnpike. Violence between some civilians and one of his recruiting parties had ended with many injured and one young woman dead. He declared to Lord Downshire, *"I believe drunkenness has been the occasion of all this misfortune ... whiskey is the curse of this country and in [the] recruiting business it is impossible to keep them from it."* [1]

We may assume that he was referring more to the troopers than to civilians. The recruiting business was not just a matter of showing the scarlet coat and sounding the side-drum to entice young men to take the King's Shilling. It often operated more like the better known press gangs finding able bodies for the navy. Often the only successful inducement to join the King's men was a knock on the head. In both cases, once in the service, the iron-hard discipline and the severe punishments for running would keep a man there.

The perceived state of the country now prompted the administrators and the gentry to initiate a less hard-line, but still urgent, recruitment drive in their local areas. In a familiar fashion they argued that the mixed corps of Militiamen were fine for supporting the Fencible and other regiments in garrisoning the country, but that a regional Protestant force, the members of which knew their own backyard and more importantly the troublemakers within it, was the only answer to local insurrection. Because of the predominantly rural nature of this force these part-time troops were to be called Yeomanry.

Thomas Knox MP and the Reverend William Richardson promulgated the Dungannon Resolutions of June 1796, which led directly to the formation of these corps. They declared their resistance to all enemies, "foreign and domestic," and could not have identified the French and the United Irishmen better if they had named them.

Yeomanry regiments were formed all over Ireland, but most enthusiastically in Ulster. They could be infantry or cavalry. They were always recruited locally, but were administered by the Yeomanry Office in Dublin Castle. They could be used for everyday patrols when the regular forces were needed for some particular duty, or they could be used as a kind of para-military police force in support of the local magistracy.

Everyone in the country knew there was discontent. Anyone who did not share it recognised the need for measures to be taken to prevent it escalating into open anarchy. Lord Londonderry, on his way to worship one Sunday, was met by his agent, the Rev. John Cleland, who told him a disquieting story. This so horrified His Lordship that he rushed home to Mount Stewart to compose an urgent letter to the County Governor, the Marquis of Downshire:

> On coming to Town this forenoon, I was informed that last night, about seven o'clock, as Mr. Cleland was coming from my Office, a person, as he passed a Lane, snap'd a Pistol, at him, of which he heard the Noise, & saw the spark of the flint, he believes he was attempting to cock it again, but Mr. Cleland having discharged a Pocket Pistol at him, he fled.[2]

This was not the only attempt on Cleland's life. He had discovered that five men, some from his own town, had cast lots to assassinate him by firing a pistol through his office window.[3] The Rev John Cleland seems to have been the most disliked man in Down. Even

Lord Castlereagh, who knew him all his life, said of him, *"Cleland richly deserves to be tossed in a blanket ...I will take a corner."*

Londonderry and his steward were now so unpopular that they were forced to spend that whole winter under constant military guard. This ardent dislike may well have been personal given the discontent prevailing in Stewart's estates, but Lord Downshire, who was not so unpopular, nevertheless was also obliged to take care. In the spring, William Drennan's sister, Mrs. Martha McTier, could not mask her feelings from her brother about the discomfiture of the two County Down aristocrats:

> Londonderry, it is said, is going to sneak into Newtown after being guarded by soldiers all the winter at Mount Stewart. His father seldom bolted his windows. Not a penny of rent is paid him. ... The Marquis of Downshire was at a ball at Purdysburn the other night, where he looked like the Devil, and I heard it said he owed his life to a mistake in the hour of leaving it.[4]

Downshire was so alarmed by his own experiences and by those he had learned of in north Down that he passed the matter to the Chief Secretary of Ireland, Thomas Pelham:

> My dear Sir,
> Assassinations are still getting more frequent in this Country. . Mr. Price [of Saintfield] is seriously threatened, and they say I was within 200 perches of having been shot at had I gone that length upon the road where I was expected, but as my time was not yet come I turned by another road.[5]

Not all of these loyal citizens agreed that the enrolment of a part-time Yeomanry was the best measure to be taken. Lord Londonderry was adamant that, because of the state of the country, regular soldiers were the best answer:

> In the state the country is in, my house, & Family are not safe, without an armed force, especially if I have to act as a Magistrate, & become an Object of Resentment. A Troop divided between this Place & Comber, I believe, will be requisite -- another between Castlereagh & Killinchy. ... they can be accommodated in the Public Houses, & upon the Inhabitants, till Beds are got. My Son & I will give every Assistance in our Power.[6]

There was not even general agreement about the grievances, which might have provoked such discontent in the people. The Customs Collector at Donaghadee, James Arbuckle, supplied Lord Downshire with a report of an argument among a few of the more influential and educated men in that town. Arbuckle reported that his deputy, William Getty, had been arguing with the wealthiest merchant in the town. The former was an Anglican loyalist like most government officials and the latter a more radical Dissenter. It clearly illustrates the bewilderment and disagreement of the times:

This foolish fellow – and there cannot well be a more foolish than James Lemon, does a deal of mischief by babbling and prating in his shop to the lower class. I sent Getty out today with the heads of the [Yeomanry] Bill. He stepp'd into Lemon's shop and explain'd the purport of the intended Act, as going merely to legalize volunteers who associate for Defence of Country and King and Constitution. Lemon said, "If we had a Reform everything would go on well"

"And what," says Getty, "do you really mean, if you have any meaning, by Reform?" Lemon cou'd not very well tell, but he said Tithes was a very great grievance and people were much dissatisfied, and that being done away wou'd help to settle men's Minds.

"Now then," says Getty, "I fix you. In the Parishes of Newtown and Comber they pay no Tithe, and in this Parish we are most heavily Tithed, yet here, bating a very few such grumbling wiseacres as yourself, all are satisfied and contented. In the former Parishes there is nothing but discontent and sedition."[7]

As subsequent events were to prove, this was not necessarily an accurate assessment of the opinion prevailing in Donaghadee, nor in the Ards district, but it is what influential loyalists such as Arbuckle naively believed.

In Hillsborough Lord Downshire quite out of the blue received a letter that must have alarmed him and all those to whom he chose to relate its sensitive contents. The information had been obtained by William Pitt's very efficient secret service and certainly put matters such as recruitment of local yeomanry at the top of many agendas. The impact of the message came not so much from what was being said as from who was saying it. The writer was the Lord Lieutenant of Ireland, Lord Camden, and the kernel of his message was, *"Some intelligence I have just received from England induces me to think it very probable the French may attempt a descent on this kingdom."*[8]

Long before the intelligence memorandum that provoked this letter had reached Camden, similar reports and rumours had been circulating. Every time a strange sail was spotted the maroons went up. As early as April 1795 a local report from Donaghadee appeared in a newspaper, announcing, *"There are four armed vessels just passed by this place standing to the northward ... we can perceive their gunports and they are carrying a press of sail."*[9] Experienced coast watchers would have known the lines of trading vessels and of British men of war, even some miles out. There is little doubt that these were foreign warships.

In August of 1796 the Marquis of Downshire sent invitations to all the landowning gentry in County Down to, *"meet me at Newtownards on Friday the 9th of September at twelve o'clock noon."*[10] At this gathering Downshire proposed that these men form Yeomanry regiments by subscription in their own localities. Not surprisingly, considering the rivalries between Lords Downshire and Londonderry, it became a fiery meeting, but a resolution was finally passed in Downshire's favour.

However, Downshire's anxieties had made him jump the gun without government approval, thus forcing Lord Camden to reprimand him and give him some diplomatic advice about always being seen to act within the law:

> If it is right to come to any resolution it should be something of the following sort, "That we are ready when called upon to enroll ourselves under officers appointed by government for the preservation of the peace and welfare of the country and for the defence of property, laws, constitution etc."[11]

When Downshire arrived back at Hillsborough that same Friday from the Newtownards meeting, Major-General Nugent, Crown-Solicitor John Pollock, the Earl of Westmeath and a troop of soldiers met him. They brought top secret news that Lord Castlereagh was to oversee the arrests of a large number of United Irish leaders in exactly one week's time.

On the following Thursday evening in Lisburn, Castlereagh enjoyed himself at one of the soirées for which Ulster society at that time had become famous. He then repaired to bed in the home of his uncle,

Lord Hertford, in the same town. Early the next morning, walking down Lisburn's main street, he met his old friend Luke Teeling, who was out for a morning horseback ride with his eighteen-year-old son, Charles. Teeling senior, like many liberals of the day, had given strong political support to Lord Castlereagh in the 1790 election and had remained quite friendly with him. The three greeted each other with all the genteel courtesy and politeness usual with such friends and they strolled up the street together.

When they reached Hertford's house Luke Teeling was beginning to take his leave when Lord Castlereagh said bluntly, but with his usual impeccable courtesy, *"I regret that your son cannot accompany you."* Seconds later, Charles Teeling found himself under guard on the wrong side of an iron gate. Teeling senior asked his old friend on what charge his son had been arrested. Castlereagh's laconic answer was, "High Treason!"

Luke Teeling was Catholic, but he was able to show that Presbyterians did not have a monopoly on stubborn pride. After giving a withering look of defiance to the man his son later described as, *"the apostate patriot and insidious friend,"* and a last handclasp with his son, Luke Teeling walked off in dignified silence. None present could have dreamt that Charles would never set foot in the family home again, or that the Teeling family would never gather together again.

A short time later on that eventful morning Castlereagh joined Downshire, Westmeath and Pollock on the road to Belfast. By ten o'clock they were riding past the Dublin Road turnpike into a city ringed by troops and artillery. Thus began what became known as, "The Siege of Belfast." The first house they searched was that of William Sampson, the prominent Belfast attorney. They had been informed they might find his friend, Samuel Neilson, there. When they pushed into Mrs. Sampson's bedroom, her husband could not resist commenting that his wife, *"was not, as some ladies are, in the habit of privately harbouring gentlemen."* This barbed jest provoked some stifled laughter since everyone in the party was well aware of the recently publicised cuckoldry of Lord Westmeath by his wife.[12]

The party found nothing incriminating in Sampson's, but within an hour or two a large number of United Irish leaders, including Russell,

Haslett and other suspects were taken up. They also found Samuel Neilson at another address. The four prime movers of this action had taken the precaution of ensuring that all arrest warrants stipulated that the prisoners were to be taken, not to the nearby County gaols of Carrickfergus and Downpatrick, but a hundred miles away to the Dublin prisons of Newgate and the brand new Kilmainham. A modern day visitor to Kilmainham Gaol will be told that the first political prisoner there was Henry Joy McCracken, but this is a story for the tourists. When Castlereagh's men had gone for McCracken, he was not at home. It would be the autumn before he and many other United Irishmen would follow the first few to Kilmainham.[13]

In a period when so many were at least part-time farmers, being arrested at harvest time was a double punishment. A man could easily recover from a spell in gaol, but if he did not get his grain in or his potatoes lifted, he and his family might starve in the winter months. Of course the whole community understood and sympathised, but with a touching generosity of spirit, they were also willing and eager to do something to help. Their enthusiasm was not, of course, due only to selfless charity. The men and women who flocked to reap their neighbours' corn or dig their potatoes did so in part to demonstrate their solidarity with their incarcerated friends and of course to take every possible opportunity to gather together to talk politics and plan possible action.

Very quickly such activities became huge social gatherings. Many hundreds would collect at a farm, equipped to work, but ready for a good time too. Picnic lunches, buttermilk and porter would be brought, the children would find a place to play and the men would organise the harvest. There might be many acres of crops to get in and no one had much time to spare from their own smallholding, their handloom weaving or other work, so such a harvest had to be done quickly.

The French traveller, De Latocnaye, observed such gatherings. Innocently he believed what he was told about it being an old custom of the peasantry to assemble at the end of the autumn and dig up the potatoes of anyone for whom they had respect and affection. He claims that he saw such work being done for persons attached to the

Government, but this does not seem very likely, unless for an unusually well-respected individual. The Frenchman was very impressed by some aspects of the business. He loved the gaiety, the best clothes people wore for the occasion, the singing and the children playing. He was astounded that such a gathering, sometimes of many hundreds, could take place with not one sign or effect of alcohol consumption. So agreeable were those present at these "potato-diggings" that De Latocnaye was provoked to comment that such gatherings in France or England could not occur without the risk of violence. He was moved to add:

> If the government would only give up at once and absolutely the attempt to Anglicise the Irish at any cost, and would lead them through their prejudices and customs, it would be possible to do with them anything that could be wished.

He was also amazed at the level of the organisation and the discipline and how authority could be given so easily on the day to one leader, who then took complete charge of the operations, *"A man, with nothing special to distinguish him, exacted obedience and directed affairs by signs with the hand or by certain calls."*[14]

Reports of such diggings came in from many parts of Ulster. North Antrim, County Londonderry and many areas near Belfast all had their own gatherings. Sometimes the harvesting was like a carnival. At times the stone-faced discipline was chilling for an observer. Occasionally the task was tackled as though trying to break a record. Belfast's *Northern Star* reported that Samuel Neilson's potatoes had been dug out in an amazing seven minutes by 1500 people and that four acres of potatoes were lifted from the fields of Gawin Hamilton by five thousand diggers, a third of them women, clearing the fields in regimented rows.[15] It does not actually say so, but any Ulsterman would know that every man there would have dug with the same foot.

Always, if challenged, the potato-diggers responded agreeably and made no show of resistance.[16] Sometimes the proceedings were attacked by the authorities and their henchmen. The *Northern Star* reported on an incident near the town of Lisburn:

The Rev. Philip Johnson, attended by a troop of Dragoons and a number of armed men, who are reported to be Orangemen, marched to the potatoe-field and attacked the unoffending multitude … a great many were wounded … and forty-eight of the potatoe-diggers were taken prisoner and brought to Lisburn tied in pairs… . Many of those that were liberated were afterwards beat and abused by the Orangemen who guarded them.[17]

Pharis Martin of Magheradroll near Ballynahinch was concerned enough on hearing stories about potato digging in Mr. Hamilton's field that he wrote to Edward Cooke about it:

The Revd. Mr. Forde, Vicar of Magheradroll, whose Glebe immediately adjoins Mr. H's Farm told me he seen the people assembled & in the act of raising pota-toes … . in his opinion there was not less than 300 people there assembled… . My father happened to be riding through the Town of Ballynahinch at the time the[y] were parading at the door of James Armstrong's with one Fifer or more playing & a man carrying a green bough. He, my father, was pressed by one of the Party, viz. Thomas Murry, a tenant of Lord Moira's to Drink with the Potatoe Diggers which he declined.[18]

He certainly would have been in no doubt about the significance of the green bough, symbolic as it was of the Tree of Liberty and long-recognised as a United Irish badge.

In the month of November Lord Castlereagh stumbled upon such a potato-digging gathering near Comber. In as innocent a fashion as that other young observer, De Latocnaye, the 27-year-old Castlereagh was charmed by the rural idyll. He could not wait to write about it to his wife in England:

I had the opportunity of seeing this morning a large body of potato-diggers – it was a pretty sight; a great number of young men marching along with smart girls on their arms – they were going towards Comber to dig Maxwell's potatoes. I rode some distance with them and had a good deal of funny conversation; you may easily conceive I neither scolded, nor attempted to argue them out of their intentions. We had a great number of jokes and nothing could be more good-humoured than they were to me.[19]

One imagines that had Castlereagh, or the diggers, been able to look in their crystal balls, the conversation that day might not have been so relaxed. The incident had happened on the very day that Camden and the Privy Council in Dublin had issued a Proclamation prohibit-ing such diggings. The Comber potato men would not have heard of it yet, but like their fellow-Ulstermen and possibly Castlereagh too, they would have ignored it anyway. A Portaferry magistrate, *"who dispersed the potatoe-diggers of Mr. McKibben, fifteen in number, under the late Proclamation, had himself, the day following, twenty-two digging his own."*[20]

Much had been said over the autumn months about forming yeomanry regiments, with much to-ing and fro-ing between the homes of those gentlemen who were enthusiastic and those who were less so. However, possibly because the threat of French ships had lost some of its urgency, little had been done. People considered the threat to be real enough, but it was not very worrying because it did not necessarily appertain to the locality where they lived. Lord Pelham also seemed fairly relaxed when he wrote to Downshire in September to say that Camden:

> ...agrees with you in opinion that about 500 [Yeomanry] cavalry would be sufficient for the internal defence and protection of the county of Down, and that it would be better to form each troop out of a barony or half-barony instead of establishing one in each parish.[21]

The following month Patrick Savage of Portaferry was so concerned about the difficulties of raising a decent yeomanry force that he rode through Kircubbin and Greyabbey to Mount Stewart to compare notes with Lord Londonderry. Each man discovered that his difficulties were very similar. Although it was Savage who actually wrote it, the two men composed a letter together to Lord Downshire to make their excuses:

> For as to the success of raising the cavalry, it is totally out of the question at present, and I am sorry to say we have found the state of this barony to be miserably bad indeed. I have a number of tenants at this moment loyal and friends to government, but they have told me themselves that they are afraid to come forward and show themselves, as they would be marked out by the United Irishmen and have themselves, their families and property destroyed.

The men were agreed that more professional troops such as Militia were what was needed:

The immediate sending of troops into this barony is the only thing can save it from total destruction of principles. I am certain it will require 50 men at Portaferry and Lord Londonderry seems to think as many will be necessary at Newtown, but he will give you his sentiments on those matters himself. In my opinion there is not a moment to be lost in sending the troops to us.[22]

Savage wrote the following day to add that when he returned home and questioned his loyal tenants he found that it was even worse than he had first thought:

The people [in Portaferry] are completely unhappy and miserable in their situation; they are actually afraid to go to bed for fear of being taken asleep and left at the mercy of lawless ruffians who take every means of frightening and seducing them.[23]

A day or two later Savage informed Downshire about a rebellious meeting held in Kircubbin. This had suggested to him why yeomanry enrolment was not going too well. It also confirmed that the United Irishmen were very well organised in the Ards, that their ranks included men from all stations in society and that they were making ready for serious business.

A man of the name of Bailie, a clockmaker of this town, (formerly of Belfast) and some others held a meeting at Kircubbin and read out on Friday last the order from the County monthly meeting. … The privates are to meet in barns to exercise, in small parties, and books of discipline are to be left with those who can read, for the instruction of those who can't read. A cutter is to be off this coast in a fortnight with 9000 stand of Arms and Ammunition equivalent for them. The arms in Donaghadee, Bangor and Castleward to be seized on the getting those on the cutter.[24]

Savage was still riding round the Ards Peninsula for some days after. One day he had an encounter that gave him first hand confirmation of what had previously only been hearsay. He instantly wrote to the Donaghadee Customs Collector, James Arbuckle, informing him of exactly what he had seen and to suggest that the Donaghadee armed Customs Barge might look into some of the peninsula's harbours and creeks. He then dutifully passed all the details on to Lord Downshire:

...I wrote to Mr. Arbuckle of the Barge &c. As I returned I met at least a hundred men marching regularly out of Kircubbin. A man with them, seemingly their Cap[tain], and two fifers playing a French tune as a quickstep for them. We passed each other sans ceremonie. I also met Frank Savage, who says Ballywalter would require troops. I spoke to Charles [Matthews of Inishargie?] about Kircubbin. He thinks thirty men and an officer sufficient for the accommodation they could get there and if thirty more in the same way were sent to Ballywalter it would be requisite, as those potatoe gentry, with their fifers, came from that neighbourhood to within a mile of this on the great road through the barony and returned in the same order, the same way.[25]

The Customs officer for Groomsport, Humphrey Galbraith, wrote to Downshire around the same time with a similar story from his man on the spot:

Mr. Johnston, a Coast Officer of Groomsport, was with me just now to have his diary signed and tells me there is a nightly meeting of Ragamuffins exercising in the House of one McKan, who, he says, sells drink in Groomsport without Licence, but he cannot speak with certainty, and says Revenue Officers in his Neighbourhood cannot venture abroad to do their duty for fear of being knocked on the head.[26]

Galbraith's superior officer, Arbuckle, actually seemed to be having more success in Donaghadee, in spite of his oft-stated claims that the region had become seriously disaffected in those late months of 1796. In his letter he is more worried that the yeomanry will not be properly equipped, but even before he has signed up one yeoman, his principal concern seems to have been how they would look on display and how giving the men a good appearance need not be too expensive:

I have sounded Catherwood [of Ballyvester House] and two or three others on adoption of yeomanry cavalry, and I am of the opinion that I shall not find much difficulty in enrolling even more respectable yeomen than your Lordship would require from this parish. I have presumed to say that government will provide Arms & Accoutrements.... A blue jacket and waistcoat are of very little expense, all have leather breeches and I hope that uniformity of colour or sex of the beasts will not be minded. Utility and not show should be the object of the occasion.[27]

A week later he was able to boast ten promised enrolments in his district to Lord Downshire. His list is almost, but not quite, a roll call of the gentlemen and wealthy merchants of Donaghadee. He has left out one or two like Daniel Delacherois and William Getty on account of their age and James Lemon, possibly because of his suspected republican sympathies. Other 'recruiting sergeants' were probably submitting similar lists, but these have not always survived.

Arbuckle's list reads:

Underneath are the names of such as might enroll, and shall mark thus -- X, those who either have promised or will enroll. The doubtfuls I shall distinguish by a D.

	X	Jas. Leslie	)	
	X	J. Arbuckle Jr.	)	
	X	Ed. Hull	)	
	X	Dobson (Garager)	) Town	
	X	Russell (Court Officer)	)	
	X	Tomb (Distiller)	)	
	D	John Nevin (Brewer)	) but not applied to	
	D	Sam. Smith	) "	
	X	Alexr. McMinn Jr.	)	
	X	John Catherwood	)	
	X	William Kelly	)	
	X	Nevin Logan	)	
	X	Nevin Taylor	) Country	
Not yet	(	Robt. Patton	)	
applied	(D	Adam Orr	)	
to	(	Rt. Pitcon	)	
	(	Jas. Shaw	)	
	(	Prt. Pitcon	) [28]	

The widely spread fears of the loyal population of the Ards eventually reached the ears of the commander of the Crown forces in the north of Ireland, Lieutenant-General Gerard Lake. He delegated the movement of the troops in Down to his second-in-command, Major-General George Nugent.

Sending troops was not just a matter of detailing a certain number to march somewhere. Troops would have to be quartered and fed. Nugent had enough sympathy with the people, enough intelligence about the nocturnal and other activities of the United Irishmen and enough misgivings about the dependability of the Yeomen to warrant some new orders taking substantial numbers of troops across the Strangford narrows:

> York Fencibles to march two companies from Downpatrick to Portaferry, Kircubbin, Comber and Killinchy tomorrow, and [I] have written to Mr. Savage to procure accommodation for them at the two former places and to Mr. Cleland to do the same at the two latter places. ... A troop of the 22nd Dragoons will be sent to Newtownards and Comber immediately and houses will be taken and fitted up for them as well as stabling for their horses.[29]

When the young French traveller, De Latocnaye, was entertained at Mount Stewart towards the end of 1796, he knew he was in prestigious company. The Earl of Londonderry was second only to Lord Downshire in the county and the Countess was the sister of Lord Lieutenant Camden. Londonderry's coercion of his wealthier tenants to sign the Oath of Allegiance and to join his son's Yeomanry Cavalry provoked William Drennan's sister, Martha McTier, to write to him highlighting the difference between Stewart the principled Presbyterian and Londonderry the swaggering peer:

> When the King let *Mr. Stewart* know that he intended to godfather his son, the Dissenter was not flattered out of his principles, but returned for answer that he christened without sponsors. He then pledged himself by a fine of £1500 to his country friends that he would ever be the same Mr. Stewart; yet as a *lord*, he threatens a poor country parson with the loss of six guineas stipend and his fields if he did not take the oath.[30]

The young honorary colonel of this regiment, Castlereagh, had taken time off from his increasingly pressing duties in London and Dublin to assist with both the enrolment and the administering of the oath. In a letter to his wife he described how his father's tenants had been won over at a dinner held in Newtownards Market House for that express purpose. He implies that there was no stinting of hospitality at the gathering. He even boasts that his father, Lord Londonderry, James Clealand, the serving colonel of the Newtownards Yeomanry and the Rev. William Sinclair, the Presbyterian minister referred to by Mrs. McTier, were all the worse for wear at the end of the day:

Between three and four hundred took the oath of allegiance yesterday. They did it with every mark of sincerity after the ice had been broken and their panic a little removed... . We had a very jolly dinner. Cleland quite drunk, Sinclair considerably so, my father not a little, others lying heads and points, the whole very happy.[31]

De Latocnaye seems to have known of this meeting, but his representation of the wooing of Londonderry's tenants was a little different, *"Man is a sheep everywhere; they had much trouble getting the first ten or twelve to join and in the days following, seven or eight hundred came forward."*[32]

Londonderry managed to engineer a Declaration of their loyalty from the citizens of Newtownards at this time, but he did not receive the endorsement of government policy he would have liked. The freethinking men of Ards had added their own qualifications to their commitment:

We, the inhabitants of the town and parish of Newtownards assembled ... when a foreign enemy threatens our shores ... declare that we consider the constitution in its purity as one of the noblest systems that was ever created by the wisdom of man, and we are willing to take up arms in its defence, but at the same time we would be wanting in duty to ourselves ... did we not declare our convictions that many abuses and corruptions have crept into the constitution.

In the Declaration the 68 signatories confirm their recent disagreements with Lord Londonderry, but assert their attachment to his Lordship as a landlord and their esteem for his character as a magistrate and as a man. This seems to be no more than an insurance against any future unpleasantness, because they insist on their determination to continue seeking every constitutional method of granting an ample reform of parliament that would include all religious persuasions. They declare they have no objection to signing the Oath of Allegiance necessary for forming a Yeomanry corps, but only when the requirement to do so becomes universally applicable.[33]

Lord Londonderry took this to mean that the tide seemed to be turning in his favour. He was soon complaining to Lord Molesworth at the Yeomanry Office in Dublin that proper equipment for a soldier was difficult to obtain. There is also a hint in his letter that a number of his yeomen were not quite full-grown:

> I am afraid that I shall be disappointed, of arms, for my Troop. On applying, in Belfast, no Pistols, or Sword Belts, were to be had; and the Swords, arrived from Dublin, instead of being light, handy Dragoon Swords, were large Basket-hilted Broadswords, such, as the heavy Horse, and Highlanders, formerly used; and could, only be handled by a Man, of great size, and Strength; but, I am sure, cou'd not be wielded, by many of the young Men I have in my Troop.

Londonderry explains that he has tried requisitioning equipment from the military stores at Newry and Charlemont without success and makes a formal request for Light Dragoon swords and pistols. In the same letter he demonstrates his serious-minded determination (not to mention his love of commas and capitals):

> My Commission only empowers me to enrol 52 Yeoman Cavalry and three Officers, but in the present State of things, it is highly expedient, to join to them, some Infantry; and I find on my Estate, I can call out, from 50, to 100, well affected, and zealous Friends, to governm't, and the defence of the Country. I would therefore wish to have a New Commission, enabling me to add a Body of dismounted Men, to my Troop; and if you will leave two Blanks, for Officers' Names, I will fill them up, then Return their Names, as I am not yet decided, who they are to be. -- You may rely upon it, I will not put a Firelock, into the Hands, of any Man, that I am not positively certain, may be depended upon.[34]

The loyal landowners of the county were not all as determined as the Stewarts. As the old year died Downshire decided to increase the pressure on such gentry and their officials. He called a meeting for Tuesday, 3rd of January 1797 for a progress report. This was not a friendly request as can be seen from a comment made to his Lordship by Patrick Savage:

> Poor Trevor, my Seneschal, is dreadfully afflicted with gout and afraid of being fined for non-attendance at Hillsborough Tuesday next. Attempting such a thing wou'd I really believe cost his Life. I shou'd hope your Lordship will be so good as to have him excus'd on the acct. of his ill State of Health.[35]

In this letter, after telling Downshire that he has had, *"the Necessity of committing another of my Tenants, to God for high treason,"* (viz. Hugh

McCleary, a Baker in Portaferry), Savage tells him that he will be able to enrol infantry but probably not cavalry.

What Savage had to an extent and Londonderry had almost completely, was the power to demand allegiance and the will to insist upon it. John Gray, a friend of the Londonderrys explained this very well with these words:

> This business has got to the alarming head it now is at, entirely by the absence of the great Landed Gentlemen for where They are settled on their Estates and have been active, the Country round them is quiet ... Mr. Stewart of Ards was at the time the French attempted a landing in the south confined to his room by a severe rheumatism and I spent many days there in my feeble attempts to sett the people around him right. I never saw more unwillingness to come forward and take the oath of allegiance than appeared among them, yet the moment he was able to show himself ... they vied in being fore [most] in acts to express their loyalty to their King and attachment to their landlord.... . This shows what may be done by a landlord that lives among his Tenants and by his example shews them the good consequences that may result from obedience to the laws -- I was personally known to them all and they knew I spoke the sentiments of Mr. Stewart, but I was not their landlord or the man they could look up to if in danger or trouble.[36]

Arbuckle would not readily have agreed with Gray. He was not a landlord himself, but his secure confidence in his position as Customs Collector often made him ready to lay criticism at what he considered the appropriate door. Londonderry's aggressive and provocative approach was not what Arbuckle thought the wisest way to proceed:

> Lord L[ondonderry] in part by his unguarded and precipitant folly did much harm. Had he quietly convoked his own tenantry at the Town Hall or at Mt. Stewart with any management of conciliation he might have done what he pleased, but the meeting being announced to be held, and its purport to be discussed at the Meeting House, it was fill'd by the ruffians of Comber and Killinchy and his treatment was such as to have been looked for from such interlopers.[37]

Arbuckle himself was still trying his best to recruit men for the Yeomanry in Donaghadee, but he only had authority over the few Revenue workers and the goodwill of some friends. The local landlords, Delacherois, Catherwood and Ker and Blackwood in Bangor, had lost the edge of their enthusiasm and the impetus for enrolment had gone. Providing one's own horse was proving difficult for all but the wealthier men, so an infantry corps seemed to be the only likely outcome:

> I am just returned from the Yeomanry meeting. Twenty have signed the resolutions but with hard tugging and lugging for cavalry -- I have not a doubt of raising a very respectable Corps of Infantry if your Lordship will give your sanction to the measure. Mr. Ker [of Portavo] came in solus - not a tenant of his wou'd join us - the utmost he cou'd obtain of a few was to say that if Colonel Blackwood cou'd raise a Corps, they wou'd join him. Possibly they depend on his not raising one, but of this I know nothing.[38]

In late 1796 stories were being carried to Camden by the informer, Leonard McNally. Not only were they correct, but the dreaded news they were bringing was that the long-expected invasion fleet, that could alter the whole course of history in Ireland, was preparing to sail. In November Bernard McSheehy, an Irish Officer in the Grande Armée, had been sent to Ireland in order to ascertain just what support a French invasion could count on. He was led to believe that there were 50,000 Irishmen trained and ready for insurrection. They already had 15,000 muskets, half as many horses, 20 cannon and capable leaders. All they were waiting for was the arrival of French forces and more weapons.

The authorities had been alarmed when General Allen's cutter, the *Olive Branch*, carrying 20,000 stand of arms and a train of artillery and camp equipment on board, had been captured by the *Audacious* a few days earlier in that December of 1796. The relief that such ordnance had been kept out of the hands of dangerous rebels was tempered by the fears that the ironically named *Olive Branch* might not be the only vessel supplying arms to Ireland. It might presage something worse.[39]

These fears were justified. On the 16th of December 1796 l'Amiral Justin Bonaventure Morard de Galles, with a fleet of seventeen ships of the line, thirteen frigates and numerous tarzeur transports, slipped past the British blockade of the Gullet of Brest and out into the Atlantic aiming for a landfall in Ireland. The transports were carrying enough muskets to arm the entire Irish contingent when they met. Scattered through the fleet were 15,000 seasoned French troops and two gentlemen named General Lazare Hoche and Adjutant-General Smith. The former was at the time the most famous soldier in France in those days before Bonaparte had won his first great victories. The latter was better known in Ireland as Theobald Wolfe Tone.

Hoche, the French hero of the campaigns in Brittany and the Vendée, was eager to help the United Irishmen, the French Directory and himself by attempting a sea-borne invasion. All he and de Galles had to do was avoid the Royal Navy and make a secure landfall in Ireland. This island would quickly cease to be British and would become an outpost of the French Empire.

But the insular character of the British kingdoms has preserved their integrity innumerable times in history. Neither prehistoric invaders, Julius Caesar, Celts, Angles, Saxons, Vikings, William of Normandy, Philip of Spain nor William of Orange had been able simply to march across a land frontier when it suited them. For a continental European to invade England, Ireland, Scotland or Wales they had to cross the North Sea, the English Channel or the seas west of the Scilly Isles and around Fastnet Rock. This last stretch of water is infamous and not without reason.

De Galles's French fleet was in trouble from the start. The *Fraternité* collided with other ships; the 74-gun *Séduisant* ran on to the notorious Pointe du Raz in Brittany with the loss of 1300 men; and many ships became separated from the main convoy by fog and storm. It has been suggested that the famous, 'Protestant wind' was not the only factor responsible for the difficulties of the French. Not every captain was as enthusiastic to help Ireland or fight 'les Anglais' as Hoche was and for them such reluctance could have caused as much delay as the storm.

Hoche was convinced that his own Captain had deliberately become separated from the rest of the fleet. Amazingly too, not one British ship had been sighted the whole way from Brest to Ireland. The squadron of seven British frigates and the 74-gun *Powerful* based in Cobh were all embarrassingly unfit for duty in those crucial days.

In separate near-actions the *Druid* and the *Powerful* did try to draw French ships into battle but the latter had stood off and declined action. It would take some time before the British could mount a force sufficient to deal with this French menace. Messages of despair were being sent from Cobh to the Admiralty, *"Every man in the Harbour is working to get the Ships ready, but unfortunately they are in a bad plight -- scarce a rope or sail fit to go to sea with."* [40]

Three days before Christmas, fifteen ships reached Bantry Bay in the south-west corner of Ireland and apparent safety. That night the weather changed. Snow came in on a biting east wind and no landing could be contemplated. Richard White of Seafield Park, near Bantry, took command of the local Yeomanry corps and sent horsemen to alert local military commanders such as General Eyre Coote, commander at Bandon. His simple message that the French had arrived would later be incorporated into a rebel song:

> The French are in the Bay! They'll be here without delay.
> And the Orange will decay, says the Sean Bhean Bhocht. [41]

General William Dalrymple, who was now in command in Cork, was as agitated as anyone in Ireland to hear this news. Hurry, doubt and confusion were the order of the day. The cavalry suddenly found that they did not have enough horses; the artillery discovered that they had been supplied with nine-pound shot for their six-pound cannons. Dalrymple's main concern in his posting seems to have been to procure every delicacy he could for his dinner table. Yeomen attached to his forces were often, *"obliged to ride express ten or fifteen miles to procure Cayenne pepper for his soup and capers for his favourite sauce."* [42]

There was great division, then and later, about the wisdom of the choice of Bantry Bay for the French landing, so remote was it from the real seat of discord in the north. Just a few days later one observer recorded his relief, *"I fear had they appeared in the Lough of Belfast instead of where they did, it might have been otherwise."* [43]

Tone himself had always been in favour of a landing in the northern counties of Down or Antrim, with a preference for Belfast. Later, in his Journal, on 14th of August 1797, he wrote:

> It was indispensable that the landing should be effected in Down or Antrim, but especially the former where there were in June last twenty-four regiments of a thousand men each, ready organised with their officers and sub-officers. [44]

By the 27th of December most of the French ships had weighed anchor and sailed for their home ports while others had been blown far out into the Atlantic by the storms. Richard White was honoured with the title of Lord Bantry for his good work while the French were in the Bay; and all over Ireland lessons to take into 1797 were being learned. The threat of invasion was over, at least for a while.

Many in Ireland had not even heard of the presence of the French until they had sailed away. On New Year's Day James Arbuckle wrote an indignant letter from his Custom House to Robert Ross at the Customs Board. Making it abundantly clear how important he considers his post to be, he fulminates that the first he had heard of the intended invasion was from the official State Bulletin he had received that morning. He declares that had it not been for this paper:

> I shd. have known just abt.as much of our Invaders as if I had been an Inhabitant of Shetland or St. Kilda – no Dublin paper arrives at this Hamlet. It is a shame … that Government don't supply their Collector with a newspaper favourable to monarchy and our blessed Constitution… . I deem it somewhat singular, that at such a Crisis, neither Castle nor Board shd. intimate Instructions to Collectors.[45]

It is instructive to see how comparatively quickly word of the attempted landing had reached the rebel leadership in the north of Ireland. The Rev. Doctor Steel Dickson of Portaferry would later deny it, but he had received the news that the French were in Irish waters some days before Arbuckle and had already set out for Dublin on Christmas Day. According to rumour he and others were assembling there to attend a National Meeting of the United Irishmen to plan how best to conduct the conquest of Ireland. The well-informed Londonderry received a letter on the subject, which caused him sufficient concern to write immediately to Lord Molesworth at the Yeomanry office in Dublin:

> I hear, this day, from Portaferry, that Doctor Dixon, the dissenting Clergyman, of that Place, is now in Dublin, as a Delegate, of the United Irishmen, from this Part of the Country, to attend a National Meeting of the Body, now assembled in Dublin, and will remain there a Fortnight. He is a dangerous Man, deep in their Secrets. – and if not laid hold of, immediately; shou'd be well watched.[46]

The message to Londonderry was probably sent to him by Patrick

Savage, the son of Dickson's great enemy, Charles Trotter Savage of Portaferry, who would have been keeping a close watch on Dickson's movements. Savage had written to Lord Downshire with the same information:

> Portaferry, 26th December 1796.
>
> The Revd. Doctor Dickson, I have just now heard, set off yesterday even'g for Dublin; I think it wou'd be a good thing to have him watch'd, and by no Means be allow'd to see, or hold any Communication, with any of the close prisoners … now in Kilmainham.

Downshire was in no doubt what could happen if Dickson and other colonels met with the thinkers and planners in the Dublin gaols. He had never been happy with their status as political prisoners, with decent standards of comfort, visits from friends and family and access to materials for publicising their views outside. Enclosing Savage's letter to the now re-appointed Under-Secretary Cooke, Downshire cannot resist adding a piece of advice for Cooke to pass on to Castlereagh and Camden:

> My Dear Cook,
>
> The enclosed came to my hand last night. I think it of consequence, but if your Belfast gentry [in Kilmainham] are allowed to see their friends, have pen and Ink, and walk about, no watching will prevent mischief.[47]

Steel Dickson told a totally different story about these few days. He claimed that in October, a number of his congregation members had been taken by Castlereagh and Colonel Savage as prisoners to Portaferry House and thence to Downpatrick Gaol. One of these, a poor weaver called Carr (a man Dickson claimed was personally unknown to him) had been taken directly to Kilmainham because it was thought likely that his evidence could convict Dickson of treason.

Dickson's story was that, as a conscientious parson, he visited those of his flock in Downpatrick every week until December, when a similar pastoral responsibility obliged him to journey to Dublin to see the prisoners at Kilmainham. Whilst in the new gaol he was told that Carr was being badly treated in solitary confinement because, *"his information fell short of his promises."*

The remand prisoners took Dickson into the exercise yard, where they threw a ball through a high open window into Carr's cell to bring him to the bars of the window. He had no reluctance to speak with Dickson, because he did not know him at all. To Dickson's astonishment, the prisoner declared before a number of witnesses assembled in the yard that, *"a thousand pounds was to be his reward"* upon Dickson's conviction.

Buoyed up by the knowledge that the other prisoners would keep reminding Carr that they had all witnessed what he had confessed, Dickson returned north and continued with his usual work. If Dickson and others really did have a National Meeting in Dublin at that time, it is not recorded anywhere as such.

1. Maj. Geo. Matthews at Hillsborough to Downshire in London, 9th May 1796, (Downshire Papers, PRONI, D/607/D/058).

2. Lord Londonderry to the Marquis of Downshire, 2nd November 1796, (Rebellion Papers, NAI, 620/26/5).

3. Rev. John Cleland, no date, (Lytton White Papers, PRONI, D/714/2/24).

4. Mrs. M McTier at Belfast to Dr Wm. Drennan in Dublin, March 17th 1797, (Drennan Papers, PRONI, D591/652).

5. Marquis of Downshire, Hillsborough to Thomas Pelham, 22nd November 1796, (Rebellion Papers, NAI, 620/26/11).

6. Londonderry to Downshire, 2nd November 1796, (Rebellion Papers, NAI, 620/26/5).

7. James Arbuckle, Donaghadee, to Downshire, 20th October 1796, (Downshire Papers, PRONI, D/607/D/243).

8. Lord Camden to Downshire, 3rd August 1796, (Downshire Papers, PRONI, D/607/D/110).

9. *Northern Star*, 16-20 April 1795, p. 2.

10. Lord Downshire in a circular letter to all Down gentlemen, 31st August 1796, (Downshire Papers, PRONI, D/607/D/63).

11. Lord Camden, Dublin Castle to Downshire, 11th September 1796, (Downshire Papers, PRONI, D/607/D/110).

12. H. Montgomery Hyde, *The Rise of Castlereagh*, London, 1933, p. 153.

13. Charles Teeling, pp.12-15, and A.T.Q. Stewart, *The Summer Soldiers*, Belfast, 1995, pp. 23-25.

14. The Chevalier de la Tocnaye, pp. 208-210.

15. *Ibid*, 7-11 November 1796, p.2.

16. A.T.Q. Stewart, pp. 26-29 and Jonathan Bardon, *A History of Ulster*, Belfast, 1992, p. 230.

17. *Northern Star*, 11-14 November 1796, p. 3.

18. Pharis Martin, Magheradroll, B'Hinch to Dublin Castle, 16 November 1796, (Rebellion Papers, NAI, 620/26/55).

19. Lord Castlereagh from Mount Stewart, to his wife, Emily Hobart, daughter of an earlier Lord Lieutenant, quoted in H. Montgomery Hyde, *The Rise of Castlereagh*, London, 1933, p. 165.

20. *Northern Star*, 18-21 November 1796, p. 3.

21. Thomas Pelham, writing from the Viceregal Lodge, Phoenix Park to Lord Downshire, 29th September 1796, (Downshire Papers, PRONI, D/607/D/206).

22. Patrick Savage from Mt. Stewart to Lord Downshire, 19th October 1796, (Downshire Papers, PRONI, D/607/D/241.

23. Patrick Savage, Portaferry to Downshire, 20th October 1796, (Downshire Papers, PRONI, D/607/D/245).

24. Savage to Downshire, 24th October 1796, (Downshire Papers, PRONI, D/607/D/252).

25. Savage to Downshire, 29th October 1796, (Downshire Papers, PRONI, D/607/D/264).

26. Humphrey Galbraith, Donaghadee, to Downshire, 13th October 1796, (Downshire Papers, PRONI, D/607/D/232.

27. Arbuckle to Downshire, 11th October 1796, (Downshire Papers, PRONI, D/607/D/230).

28. Arbuckle to Downshire, 18th October 1796, (Downshire Papers, PRONI, D/607/D/240).

29. General Nugent, Carnbane to Downshire, 6th November 1796, (Downshire Papers, PRONI, D/607/D/289).

30. Mrs. Martha McTier to William Drennan, 29th November 1796, (Drennan MSS, PRONI, D/591/640), quoted in Stewart, pp. 17-18.

31. Castlereagh to his wife, quoted in H. Montgomery Hyde, p. 169.

32. De Latocnaye, p. 225.

33. Newtownards Declaration, No date, (Lowry Papers, PRONI, Mic. 506 Reel 1. D/1494/2/24R).

34. Lord Londonderry to Lord Molesworth, Not Dated but certainly December 1796, (Rebellion Papers, NAI, 620/28/2).

35. Patrick Savage, in a letter to Downshire, which the latter passed on to Under-Secretary Cooke at Dublin Castle, 26th December 1796, (Rebellion Papers, NAI, 620/26/159).

36. John Gray, Letterkenny to Rt. Hon Sackville Hamilton of Merrion Square, Dublin 27th March 1797, (Rebellion Papers, NAI, 620/29/116).

37. Arbuckle, Donaghadee, to Downshire, 20th October 1796, (Downshire Papers, PRONI, D/607/D/243.

38. Arbuckle, Donaghadee, to Downshire, 6th February 1797, (Downshire Papers, PRONI, D/607/E/083).

39. Thomas Pelham, Phoenix Park to Lord Carhampton, Carhampton and Robert Ross, Dublin to Lord Downshire, (all Downshire Papers, PRONI, D/607/D/383, D/607/D/388 and D/607/D/386).

40. Despatch from an anonymous Naval Officer to the Admiralty, 1st January 1797, 11 o'clock, Sunday Morning, Cove of Cork, (Rebellion Papers, NAI, 620/28/4).

41. Georges-Denis Zimmermann, *Songs of the Irish Rebellion: Political Street Ballads and Rebel Songs, 1780-1900*, Dublin, 1967, p. 133.

42. Teeling, p. 39.

43. James Brownlow in a letter to Lord Darnley, 29th December 1796, (Collection of Manuscript letters, NAI).

44. Wolfe Tone, his private *Journal*, 14th August 1797, quoted in Charles Dickson, *Revolt in the North, Antrim and Down in 1798*, Dublin and London, 1960, p.102.

45. Arbuckle to Robert Ross at the Customs Board, 1st January 1797, (Downshire Papers, PRONI, D/607/E/1).

46. Lord Londonderry to Lord Molesworth, Not dated, but end of December 1796, (Rebellion Papers, NAI, 620/28/2).

47. Lord Downshire to Edward Cooke at Dublin Castle, Not dated, but 27th December 1796 from its context, (Rebellion Papers, NAI, 620/26/159).

A Harp
New-Strung

From the east to the west blow the trumpet to arms!
Through the land let the sound of it flee;
Let the far and the near all unite with a cheer
In defence of our Liberty Tree.

Thomas Paine,
The Rights of Man, Part 2, 1792

By early 1797 the atmosphere in County Down had become very tense indeed and anti-government feeling was at its highest level. With the benefit of hindsight the conclusion is inescapable that if the United Irishmen were ever to succeed in overthrowing the Dublin government, it should have been in the spring or summer of that year. The people were ready; the government was at its lowest ebb; the French had come once (and had given the rebels the encouragement that they could come again) and, given that some of the strategists were locked up in Kilmainham or elsewhere, the command structures were as organised as they would ever be.

Had the rebellion broken out in earnest a year earlier than it did, there is little doubt that the nature of it would have been quite different. With the support of the French, the rebels might have been able to declare a Republic within days and, just as with successful leaders like Washington and Bonaparte, the world would have remembered Wolfe Tone, Robert Simms and Steel Dickson as the men who had ushered in a new dawn.

Of course, even with French support they may still have failed. However, it is certain that they would have been much more difficult to defeat in that year of 1797, especially in the North. The Crown forces were still inefficiently organised due to their complacency and the strength and vigour of the United Irishmen had yet to be emasculated by the ravages of the legion of informers. Either way a rebellion in 1797 would largely have been fought in counties Antrim and Down and would undoubtedly have had a strongly Presbyterian flavour.

When the rebellion did begin in May 1798 it surprised everyone, even United men, by starting in Dublin and even more startlingly, by breaking out soon afterwards in such enormous numbers and ferocity in County Wexford. Until the summer of '98 neither had been considered to have a large enough groundswell of popular support to be worrisome.

Just over a year earlier things had been much different. During those fraught months of early 1797, it was the Ulster-Scots counties of Down and Antrim and, most especially, the hot-beds of disaffection of the Ards and north Down that formed the kernel of discontent.

When General Lake spoke to Lords Downshire, Londonderry and Castlereagh he discovered that all three of them had been in frequent and regular correspondence with Ireland's Chief Secretary, Thomas Pelham. Indeed, it later became apparent that the vast bulk of the correspondence Pelham had received about rebellious activities had originated in the Ards.[1] Londonderry, of course, was in regular contact with his brother-in-law, Lord-Lieutenant Camden. Lord Downshire's regular correspondents had always kept him up to date with happenings in their home localities and in turn Downshire passed on to Dublin Castle anything he considered of interest.

One of his regular correspondents, James Arbuckle, let his Lordship know everything of interest in the Packet port and anything concerning cross-channel activities. In February 1797 he wrote a hurried letter to Downshire telling what he had recently learned:

> Every appearance announces a very speedy explosion of violence in this part of the country. I am sure it is the same all over. The preparations being made are both great and rapid. I think it is very silly to fritter away the military force as men has happened lately – 15 or 16 here, as many at Bangor, the same at Kircubbin, the same at Comber. Should the rebellion break out each detachment of troops will fall in turn and their arms will go to the rebels.

I heard today that the rebels propose to rise even should the French not invade, in less than 3 weeks. Pikes and pike shafts are being made in large numbers. Within the last week more than 100 ash trees have been cut in Mr. Ker's plantation at Portavo, some on Finlay's farm, and 9 large ash poles were carried off one night out of my own farmyard at Ballywilliam House. On Thursday night a large barrel of long ash poles was taken away off the Parade at the end of the pier, all I am certain for the making of pikes.

I am very worried about the safety of the Arms chest and the Valuables chest on board the Packet boats, and about their three-Pounder guns. For the present I request your Lordship not to send gunpowder for the cannons in quantity more than one barrel at a time.

I think I shall ask Hull to have the powder and the guns taken to the Barrack on Millisle Road for safe keeping.[2]

The Marquis was hearing similar stories from a number of correspondents, usually conveying their trepidation, alarm and fear. A day or two after Arbuckle's letter Downshire heard about the re-arrest of Thomas Maxwell, a hugely popular leader of the United Irishmen in Comber. Six hundred armed men had blocked the Killinchy road from Comber to Downpatrick, forcing the authorities to take Maxwell to Belfast. What Arbuckle and Downshire were both all too aware of was that this man had been imprisoned the year before. Lord Castlereagh himself had seen the crowds that had assembled to pick his potatoes and now some months later he had an even greater degree of popular support, which was of great concern. Downshire wrote all of this to Edward Cooke on the 24th of February. The whole tone of his letter is gloomy, but his closing paragraph is a superb construction of contempt for the complacency and ignorance of the officials safe in Dublin, together with unmistakable directions for their immediate course of action:

...I wish you and your Privy Council were obliged to live here for three weeks. You would all by acclamation, and I dare say in the utmost haste and irregularity, and without attending to precise words or form, be for proclaiming not only this county but also Belfast and the Province of Ulster. If there is a Rebellion and His Majesty's loyal subjects murdered, let it be on Your Heads who are comfortably sitting in your closets in Dublin and pretending to decide without knowing really how bad we who reside in this country know the state of it to be.[3]

Downshire's letter to the Castle was a large load of straw to be put on the camel's back. Four days later the last straw arrived.

On the 27th of February Downshire's old political rival, Lord Londonderry, wrote directly to Lord Camden. He told him what he thought of a system of law enforcement that would permit a band of armed ruffians to close the King's highway as had happened upon the arrest of Maxwell. He added some instances of yeomen being threatened with death for enrolling. The night before he wrote, one of his own yeomen, a wealthy farmer called Cumming, was attacked at his home of Unicarval House, also near Comber. The rebels had demanded any weapons he possessed and when he supported his refusal to give them up by rashly pointing a blunderbuss at them, they had beaten his brains out with the butt end of a musket.

Lord Londonderry was in no doubt as to the solution to the problem:

> A Large Body of Troops must be marched into this Part of the Country and the Inhabitants disarmed; and made sensible of the efficacy of Martial Law, for be assured, the Civil Power is now, set at defiance here; and they think they are able to cope with the Military... God send us better times.[4]

If Londonderry was in a state of apprehension, then notice would have to be taken. If he was speaking in concert with a man such as Lord Downshire, the man government most respected in the north and a man with whom Londonderry regularly disagreed, then action was certainly necessary. Possibly the close family ties between the Lord Lieutenant and the Stewarts helped expedite matters, because the day after Camden received Londonderry's letter advocating Martial Law, Pelham sent General Lake instructions to Proclaim the North.

Pelham's written orders are a clear indicator of the Castle's concerns about the north of Ireland and the discontent in the country of the Ards in particular. They show that both he and Camden were indeed worried and that they realised that whatever unease there was, it must be dealt with strictly and soon. Pelham's letter, which conveyed the Lord Lieutenant's views to Lake, also contained the formal text of the Proclamation. This effectively was to put large parts of the north of Ireland under very strict control, although not quite Martial Law. The only permitted arms in those areas were to be strictly in the hands of the military. Pelham's words to Lake instructed him thus:

> His Excellency [Lord Lieutenant Camden] has commanded me to communicate to you his positive orders that you take the most immediate and decisive measures for disposing of the military force under your command, aided by the Yeomanry Corps for immediately disarming all persons who shall not bear His Majesty's Commission or are acting under persons so commissioned or persons holding commissions under the authority of the Yeomanry Act.[5]

However his accompanying letter to Lake, in contrast, is less formal. Pelham tacitly admits where his information has come from, but implies that the situation, whilst serious, is containable. He considers that most of the North must be proclaimed. When he suggests to General Lake that he take advice from the three most influential lords in north Down and the Ards and only these three, it seems clear that he considers that the best organised and most determined dissent is very localized there:

> The Marquess of Downshire and Lord Londonderry are on the spot and Lord Castlereagh will be with you tomorrow. They will be able to give you the best advice with regard to the best places.[6]

Lake's second-in-command, Major-General George Nugent, wrote to Downshire a week after the Proclamation confirming the view that the crucible of discontent was in the Ards area and explaining how the instructions from Dublin were to be implemented:

> It is General Lake's intention to search every suspected neighbourhood for arms &c in the first place and then the other parts of the district. Your Lordship's and Lord Castlereagh's advice determined him to begin with the Ards and the other side of Lough Strangford.[7]

The Proclamation, enunciating its severe measures, was issued on 13th March in Belfast. Posters and handbills shouted the warning that every person must be off the streets by 10 o'clock each night and that soldiers had the right to enter property after that time to establish the observance of the curfew and to search for arms. Anyone found breaking the curfew was liable to be fined the considerable sum of five shillings. If they could not pay they could expect to receive one hundred lashes.[8]

On a visit home to Mount Stewart, Castlereagh wrote about the calming effects of the Proclamation, although he warns that the principal actors in the drama had not been noticeably affected:

> At first the banditti were actively employed every night in taking arms, but since the sweep made by General Lake, a few transmissions to the [prison] tender, and some apprehension of a still more severe rebuke if the violence was persisted in, matters have subsided at least in this neighbourhood…. the leaders of the disaffected party do not seem at all dispirited, which arises I conclude from expectations they have of another effort being made in their favour on the part of the enemy.[9]

James Arbuckle too was anxious to have the stings taken out of the rebels' tails. He was extremely critical of the way the Lord Lieutenant's Proclamation was being enforced. He complained to Downshire that with the loyal farmers, persuasion was preferable to coercion:

> This disarmament, I fear, will be unproductive of intended effect – the military glean but few arms. I have had nearly forty firelocks voluntarily brought in… I really am of opinion that the farmers in this area are well disposed and wholly adverse to insurgency.

Arbuckle may have been too complacent about the loyalty of his neighbours and his criticisms may have been prompted by the gross insult he felt that a senior government representative like himself had been lumped in with the general herd, *"When I shall have the pleasure to see General Lake I will take the liberty to intimate, that in his proclamation for disarming the country, he ought to have excepted the Officers of Revenue."*[10]

Writing yet another letter to her brother, Mrs. McTier unwittingly gives strong support to what Arbuckle was telling Downshire, *"Murders and assassinations are dreadful subjects, but common here… The country people treat the officers well, ask them to breakfast &c. and give them old rusty guns."* Mrs. McTier can always be relied on to show a little sympathy with the plight of the ordinary people who had become embroiled in the conflict, especially when their own sympathies appear to chime with her brother's political views. A fortnight after the Proclamation she was telling Drennan about the activities contingent upon discovering weapons and expecting neighbour to inform on neighbour. She does not like the daily interning of suspected, but unconvicted, rebels on the prison tender, *Postlethwaite,* in the Pool of Garmoyle. As a touching example, she tells her brother a story:

> On the quay a decent man who was seeing others shipped off was asked, "What has that man now going done?" "Nothing," replied the other, "but lived in peace and union with his neighbour. I have the honour of being his father."[11]

Almost in the same postbag Lord Downshire expressed his derision while informing Pelham that the arms in the countryside have been taken in great quantities – most of them unfortunately from the wrong people:

> The well-affected & good subjects was the great contributor, many brought the arms voluntarily. …The Papists, the United Irishmen, the turbulent, the disaffected, the Vagabonds concealed & denied having arms & are left now in the liberty of destroying the property, murdering the innocent & good subjects.[12]

In a scarcely veiled criticism of Lake's method of application of the measure he himself sought, Downshire goes on to tell Pelham that he has decided that it is better to return arms to those men he considers sound – telling them the arms were only taken from them to save them from attack by robbers.

It would be wrong to think that all thoughts were of arrests and disarming. The same day, or possibly the one following, Downshire wrote to Pelham about some of the logistical difficulties of conflict resolution. From his position as patron of the Donaghadee Packet Service he is able to answer Pelham's enquiries about capabilities and tariffs for transporting troops to the province of Ulster. He explains that their Post Office duties must be maintained, but that every effort could be made to keep the fast sailing cutters plying to and from Scotland continuously, wind and tide permitting, *The [two] Packets can conveniently carry in moderate weather from 80 to 100 men, but cannot contain more than 8 horses, the price is fixed.*

He wisely does not commit himself, but this would have meant a maximum of three return journeys per ship per day, or six hundred troops each day and with the vagaries of weather often a good deal less than that. He does not press the matter, probably because he recognises that Dublin Castle is still only exploring contingencies. He concludes his long letter with a warning that a large number of young men of suspect loyalties have disappeared for some past days, probably training:

> to form a corps either of guides to the United Irish army or to the French army in case it comes to Ireland. Where the most vulnerable part of the country is where the most obnoxious People live. I think this Hint is worthy of attention. I have discovered letters are conveyed by a beggar woman and a little boy to different parts to and from very suspected characters.[13]

In their later years many rebels who survived the rebellion when it did eventually break out, must have believed that had they taken the tide when it was at its flood in late March 1797 it would have been better able to take them on to inevitable victory. Government officials who were privy to the relaxed state of preparedness in Ulster at the time of Proclamation in March 1797, with a similar sharpness of hindsight, might privately have confessed that they were extremely lucky to receive what the following month brought them.

The news of the sighting of the French fleet in Bantry Bay had almost scared the life out of the loyal population of Ireland. Simultaneously it had given all the island's rebels a surge of encouragement. When the French had then sailed away again the rebels initially were distraught and the loyalists relieved. Then everyone stopped to consider what such an occurrence really meant. It was the view of both sides that if the Directoire were interested enough to send a French fleet once, they could probably be persuaded to do so once again. The United Irishmen met frequently to organise a full readiness for that happy day and Government and Dublin Castle began to plan carefully how they could best deal with such an event if and when it did happen.

Pitt and his government in London felt beleaguered. The French seemed to have defeated most of continental Europe and made peace with the rest. The British felt as though they were standing alone. Now on top of all, their great enemy was conspiring with elements no longer loyal to King George in order to sneak round behind his back. The

Royal Navy still had command of the sea, but the recent French expedition had shown that Britannia's rule over the waves was no longer as all-powerful a command as many had once thought it.

For so long had they thought of the French as their deadliest enemy, that the governments in both London and Dublin both assumed that the dissidents in Ireland could pose a real threat to the kingdoms only if France provided the bulk of the brains and brawn. They were well aware that there were many in Ireland who were very discontented with their government, but seemed not to have recognised how resolute and determined the United Irishmen were to overthrow it. Nor did they recognise just how widely organised the System was. They would soon find out.

1. Thomas Pelham, Dublin Castle to General Lake, 3rd March 1797, (Downshire Papers, PRONI, D/607/E/148 & 149).

2. James Arbuckle to Downshire, 19th February 1797, (Downshire Papers, PRONI, D/607/E/110).

3. Marquis of Downshire to Edward Cooke, 24th February 1797, (Rebellion Papers, NAI, 620/28/295).

4. Lord Londonderry, Mountstewart to the Lord Lieutenant Earl Camden, Sent 28th February 1797, Received 2nd March 1797, (Rebellion Papers, NAI, 620/29/3).

5. Thomas Pelham, Dublin Castle to General Lake, 3rd March 1797, (Downshire Papers, PRONI, D/607/E/148).

6. Pelham to Lake, 3rd March 1797, (Downshire Papers, PRONI, D/607/E/149).

7. General Nugent to Downshire, 11th March 1797, (Downshire Papers, PRONI, D/607/E/173).

8. Trevor McCavery, *Reformers, Reactionaries and Revolutionaries: Opinion in North Down and the Ards in the 1790s*, Ulster Local Studies, Vol. 18, No. 2, Belfast, 1997, p. 86.

9. Lord Castlereagh to Thos. Pelham, 7th April 1797, quoted in H. Montgomery Hyde, *The Rise of Castlereagh*, London, 1933, pp. 180-181.

10 Arbuckle to Downshire, 15th March 1797, (Downshire Papers, PRONI, D/607/E/192).

11. Mrs. M McTier, Cabin Hill, Dundonald, near Belfast, to Dr Wm. Drennan in Dublin, March 17th 1797, (Drennan Papers, PRONI, D/591/652).

12. Lord Downshire to Thos. Pelham, Sunday morning, 26 March 1797, (Rebellion Papers, NAI, 620/29/114).

13. Marquis of Downshire to Thomas Pelham, 28th March 1797, (Rebellion Papers, NAI, 620/29/119).

THE DONAGHADEE RESOLUTIONS

Society in every state is a blessing, but government,
even in its best state is but a necessary evil;
in its worst state, an intolerable one.

Thomas Paine,
The Rights of Man, 1791.

At 8 o'clock on the evening of Friday the 14th of April 1797, three officers of the Royal Artillery Company went into Alexander's Public House in Belfast. Colonel Barber, Lieutenant Ellison and Mr. Fox, the Storekeeper of the Ordnance, were not there to enjoy the crack. They had with them a platoon of soldiers and Mr. Atkinson, the High Constable of Belfast and they had come to make some discoveries.

In addition to his Artillery responsibilities, Colonel Lucius Barber had another position with the army. Secretly he was the head of Intelligence gathering and he had just received orders from the army's northern commander, Lieutenant-General Gerard Lake.[1] These orders were the result of a message that had come from two informers, Edward John Newell and Robert Murdoch. Newell, who was originally from Downpatrick, was a painter of portrait miniatures and Murdoch was a hearth-money collector from Belfast. Newell had at one time been an enthusiastic member of the Catholic Defenders and in 1796 both he and Murdoch had joined the Belfast Society of the United Irishmen. Some time early in 1797 they had been 'turned' by an unknown agent of Dublin Castle. Incredibly quickly the two men became very important to the authorities and were given ever-growing support. By April they had become the Belfast eyes and ears of Thomas Pelham, the Chief-Secretary to the Lord Lieutenant.

Newell sometimes worked with informers other than Murdoch, most colourfully with a Portaferry girl called Bell Martin. Bell, Bella, or Elizabeth, was from a poor family, but had been blessed with a most comely appearance. In the time-honoured fashion for such favoured girls, she had moved to Belfast and gone on the streets. When Newell was associating with her she was consorting with the soldiers of Blaris Camp, first selling herself to them and then selling on their disloyal boastings, through Newell, to Colonel Barber.[2]

Newell had great confidence in his privileged position because he had in his possession an amazingly frank letter from the Under-Secretary for Ireland, Mr. Edward Cooke. This told him with emphasis, *"You shall have unlimited powers, take up all you know, no matter about warrants, you can get them afterwards when you know their names. Gen. Lake and Col. Barber will assist you in anything."*[3]

This carte blanche was remuneration for services rendered. Another common reward for such service is the alienation of friends and family. Robert Newell wrote to the *Northern Star* disassociating himself and his family from his brother and alerting the people of Belfast that Edward was, *"in the practice of going through the town of Belfast disguised in the dress of a light horseman, with his face blackened and accompanied by a guard of soldiers, pointing out certain individuals who have in consequence been immediately apprehended and put in prison."*[4]

The relationship between the Castle, Newell and Murdoch was not one of mutual respect and admiration. In his book, Newell is most uncomplimentary about Under-Secretary Cooke and colleagues such as the Privy Councillor, Lieutenant-Colonel Robert Ross. He describes a visit to: *"that arch betrayer of every honest heart, the diabolical agent of the sanguinary Pitt, – the damned insinuating Cooke."* Newell also tells of the occasion when he was conducted to Cooke's office by, *"that old pander of iniquity, Col. Ross, there I met with all that sweetness of reception, that cringing servility and fulsome flattery such sycophants ever use to those whom they wish to seduce to their own ends."*[5]

Some time later an unknown witness described Newell as using in conversation the words, *"such a set of old whores as composed the Committee of the Lords."* [6]

Newell and Murdoch were shrewd enough to use a go-between to take information to Barber. Newell even boasted that the information for the raid on John Alexander's had been carried to Intelligence by Robert Kingsmill Esq., an acquaintance of Lord Downshire's. With his usual bluntness of description, Newell depicts this man as, *"the cowardly commandant of the Castlereagh [Yeomanry] cavalry, who is an honest Orange-man."*

When Barber's men entered Alexander's pub on the evening of the 14th of April they discovered three simultaneous meetings of United Irish Committee. Fox and Ellison each found a room where a committee was actually meeting, their papers still on the tables before them. Simultaneously, Belfast's High Constable, Atkinson, found papers purporting to belong to another Committee or Society, viz. the eightieth Society.[7]

A number of the United Irishmen present were taken up and put into temporary custody. Lake was informed of the arrests and the seized papers. He immediately passed on his prisoners and papers to his Commander-in-Chief, Lord Carhampton, and wrote to Pelham at the Castle. It is clear that Lake did not at first realise the full significance of what he had found:

> In consequence of Newell's information I searched the house of Alexander, a publican, in Belfast, & took up thirty-one United Irishmen assembled for their treasonable practices, as the papers which Lord Carhampton will give you will convince you.

Lake moans that he was frustrated that they had not arrested some senior United Irishmen at Alexander's, because he was not overly impressed with the calibre of the men who had been captured and that he now had to deal with, *"I presume they should all go on the tender as they are low people. ... I ... wish we may find the papers of these [other] gentry, as I think from some of them very material intelligence must be gained."* [8]

Putting those suspected of being United Irishmen on board the tender in Belfast Lough was to hold them there until they could be taken to The Nore or Spithead to be pressed into naval service. Lake was not happy with this arrangement. He explained to Pelham that some of the prisoners were heard to boast to their guards that they would subvert the Royal Navy as soon as they were on board a man o' war.

In Dublin Castle, Pelham soon realised that the papers taken from Alexander's were much more important than Lake had realized and more important too than the men destined for the navy. He set some intelligence operators to appraise the information contained in the papers. It was soon realised that what was contained in them was sensational. They comprised:

1. The printed Declaration and Constitution of the United Irishmen.
2. Minutes of the Proceedings of two of the Societies.
3. Reports from Provincial and County Committees.
4. A Report from the Military Committee.
5. Forms of the Oath of an Officer and of a Soldier.
6. Names of some of the Society, with the Arms that they possess.
7. Size Roll of the Society.
8. A List of the Families that have received Relief.
9. Resolutions of the united Societies of Donaghadee and its Vicinity.

Other loose Notes and Papers of their Proceedings.[9]

Two weeks later the appraised and annotated papers were back on Thomas Pelham's desk. It did not take him long to react. He was well-aware that his generals in the North felt ham-strung because they considered that the measures stated in the March 13th Proclamation were neither strict enough nor would they be effective. In the same letter that informed Pelham of the seizures at Alexander's, Lake had declared:

> The situation of this country is really most wonderfully alarming. …with Martial Law proclaimed I trust we should very shortly have all the arms in the country & put an immediate stop to the rebellion. … Genl. Knox, who is sitting by me, agrees with me entirely & says we ought to have six thousand more men than we have.[10]

Pelham may have been genuinely frightened for the safety of the country, or he may have decided quite cynically to exaggerate the significance of the seized papers for his own pragmatic reasons, but he chose to confide only in Parliament. He appears never to have put his private opinions of the importance of the papers in writing.

What is undeniable is that within days of having the contents examined by the Committee of Secrecy he was reporting their significance to the House of Commons at College Green. Reading Pelham's Report is quite extraordinary to the modern reader. Even allowing for the Secretary's having to state well-known facts for the record, what comes through is a previous lack of awareness of many things that had been going on for months in Belfast, Down and Antrim. One could readily understand government's state of ignorance as indicated by the comments below as early as 1795 or 1796, but when they are clearly dated April 1797 one can only wonder at the complacency of the Government of Ireland and Dublin Castle in the days just before these papers were discovered:

> It appears that soon after the French Revolution certain Individuals, encouraged by the Example of France, aimed at the Overthrow of the existing Laws and Constitution of this Kingdom, and the Establishment of a Republic unconnected with Great Britain.
>
> It appears to your Committee that in the original Formation of this Society, its Authors . . . held forth Catholic Emancipation and Parliamentary Reform as the ostensible Objects of their Union: but their real Purposes were to separate Great Britain from Ireland and to subvert the present Constitution.
>
> It appears to your Committee that their Hopes of Success in this apparently improbable Design are derived from their Expectations of being able to infuse into the Minds of the lower Orders of the People an Idea that they are in a State of Oppression and Misery.[11]

The information that so startled the establishment was not co-ordinated. It was a jumble of information from three different Committees, who had been meeting separately in what they thought was a safe house. Three separate United Irish Committees meeting in the one house must have included at least one County Committee (Down, Antrim or both) and an Ulster Provincial Committee. The leaders of the United Irishmen had not had time to organise and collate all the scraps of material and data, so the Secret Committee did so. What they discovered seems genuinely to have terrified most of them.

Pelham had realised that the situation was such that he must act in a number of different ways. The very next day after the seizure of the papers from Alexander's he wrote to General Lake, *"I sent this morning a Despatch containing certain Warrants which are to be executed at Belfast & which I hope may be of some service."*[12]

As General Lake wielded the iron fist, his friend, Brigadier-General James Knox, was voicing a softer word of caution about the legality of the military actions:

> General Lake can have no authority to proclaim Martial Law – The Order must come from the Lord Lieutenant & Council – All Civil Power then ceases ... nothing less... will ever disarm & subdue the North of Ireland.

Knox then tells Pelham that he has had a conversation with an influential local man who suggested that he might be able to provide some help to the beleaguered troops:

> Mr. Verner has informed me that he could enrol a considerable number of men as Supplementary Yeomen, to be attached to his Corps without Pay, if Government would give them arms - They would consist of staunch Orangemen - the only description of men in the North of Ireland that can be depended upon. He reckons upon two or three hundred.[13]

By the end of the month, Order in Council or not, Lake was sending returns of Prisoners taken in Belfast by Colonel Barber. He had been taking up strange captures, in even stranger places. One note to Pelham lists the names of 10 prisoners and, *"Four Drums taken in a house of disrepute last night, two of them large size."*[14]

In spite of all the intelligence that had been collected and the steps taken before and after the Proclamation, it was apparent that the true import and extent of what they were dealing with had not dawned on government until the discoveries in Alexander's public house in April 1797. Once they had been properly studied, these papers told Pelham that 22,922 men of County Antrim, 16,000 from Down and a total of 68,000 from the province of Ulster had sworn oaths to support the United Irishmen in an armed struggle. If they had seen other Down estimates that did not turn up until later, they would have found that there were as many as 28,597 rebel supporters recorded there.[15] These totals of eager rebels cannot be taken as entirely accurate, but they would have been considered so at the time and their magnitude was to cause great consternation.

Details of the objectives of this huge movement and their proposed methods of achieving them were also included. The Chief Secretary realised that he must bring them to the attention of the Secret Committee of the Irish House of Lords immediately. The papers were annotated, possibly by Pelham, as being, *"of great importance although neither dated nor signed, … obviously the Composition of a Person of Intelligence, who seems to have wished to conceal his being so."* Other points found among the papers included:

> Rents and Tithes are sentenced to be seized, the latter to [be] abolished after the present emergency.
> A <u>Requisition of Provisions</u> and a Revolutionary Committee resolved on.
>   … Provision to be made for the Families of those who may suffer in the War
>   … that all married men lay in Provisions for their Families for one Week,
>   … that the Society support them for four weeks longer,
>   … that Money ought not to be the principal object,
>   … but that lives ought to be freely sacrificed for Liberty.
> <u>No Person to insult Yeomen</u> as some of them may turn out <u>useful</u>.
> To set their faces against Bank Notes in order to harass Government.
> To make friends of Catholics and Orangemen, as that Plan has been adopted with success at Armagh.[16]

Of the papers seized in Alexander's the one which caused most of the agitation in Dublin Castle and which had impressed the urgency of the matter on Pelham, was the one he numbered, '9'. It was entitled, "Resolutions of the united Societies of Donaghadee and its Vicinity." and Lieutenant Ellison of the Artillery had attested in writing that the paper was genuine.

There had been such papers discovered earlier. Just three months before the seizures in Alexander's, a document entitled *The Belfast Resolutions* had been sent to Pelham. The sender was John Brown, the Sovereign of Belfast and the paper had been formally presented to him by William Sampson, one of Belfast's senior barristers. Brown had decided that it should be brought to Pelham's immediate attention. The paper had been drawn up at a "Meeting of the Inhabitants of Belfast" on 2nd January 1797. When the meeting's resolutions were read by members of the Irish establishment they did cause some anger, but largely because the thoughts expressed by the educated men of Belfast who had formulated them were so radically different from their own.

In essence the *Belfast Resolutions* stated that the representation in the Irish Parliament was the real cause of discontent in Ireland and were advocating some measure of reform. The only threat mentioned in the paper can hardly have terrified anyone. It cautioned that the citizens of Belfast were ready to arm, *"in like manner as the Volunteers,"* but only, *"if permitted by Government."*[17]

The Donaghadee Resolutions were entirely different. When they were brought to the Committee of Secrecy they caused a sensation and provoked much heated discussion. When they became more generally known to the loyal gentlemen of the country they added greatly to the sense of alarm. The Donaghadee Resolutions had suddenly raised the stakes in the game of politics. They showed that the days of radically minded democrats gently prodding the government with a few containable local disturbances of the King's Peace now appeared to be over. Here in these seized papers were militant men advocating revolution on a national scale, prepared to take the field to achieve it, requisitioning foodstuffs, proposing their own 'lawful' rents and taxes to pay the costs, threatening to confiscate the property of landed gentry and talking openly about the details of the new society they were about to achieve.

When Newell was asked to comment on what was found, he confirmed for his masters that matters really were that serious. He added that the reports of the existence of an Assassination Committee were true and even insisted that he had been a member of that secret committee of twelve United Irishmen. Their group had, he said, been formed for the purpose of assassination of Society members who were suspected of betraying it to the Government. With chilling echoes of more recent times, he added that the suspected members would not have been present at their 'trial', but if those present found a man guilty, one or two members of his 'jury' would be chosen by lot to be the instruments of his destruction. He even gave an instance of a soldier, first made drunk and then tipped over the parapet of a bridge into the River Lagan, with weights in his pockets.[18]

Pelham realised that if there really was this level of sedition then the army's state of readiness was not sufficient to counter it. Had he been privy to the then unpublished thoughts of the new commander-in-chief of the land forces in Ireland he might have been even more worried.

Sir Ralph Abercromby some time afterwards told a friend that when he arrived to take over his new command from Lord Carhampton he had found an army of over 40,000 soldiers in no state for any real military action. The cavalry did not have enough horses and the artillery had none at all for pulling the cannon. What bits of effective army did exist were scattered in very small detachments throughout the country, especially in the north, each in serious danger of being overwhelmed by a small force of rebels.[19] The papers found in Alexander's and the gravity of the inferences taken from the Donaghadee Resolutions, meant that the country was in the utmost danger, even should the French not come.

There is no record of exactly when any meeting sufficiently influential to draft such Resolutions was held in Donaghadee, who was present, nor of how the Resolutions passed at such a meeting came to be tabled at a number of Committee Meetings of the United Irishmen in Belfast. Pelham was probably wrong in his opinion that the Resolutions were the creation of one, "Person of Intelligence." It seems more likely that they were the product of a number of able but secretive minds.

Another question left begging is, "Why Donaghadee?" The small seaport was only really significant as a Packet Service terminal. There was certainly much popular support for the ideals of the United Irishmen in the town, but there was also a vigilant core of loyalist gentlemen ready to report anything untoward to the Marquis of Downshire and Dublin Castle. There had been no advertisement of any public convention held in the town, although there undoubtedly would have been secret meetings there.

The Donaghadee Resolutions were of sufficient import to have been conveyed to the County and provincial Committees of the United

Irishmen for consideration and possible adoption by them; and they had an undoubted and profound effect on Camden, Pelham and the Castle. It seems reasonable to think that, had government not discovered them when they did, the papers might later have become known nationally, perhaps as the Ulster Resolutions. They state very simply what the intentions of the United Irishmen were:

Resolutions of the United Societies of Donaghadee and its Vicinity

1stly. Resolved, that it has always been the invariable opinion of all sound philosophers, statesmen and divines, that all power is radically in the people.

2ndly Resolved, that when Tyrants, Usurpers and Oppressors, grasping at domination, or even such as are legally delegated by the People, degenerate into Tyrants, or act contrary to the trust committed to them, in that case the people ought to claim their Right and the power return to its original channel.

3rdly Resolved, that at the present Crisis the People being united should also arm, choose their Officers, and take a first, second and third Requisition of such as are able to go forth to war in defence of their rights as men. 4thly Resolved, that our Brethren in Arms be duly provided for with such things as their case and situation requires, and that means be adopted that their families may not suffer in their absence.

5thly Resolved, that to answer such emergencies a contribution be imposed upon the People in general according to their respective circumstances; Rents and Tythes shall also be considered, the latter of which, except in the present emergency, shall for ever be abolished.

6thly Resolved, that there are a great many inimical and will no doubt prove hostile to the cause of Liberty; their Estates or Property shall be confiscated and converted to the National Benefit.

7thly Resolved, that the Civil Law must always be kept up and proper men appointed to prevent Outrage in the Country and these men to be assisted by a military force when called upon and that said men shall take proper measures to support both the Inhabitants and Military with proper necessaries.

8thly Resolved, that there shall be a National (or if it be thought more eligible) a Provincial Fund where the Property of the Enemy shall be deposited and that Drafts for the above purposes shall be made as necessity shall require.

9thly Resolved, that any avowed enemy to the cause shall not have admittance when it makes its appearance, but shall be taken as Prisoners and tried by a Jury according to the law then existing and if found guilty their Property disposed of according to said Law.

10thly Resolved that Farmers or such as possess a Redundancy of victualling shall bring it forward to sale, and that the Families of such as are called off in the cause of their country shall be supplied thereby at a moderate price which shall be agreed on by the Revolutionary Committee of fit men delegated by them.

11thly Resolved, that the Wounded, the Widow and the Fatherless of such that have fought in the Cause of their Country shall be provided for or supported from the aforesaid fund.

12thly Resolved, that there shall be an Association under the name and designation of a Revolutionary Committee, composed of the best qualified and most respectable Characters, viz. one man chosen from each Society, and delegated by said Society to meet together, who shall keep and enforce the above Resolutions and take care that they be carried into effect and duly executed whenever the cause shall require.

13thly Resolved, that to act in concert with the Revolutionary Committee there shall be Magistrates appointed and vested with Executive Power which shall continue in Office for the space of six months only except in case of re-election, but if a Revolution be accomplished an annual election shall take place.

Paper-writing seized and identified by Mr. Atkinson. [High Constable of Belfast] [20]

It was immediately agreed that a Statement be made before the House of Commons to put the Members and thence the entire country, fully in the picture regarding what these United Irishmen really intended. Naturally the Resolutions themselves were not made public, neither to the House nor to the people of Ireland. In the discontented atmosphere of the day, which the members of the Secret Committee recognised, such a step would have been too risky. Better that the House should discuss a version that had been carefully edited for them.

A barefaced Pelham informed the House of Commons that the Donaghadee Resolutions and the other papers from Alexander's had come as proof of what had long been known. The United Irishmen, he affirmed, had been in contact with the French for some time and had in recent times achieved a worrying degree of influence with the Directoire and the military. Their design was:

Complete Revolution upon the French Principles and assisted by a French Invasion;

… Parliamentary Reform and Catholic Emancipation are pressed merely as means, not as their ultimate object, … [which is] subverting the Government, [and] breaking the connexion of Ireland with Great Britain.[21]

Although there is no actual mention of these objectives in any of the seized papers, Pelham stated that among their means for carrying their purpose, the United Irishmen would abolish tithes, spread false reports, destroy jurymen, *"distress government by refusing Bank Paper, engage women to attend their meetings for Potatoe digging,"* and *"wear green Ribbands and crop their hair."*[22]

There is a clever mix here of observed activity, popular perceptions and a playing on oft-expressed fears. For the Protestant gentry who were the Members of the Lords and Commons, the Donaghadee Resolutions must have raised echoes of the newspaper stories of Danton, Robespierre and Marat. What for some time had been thought of as the rumble of discontent due to liberal ideas learned from their cousins in America must now have sounded like Jacobin thunder from France. What first came to the attention of many complacent loyalists with the publication of the Donaghadee Resolutions would, over the next two years, become the dread of an Irish Reign of Terror.

That month of April 1797 had raised quite a number of concerns, all of which contrived to agitate the minds of those privy to them. The man who had led the raid on Alexander's, the Chief of Military Intelligence, Colonel Lucius Barber, had almost simultaneously received some more information from Edward Newell's friend, Bell Martin. Unaware of the extent of the connotations for the United Irishmen of the location, she had told Barber that a public house called Peggy Barclay's in Sugarhouse Entry in Belfast was the meeting place of an Assassination Committee of the United Irishmen and of the Muddlers' Club, which comprised many well-known Society members. She also had told about the attempted murder of a man called Lee in that tavern and on her evidence Lords Carhampton and Castlereagh had arrested a tailor called Joseph Cuthbert. This man was later indicted at the County Antrim Spring Assizes in Carrickfergus.

Joseph Cuthbert was never a major figure, but his trial proved to be interesting for a number of reasons. Given her well-known profession, Miss Martin was able to call an impressive collection of witnesses to attest to her good character. These sensationally included Lords Londonderry and Castlereagh, their land-agent, John Cleland and the Rev. Dr. Steel Dickson. All these men were said to have known her in the Ards before she went to Belfast. Of the four men we only know the details about her connection with Steel Dickson, because it is recorded that he had counselled her through some bad times before she had left Portaferry.

Lord Castlereagh only turned up for the first day of the trial and then pleaded a cold and excused himself thereafter. Bell Martin, although having been placed under guard, could not be found either. Cuthbert's case had to be dismissed for lack of evidence and rumour abounded. Castlereagh's political enemies quickly circulated the story that he had been more intimately involved with the young woman than was publicly admitted and that he had promised her money to help him satisfy a private grudge by convicting Cuthbert. The story went on to explain that Martin had been spirited away from her guards because of a fear that she might have to make some embarrassing revelations about Lord Castlereagh whilst under oath.

Whatever substance there was in such prurient stories, Miss Martin was effectively and quite definitely, removed from the proceedings. It is known that she did receive payment for services rendered, but only long after the court case was over. Some months later, Under-Secretary Edward Cooke entered in his Secret Service Money Book in Dublin Castle, *"Nov. 3, 1797. Paid to Bell Martin for taking her out of town, etc., £5 13s. 9d."*[23]

Government and the establishment were now aware that a deadly discontent was widespread in Ireland and they knew where it was most intense. They had been concerned by the *Olive Branch* in early December 1796,[24] then frightened by the abortive expedition of General Hoche to Bantry Bay a few days later and by the gun-running *Amitié* off the County Down coast.[25] They had assiduously read the anti-government writings in the *Northern Star*, informers had been feeding them snippets about localised occurrences with the names of suspected dissidents and now there was the news of the papers seized from Alexander's.

But God and the Royal Navy had dealt with the *Olive Branch*, Divine protection had stopped the French fleet landing in south-west Ireland and the *Amitié* had been sunk by a storm off Ardglass. Pelham recognised that if the level of discontent was perceived to be as high as the discovered papers indicated, then in the immediate future Providential deliverance might need some assistance.

1. Lt. General Gerard Lake, Newry, to Thomas Pelham, marked "Private", 16th April 1797, (Transcript of Pelham Papers, PRONI, T/755/4B/361f).

2. Charles Dickson, *Revolt in the North*, London, 1960, p. 169.

3. Edward John Newell, *The Apostasy of Newell*, London, 1798. (The italics in Newell's writings are his own.).

4. Robert Newell. *Northern Star*, 5th May 1797.

5. Edward John Newell.

6. Anonymous witness, (Rebellion Papers, NAI, 620/23/137).

7. Edward John Newell.

8. Lake to Pelham, 16th April 1797, (Transcript of Pelham Papers, PRONI, T/755/4B/361f).

9. An Index of United Irishmen books and papers, (Sheffield Papers, PRONI, T/3465/78, original at ESRO ref ACC 2714).

10. Lake to Pelham, 16th April 1797.

11. Further Report from the Committee of Secrecy, Reported by the Rt. Hon. Mr. Secretary Pelham, Journals of the House of Commons, Ireland, May 1797, quoted in *The Decade of the United Irishmen, Contemporary Accounts, 1791 - 1801*, edited by John Killen, Belfast 1997.

12. Thomas Pelham, Dublin Castle, to Lt. General Gerard Lake, 15th April 1797, (Pelham Papers Transcripts, PRONI, T/755/4B/357f).

13. Brigadier-General James Knox at Armagh, to Chief-Secretary Thomas Pelham,

19th April 1797, (Pelham Papers Transcript, PRONI, T/755/4B/379f). There is no hint as to who this Mr. Verner was, but it is probable that he was the Thomas Verner who later was elected Sovereign of Belfast.

14. Lt. General Lake, Belfast, to Thomas Pelham, 30th April 1797, (Pelham Paper Transcripts, T/755/4B, in an enclosure).

15. Charles Dickson, p. 113.

16. An Index of United Irishmen books and papers apparently submitted to the Irish Parliament, (Sheffield Papers, PRONI, T/3465/78, original at ESRO ref ACC 2714), [A faithful copy of extracts from the index with the original explanations and notes].

17. Thomas Pelham to General Lake, January 1797, (Rebellion Papers, NAI, 620/28/14).

18. W.E.H. Lecky, *A History of Ireland in the Eighteenth Century*, 5 vols., London, 1892-96, Vol. II, pp. 78-79.

19. A.T.Q. Stewart, *The Summer Soldiers*. Belfast, 1995, pp. 51 - 53.

20. Appendix No. II to the Report of the Secret Committee of the House of Lords, 1799, (Linenhall Library, Belfast, N 648 and Sheffield Papers, PRONI, T/3465/80, original at ESRO ref ACC 2714).

21. Chief Secretary Pelham in *Journals of the House of Commons*, Ireland, May 1797, quoted in *The Decade of the United Irishmen*, Contemporary Accounts 1791 - 1801, edited by John Killen, Belfast, 1997, P. 96.

22. Reasons for making the Statement now, (Sheffield Papers, PRONI, T/3465/79, original at ESRO ref ACC 2714).

23. H. Montgomery Hyde, *The Rise of Castlereagh*, London, 1933, pp. 181-183. Hyde tells this story in detail in his family-approved biography of Castlereagh, but protests that the suggestion that his Lordship, "could possibly have had any connection with Bell Martin apart from an official one is so entirely out of keeping with the high standard of morality that he was known to preserve in his private life, that it might well be dismissed as unworthy of serious consideration."

24. Thomas Pelham, Phoenix Park to Lord Carhampton, Carhampton and Robert Ross, Dublin to Lord Downshire, (all Downshire Papers, PRONI, D/607/D/383, D/607/D/388 and D/607/D/386).

25. A.T.Q. Stewart, *The Summer Soldiers*. Belfast, 1995, pp. 30-31 and 170-171.

The Calm before the Storm

Between the acting of a dreadful thing
And the first motion, all the interim is
Like a phantasma, or a hideous dream;
The genius and the mortal instruments
Are then in council; and the state of man,
Like to a little kingdom, suffers then
The nature of an insurrection.

William Shakespeare,
Julius Ceasar, Act 2, Scene 2. Line 63

In the early months of 1797 many senior figures in the Society of United Irishmen found themselves in Dublin prisons or else transported even further away. This was a direct result of the seizure of arms and the arrests brought on by the Proclamation in March, followed by the subsequent increase in vigilance. This had been produced by the discovery of the papers in Alexander's public house in April and the amount of information being supplied by Edward John Newell and Robert Murdoch. An even more effective government spy than Newell or Murdoch in those days was Nicholas Mageean of Lessans, near Saintfield.

Mageean, sometimes spelled Magin, was a young Catholic member in the northern command of the Society of United Irishmen. He had somehow fallen into the clutches of three men we know to have been doggedly opposed to everything this society stood for. These men were Lord Londonderry, the Rev. John Cleland and Colonel Nicholas Price, the squire of Saintfield. These men had persuaded, frightened or paid

Mageean to pass on to them everything he could discover of the plans of the United Irishmen in County Down.

His first report was on the very same night that Edward Newell had led Colonel Barber to Alexander's, although this was possibly by coincidence. During the next fourteen months Mageean was to pass on to his secret employers the decisions and plans recorded at every United Irish meeting he attended, sometimes almost before the ink was dry on their papers. His rising seniority in the movement put him close to all the senior figures and made him a party to all significant discussions.

In early May 1797 Mageean passed information about another meeting to Cleland. This added even more alarm to those loyalists who were privy to the informer's letters. Having just become used to the idea of a possible insurrection across Ireland, these loyal citizens now discovered that the area of disaffection was much greater than one relatively small island. Mageean reported that Doctor David Thompson of Tullyrush had brought some cheer to a baronial Meeting in James Shaw's public house in Saintfield with the news that he had attended a Scottish National Meeting of United North Britain in Edinburgh. This brother movement in Scotland may not have been very large or even properly organised, but Mageean was later able to pass on that Thompson had brought along the Scots' expressions of support and a copy of their constitution. This document was almost word for word the same as the Irish ones.[1]

It is unlikely that expressions of Scottish solidarity would have carried much significance on their own, although it must be said that by September there were reputedly up to 10,000 United North Britons on their rolls. The Scottish firebrand Thomas Muir had even made the brash promise of the support of 200,000 Scottish rebels if the French landed in Ireland.[2]

However both Westminster and Dublin were already alarmed at the increasing spread of disaffection. They knew that among the mutineers at the Nore and Spithead there had been a number of United Irishmen spreading discontent and that there had even been rumours of support from the young United States of America. In Britain, Mageean's information about Scottish rebels brought these worries alarmingly close to home.[3]

All this greatly added to the breath of insurrection they felt becoming increasingly hotter behind them in Ireland. On top of all of this, London felt unable to turn and deal with this challenge effectively, because they were conscious that the majority of their resources were committed to action in Europe. In government circles it was increasingly the belief that each of Britannia's European allies was deserting the long-running fight against the French and that she now stood alone.

It was clear that the military as already established in Ireland could not expect reinforcement and would have to control the island as best it could. Four weeks earlier, Colonel Charles Leslie of the Monaghan Militia, based in Antrim and Down, had disclosed to General Lake how he had discovered that over seventy of his men had sworn the United Irish oath. Lake had decided that prompt action was needed and it was quickly taken. Four ringleaders were identified, court-martialled and convicted. Lake insisted that the severest sentences be carried out as an example to the rest. With an almost indecent haste the men were marched from Belfast to Blaris camp, near Lisburn, accompanied by all available companies and battalions. Once there, the condemned men were made to kneel on their coffins and were then shot to death by a firing squad.

Immediately other steps were taken to restore the Militia's name. A declaration of loyalty to the Crown was submitted to the *Northern Star*. This newspaper refused to print it because it contained a slanderous reference to the seditious nature of the citizens of Belfast. On the 20th of May, a large group of Monaghans, accompanied by some other soldiers, broke open the newspaper offices and smashed all the equipment. This has often been portrayed as a spontaneous act of angry violence perpetrated by some undisciplined Militiamen, but a request from Lt.-General Lake to Chief Secretary Pelham suggests that it was more premeditated than this and that the action had a heavy stamp of approval. Four days before this spontaneous attack Lake had mused,

> "Surely the *Northern Star* should be stop'd, the mischief that it does is beyond all imagination. May I be allow'd to seize & burn the whole apparatus?"[4]

Whatever the impetus for the attack, the result was that Samuel

Neilson's radical newspaper, which many had tried to quieten in other ways, was now silenced.

If this caused the balance of the Fourth Estate to be upset, the scales of the Judicature were also becoming a little more tilted against anyone of an anti-government persuasion. Justice's famous blindness and impartiality were to take some heavy blows as Castlereagh and his friends tried to suppress all criticism and dissension.

It was known that the Monaghan Militia were not the only soldiers being seduced into swearing United Irish oaths. The numbers being mentioned were not as high as the alarmists of the day feared they were, but the Society's avowed aim of subverting as many soldiers and yeomen as possible was having some successes. Two privates in the Fifeshire Fencibles, stationed in Londonderry during the summer of 1797, were called before their commanding officer, Colonel James Durham. Papers had been found in their barracks. These suggested that the two men, Hugh Wheatley and John Lindsay, were sworn United Irishmen and the colonel wished to hear them admit or deny it. He could not have guessed at the ramifications to come.

The story they told led to a major trial, a *cause célèbre* without equal in the decade and what can only be described as a deeply disturbing miscarriage of justice. They stated that on their way to their posting in Derry on the 24th of April they had got into some company who took them to the home of William Orr, at Farranshane, a small townland halfway between Donegore Hill and Antrim town. There, Wheatley claimed, Orr and others forced him to swear the United Irish oath, even though he did not wish to.

There are strong suspicions that when Lord Castlereagh got to hear of this, he saw to it that the minor incident was inflated to full-blown sedition and represented an attempt at corruption of His Majesty's forces. Unfortunately he could not raise the quality of the evidence given by the two Fencibles to match. The case was heard in September and to the modern reader almost defies belief.

The case certainly involved an interesting collection of legal luminaries. The judge was Barry Yelverton, the first Baron Avonmore, a former Volunteer and Patriot M.P. The prosecuting counsel was Arthur Wolfe, who five years later (as Lord Kilwarden) was to be almost the only fatality in Robert Emmet's brief but hugely significant rebellion. The defence barristers were John Philpot Curran, Ireland's pre-eminent advocate, and William Sampson, who had chaired the January meeting that had drawn up the *Belfast Resolutions*. These defence counsellors were possibly members of the Society of United Irishmen, or at least had a sympathy with their ideals. At Orr's trial they were instructed by the defence solicitor, James McGuckin, a Catholic, then secretly known to the United Irishmen as a member and, in the months after the rebellion, secretly known to the authorities as an informer.

Anyone who read about the trial, or heard of its statements and arguments, knew that Curran and Sampson's defence was impregnable. The packed jury seems to have thought so too and brought in a verdict of leaving the prisoner, "*to his Lordship's mercy.*" When instructed by the judge that there was no such verdict, they then stated, "Guilty", but with a strong recommendation for mercy. Curran then contended that Orr had been tried for treason, but under the wrong statutes and under an Insurrection Act that had expired. The judge summarily dismissed these arguments.

Before sentence could be pronounced, the foreman of the jury produced sworn affidavits to state that he had been intimidated to bring in a verdict contrary to his beliefs. He added that two bottles of whiskey, passed through an open window to the jury, had been consumed by them while they were supposedly giving sober consideration to their verdict. Judge Yelverton ruled that these were no reasons for refusing to pass sentence. He pronounced that Orr would be executed on the 7th of October.

Appeals of all kinds were lodged to save Orr. Evidence was produced to show that Wheatley was so deranged in his mind that he had tried to commit suicide and that he had even committed seduction and murder some months earlier. Even Countess Londonderry interceded on William Orr's behalf, but with little result. The efforts to save him only succeeded in extending Orr's life by an extra week.

On 14th October 1797, at 2.45 pm, William Orr was taken to the Carrickfergus common, a mile out of the town on the Belfast Road and near the sea. On this open area stood an ancient structure of three stone columns, supporting a triangle of wooden beams forming a multiple gallows. It was known colloquially as the Three Sisters. The multitudes from Carrickfergus were gathered to watch the carriage convey Orr to the gallows. The procession made its way to the Gallows Green through the ranks of soldiers and some field guns deployed by Colonel Lucius Barber. Along the way two volunteer chaplains gave the prisoner strong moral support. These were the Rev. Adam Hill of Ballynure and the Rev. William Staveley, minister both of Knockbracken and the Reformed Presbyterian Church in Anne Street in Newtownards.

At the appointed time Orr climbed the ladder to martyrdom and had the rope placed around his neck. His last words were, "*I am no traitor. I die for a persecuted country. Great Jehovah receive my soul. I die in the true faith of a Presbyterian.*"

The primeval moan which escaped the crowd as he was pushed off the platform gradually formed into a cry which was to reverberate through the plateau lands of Antrim and the drumlins of Down for eight months, until it was heard at its sharpest in the streets of Antrim and Ballynahinch – "REMEMBER ORR!" For many years afterwards, there were many houses in both counties that could produce to the right company a yellowing copy of Orr's dying declaration.[5]

There is an interesting postscript to this affair hidden among the Rebellion Papers in the National Archives of Ireland. It is in the form of a letter written some four months after Orr's death. The letter in question was written by Hugh Wheatley from his home in Maybole in Ayrshire shortly after he had had an unnerving experience. It was addressed to Edward Cooke, the Under-Secretary to Lord Lieutenant Camden. One would have thought that for many years Wheatley's best course would have been to lie low in Scotland. However, from his letter it seems that only a few months after Orr's death Wheatley could not resist taking ship from Portpatrick to Donaghadee to do a little horse-trading. Whilst waiting for the tide in Donaghadee, he had been identified to Francis Falloon, the proprietor of the public house there. Falloon was already known to many as an uncompromising United Irishman and within a few months he would feature in many bigger confrontations than the one with the betrayer of William Orr.

A measure of Wheatley's intelligence can be inferred from the letter, but it would be a shame to tell his story of the meeting in anything other than the man's own words:

To Edward Cooke Esq.
Secretary
Dublin Castle   Feberuary 8th 1798
Ireland

 Honble Sir

A few Days ago I arived here saif but I must Observe I had som litle Altrecation with one at Donachadee who on the hearing of my Neam Mentioned by a hors Dealer swor that if he had knon who I was I shd not have staid at his [Public] house Nither with so much safty. This is a Mr. Faloon, Signe of the Hors Donachadee.

I understood By his Convers that i would have gon No farder had I Bean knon the Night Befor as well as I was knon Next Day...[6]

What Wheatley probably did not know was that Falloon, or Fallon, had recently been released from confinement. In the same October that Orr was tried and executed and just across Belfast Lough from Carrickfergus, the loyalists of Donaghadee had been rejoicing that the owner of a public house in the town was now in custody and that his colleagues were being taken up. The man was Francis Falloon.

John Miskelly, the Millisle blacksmith, had been making iron heads for ash-shaft pikes provided by a man called Robison, all of them for Falloon. The latter had been recognised as a rebel for some time and, indeed, was known to both sides as 'Colonel' Fallon. William Getty, Arbuckle's deputy Customs Collector in Donaghadee, and Humphrey Galbraith, the Groomsport Customs official who lived in Donaghadee, had known Fallon and Miskelly well. As Getty described it, Miskelly had, "*made such discoveries as I hope will ensure us a quiet winter. From what I hear, he has nailed Fallon's coffin. [He has] implicated above thirty others, who will be taken up or run for it.*" [7]

Galbraith had been convinced that the arrests had been directly due to the increased activity of the 22nd Dragoons in the area and that it would produce even better results in the near future. When he tells the Marquis of Downshire about this he has doubts about linking it with the topics that had been exercising many people's minds for some months, "*I have no doubt that we may yet discover the Authors of the infamous Donaghadee resolutions and perhaps the Murder of Cummin too.*" [8] [See chapter 4]

By the time of Wheatley's visit in February 1798, Falloon had been released and restored to his status as the most significant United Irishman in Donaghadee. Wheatley's accidental meeting with Falloon may have unnerved him, but there is little doubt that it also reminded him of something that he had perhaps let slide. He concludes his letter to Cooke:

> I wrot John Lindsay but have had No Returns from him as Yet. Neither have I had any Acounts of Allan Willie…As it is parfitly in Your Honours powr to Provid for me I Beg Leaf to Depend on your well known goodness and I am perfitly at your Devotion.

From this plea there is a clear implication that the role of Wheatley and Lindsay in the Orr affair was a more sinister one than is usually thought. It is not known whether Cooke ever responded to Wheatley's request to provide for him.

The military measures and the influence of the Castle were probably greater in the home country of Lord Castlereagh than anywhere else in Ireland at the time. Any prisoners expecting a fair trial in the Ards would have been disturbed to discover that the relentless John Cleland, who was sub-sheriff in addition to his other duties, had stacked the jury lists with loyal tenants of Castlereagh's father. William Orr's leading counsel, John Philpot Curran, was hired to defend some of those charged in the Ards. Six years later this great jurist was to disqualify himself from defending Robert Emmet because he knew that the accused was secretly attached to Curran's youngest daughter, Sarah. Daniel O'Connell was subsequently to claim about Curran, "*There never was so honest an Irishman.*" [9] Curran is famous for his authorship of the much-misquoted epigram, "*The condition upon which God hath given liberty to man is eternal vigilance,*" so it is no surprise that he was appalled that the land agent of the accused's landlord and a man who had pursued and captured many of the accused, could be allowed to ravage the principles of natural justice by designating who would decide their fate. Curran railed:

He [Cleland] receives blank summonses, fills in what he deems convenient etc. Gracious God what are the courts of justice? What is trial by jury? What is the country brought to?...He ascends the pulpit with the gospel of benignity and peace, he endeavours to impress himself and his hearers with its meek and holy spirit. He descends, throws off the purple, seizes the Insurrection Act in one hand and the whip in the other, flies by night and by day after his game, – and, with his heart panting, his breath exhausted and his belly at the ground in the chase, he turns round and tells you that his mind is unprejudiced, that his heart is full of humanity and that all his hopes, fears and wishes are a pure and innocent mixture of milk and water.[10]

Amazingly, in spite of this apparent corruption, not all of the accused were found guilty. The distinguishing traits of the Ulster Presbyterian character ensured that although the Ards jurymen might be carefully selected, they could not always be bought.

Not all of those suspected of being United Irishmen were taken up. In Down a few of the senior men, or colonels, such as Steel Dickson, James Porter and David Thompson somehow evaded the net. The Rev Arthur McMahon of Holywood, Alexander Lowry of Linen Hill near Rathfriland and John Magennis of Baleely had accomplished it by leaving Ireland. The number of leaders going to prison or leaving the country over these twelve months or so was a heavy burden for the United Irish movement to carry and the men coming in were not of the same stature as those they were replacing. Ironically, in spite of the constraints, the emphasis in United Irish activities in County Down was shifting more and more to the Ards.

In Belfast and Antrim too, many of the Ulster leaders were short of enthusiasm or ability, or perhaps just of years. The hub of the Society in Ireland moved gradually from the northern theatre to the capital. In November 1797 a new National Executive was formed in Dublin – and significantly there was only one representative from the province of Ulster.[11] This shift would not have been too quickly apparent to the authorities in Dublin. What actually was alarming them most was that they could see no diminution in the overall organisation. It was recognised that it was, "*the regularity of their system which is to be dreaded more than any individual ability.*"[12] In County Down this regular structure had sustained the Society through the disappointments of failed French landings, the arrest and/or defection of many leaders, the constraints of the Proclamation and Lake's 'Dragooning' of its measures.

The people of Ireland, especially in the north, had long been familiar with the compulsory and unpaid billeting of troops in their homes, the floggings of suspected sympathisers and the ceremonials of the pitch cap. This last named delight was where a man or boy, suspected of being a rebel, or of protecting rebels, had a cap, filled with boiling pitch or tar, put on his bare head for the amusement of the soldiers and perhaps to persuade him to tell all that he knew.

Occasionally though, the cottiers and tradesmen found allies in strange places. That same month of November, Francis Rawdon-Hastings, 1st Marquis of Hastings and 2nd Earl of Moira made a passionate address to the House of Lords in London deploring the excesses he had witnessed. The name of this liberal aristocrat is to appear again later in our story when Henry Munro's army of rebels arrive at Moira's family seat at Montalto in Ballynahinch. In his speech to the Lords about government policy in Ireland he ruffled many feathers by being so graphic and critical of the resident military forces. He described the policy as, *"the most absurd, as well as the most disgusting Tyranny that any nation ever groaned under."* [13]

As the cooler airs of winter began to arrive, with them came the realisation that there might be no insurrection that year. However, there were rumours that there might be one last attempt to organise naval support. For some weeks it was widely reported that an invasion fleet was being assembled in French-occupied Holland at the island of Texel. But whatever hopes were entertained that this could lead to a successful Irish landing, they were dashed by the news of the English defeat of the Dutch at the Battle of Camperdown on the 11th October. The earliest the United Irishmen could now expect a French fleet was the early summer of 1798.

The evening after the news of Camperdown reached Newtownards, the soldiery garrisoned there paraded round the town looking for evidence that the great British victory was being properly celebrated. But as is often the way with bitter opponents, those whose spirits are lifted by a victory must exult in some triumphalism in order to demonstrate their fellow feeling with the victors. A level of disorder of course often accompanied this. A visitor from Scotland told a newspaper that the soldiers, led by a local gentleman, had smashed windows in houses in Newtownards where there appeared to be an insufficient show of enthusiasm for the navy's success and that he was disturbed to see so many windows being broken. In spite of his coyness about naming the 'gentleman' the writer could hardly have been plainer in identifying this bitter and wretched agent:

> I was also told that a gentleman whose connection with the principal landlord of the place, and whose professional character should have pointed out to him the imprudence and indecency of being one of such a party, accompanied the military mob through the whole of their perambulation and seemed to think the rattling of a glass a much more agreeable sound than that of the parish bell on a Sunday morning.[14]

Perhaps the words of Humphrey Galbraith best sum up the prevailing mood among the loyal gentlemen of Ulster at the end of 1797. He could not wait to communicate his joy to Lord Downshire for the:

> GREAT GLORIOUS, ever to be remembered, and never to be forgotten Defeat and Capture of the Dutch fleet Soli Dei Gloria we may now bid the Croppys ly down, their hopes for invasion are at an end and we shall yet have day about with them.[15]

The new year brought a significant change in the military command. The well-known Scottish general, Sir Ralph Abercromby, was appointed to succeed Lord Carhampton as Commander-in-Chief in Ireland. He soon issued a general order to all his officers, setting out exactly how, when and on whose authority they could act. No one could seriously quarrel with the order, with the exception of the clause where the general, probably through sheer frustration, had described his army as being, "*in a state of licentiousness which must render it formidable to everyone but the enemy.*"

This frankness provoked an outcry against Abercromby from all quarters. It was so great that the Earl Camden was forced to call "*this Scotch beast*" to account for his words. The general recognised that he had lost the confidence of the government and promptly resigned. General William Dalrymple had continued to be unimpressive since

Bantry Bay, so somewhat reluctantly the government gave the overall command to Lieutenant-General Gerard Lake. His northern command passed smoothly to his deputy there, Major-General George Nugent.

This career soldier, who was to feature so prominently throughout the rebellion in the north, was the illegitimate son of a respected Anglo-Irish military family. His grandfather, in a similar fashion to the Stewart men of the Ards, had married a fabulously wealthy woman. Although his influential family connections could have procured him steady advancement in the army, what he achieved was mostly through his own efforts. He was considered by almost everyone who met him to be a fine man, with an unusual humanity for a soldier and an understanding not always associated with the gentry of the day. He had served with distinction in the American War of Independence and well knew the ways of the Ulster-Scots. After the harsh military regime of Lieutenant-General Gerard Lake, his appointment was greeted warmly by almost everybody in Antrim and Down.[16]

In the month of March Lord Downshire made a rousing speech in the London House of Lords. It amounted to a rebuttal of everything Lord Moira had said about Ireland in the previous November. He justified the behaviour of the forces stationed in Ireland and singled out General Lake for special commendation. Lake saw this in the newspapers and very quickly wrote a letter of thanks to the Marquis saying how gratifying it was to read of someone who really knew what went on in the country praising the actions of the army and countering the criticisms of the people who had tried to dishonour him and his men in the minds of the public.[17]

Simultaneously in Dublin the newer leaders of the Society of United Irishmen were being taken up by the military. Emmet, Nevin, Bond, Sweetman, the two Jacksons and others were captured in Oliver Bond's house, almost certainly as a result of a tip-off. All of the many correspondents who transmitted the news to Downshire in London were ecstatic that such dangerous men had been caught, although they were unanimous that the danger would not ease until Lord Edward Fitzgerald had been killed or apprehended.[18] They did not have long to wait.

In the middle of May the Dublin Castle spies discovered where they could find and arrest Lord Edward. They had proper warrants drawn up and sent Major Sirr with two magistrates, Swann and Ryan, to apprehend him. In the scuffle which ensued Fitzgerald was mortally wounded and some days later he died. His loss was calamitous to the United Irishmen, because he had been made the undisputed commander-in-chief to oversee the campaigns in all the different parts of Ireland.

Wolfe Tone had led Fitzgerald and the other leaders to believe that a huge French force would arrive in Ireland in the early summer of 1798 with ample supplies of weapons and ammunition. They were to be supplemented by thousands of United Irish volunteers, in part as auxiliary troops and in part as an underground resistance movement. Dublin Castle, the military and the loyal gentlemen of the country all thought they had a solid grasp of the situation, but, as in '96 and '97, there was more going on than they were hearing about.

The authorities were aware of most of what was happening at the secret meetings of the United Irishmen, but they held their hand during this time because the informers, Edward Newell, Robert Murdoch, Thomas Hughes and Nicholas Mageean, had made it plain enough that their agreements were only to supply the intelligence, not to commit suicide by standing in the witness box at the court martials of any leaders who might be arrested.

The other factor which constrained government was that there was a body of opinion which said that, save in the extremely unlikely event of an overwhelming French invasion, any insurrection in Ireland was so certain to fail that the best policy was to allow it, even encourage it, to break out. The rebellion, the rebels and their supporters could then all be crushed so hard that the green flag of insurrection would not be raised again for at least a century.

There is little doubt that the atrocities of the previous year and the frustrations of an unhearing government had turned many a peaceable liberal in the United Irish Society into a committed revolutionary. What is not certain is how much the intransigence of the political leaders in Ireland was inbred, ingrained and unavoidable and how much was a deliberate policy to incite the people into a controllable revolt. But both sides on the chessboard were now committed. All that was necessary to start the endgame was a signal.

During the spring months the Colonels of County Down held a series of secret meetings, usually in public houses. These were deliberately held at a number of different locations in order to avoid detection. There were meetings in Newtownards, Greyabbey, Saintfield, Downpatrick, Dromore, Rathfriland and Lisburn. They had one meeting in "*a wrecked house of Wm. McCormick in Newtownards*," but this was an act of symbolism rather than an inability to find somewhere better.

William McCormick's public house had earlier been deliberately destroyed in order to prevent such meetings. As we now know, the efforts of these men to avoid detection were futile, because Nicholas Mageean was present at most of them. This meant that on the following day John Cleland and thence Londonderry, Price and Castlereagh, knew as much about the meetings' business as those present at them. Certainly someone in Newtownards made sure that McCormick's name was not forgotten. On the 24th of July 1798 he was sentenced to be hanged for, "*acting as a traitor and rebel and endeavouring to excite treason and rebellion in Ireland.*" [19]

Mageean usually gave the names of the men present at meetings, even when they did not contribute materially. These names change to a degree, but a few appear with significant regularity. It is apparent that Andrew Bryson of the Cottown, George Sinclair of Newtownards, David Thompson, James and David Shaw of Saintfield, Richard Frazer of Ravarra, Francis Falloon of Donaghadee, Andrew Todd, John Cowan, Andrew Maxwell and the two young clergymen, David Bailie Warden and James Townsend, were among the most enthusiastic representatives.

Two more senior clergymen, the Rev. James Porter and the Rev. Dr. William Steel Dickson, were regularly being courted for their abilities and gravitas, although the two gentlemen seem not to have been in attendance as often as the others. Indeed until the beginning of the month of May, Dickson was in Scotland and Porter, like many more anonymous others in these difficult days, seems to have been having second thoughts about total and irrevocable insurrection.

The plans of the French, suspected or known, continued to excite both sides. Robert Hunter, the Belfast shipbroker and senior member of the Belfast Society, was able to inform an Ulster provincial Meeting in Belfast that the expected French invasion could not be delayed any further than the middle of April. He said that the troops from Brest, *"were determined to try to evade the British Fleet . . .and while the British Fleet were thus employed all the rest of the troops going on board at the different other ports would make a descent on England."*[20]

No doubt Hunter's information was sincerely delivered to the meeting, but it would appear that Napoleon Bonaparte and the French Directory were treating the United Irishmen and Wolfe Tone in particular, as pawns of not very great strategic importance. Nothing happened in April, nor until almost three weeks into May, when a frigate from the English naval blockade in the Mediterranean saw that 12 French ships of the line had left Toulon, their destination understood to be Ireland. The news took a fortnight to reach Ireland and initially caused some consternation. In fact, Napoleon Bonaparte's eyes were looking, not there, but in the direction of Egypt and its treasures. The suggestion that the fleet was headed for Ireland was a deliberate piece of misinformation calculated to draw off the blockading British fleet. In this endeavour Bonaparte did not succeed, as his expeditionary force was to discover a little later when it encountered Horatio Nelson at Aboukir Bay, near the delta of the River Nile.

On the 3rd of May Dr. Steel Dickson had replied to a request made by Nicholas Mageean, David Thompson, Andrew Todd and Richard Frazer that he would prefer to have a civil station rather than take the field in an insurrection on account of his age, but that if he was elected to the office of Adjutant-General for County Down he would endeavour to fill it.[21] The men agreed to meet again on Tuesday the 5th of June.

On that very evening, acting on information, Captain Magennis and Lieutenant Lindsay of the Hillsborough Yeomanry called at the Ballynahinch inn where Steel Dickson was staying and told him they had a letter from the colonel of the regiment, Lord Annesley, to detain him. All three of the men were very relaxed about the business. Magennis even allowed Dickson to spend the night in his bed, saying that the letter, *"was only a whim of his Lordship,"* and that it would be resolved in the morning.

At around noon the following day, a Colonel Bainbridge arrived to inform his two subordinate officers that the arrest was to be carried out immediately. Dickson sent the colonel a message to request a chaise, or at least a horse, to carry him to Lisburn because he was not in the best of health and the weather was intensely hot. Bainbridge's reply to the messenger struck Dickson as not only blunt, but cruel, *"A chaise, and be damned! Let him walk, or take a seat on the car, which goes to town with the old guns."*

His stubborn pride irritated, Dickson walked the eight exhausting miles to Lisburn. There General Tom Goldie received him with the utmost courtesy. The general was concerned for Dickson's health, not just because of his obvious fatigue, but because he considered that he could not guarantee his safety at Blaris Camp because of the intensity of the fervour against United Irishmen among the soldiers. Goldie told Dickson that he was certain the only reason for Annesley's letter was the suspicion that Dickson had been promoting disaffection whilst in Scotland. He provided an armed escort and told Dickson to take a chaise to General Nugent in Belfast, where he would undoubtedly be released. When Dickson arrived at Nugent's headquarters his request to see the general resulted in a second-hand instruction to carry the Reverend Doctor to the 'Black Hole'.

In this gaol Dickson found Robert Hunter. Both men were interrogated for some time, sometimes separately and sometimes together. They were treated well by some of the Monaghan Militiamen who guarded them and extremely badly by others. The two prisoners slept the following night on filthy floorboards with only Dickson's saddlebags as pillows. The next morning brought them some relief. Hunter was allowed to order two breakfasts to be brought from his home nearby and soon after, the prisoners were taken to the Donegall Arms.

However false the news of the French sailing, forecast in May by Hunter, eventually proved, it was enough to signal the outbreak everyone had long expected. Ironically, after waiting for such a bulletin for years, it was not the men of the Ards, nor those of anywhere in Down or Antrim who were 'out' first. The first shots of the 1798 rebellion were fired, not in the north, as had always been feared, nor in Wexford as is popularly thought, but in County Dublin. As we have seen, Down was in confusion in those May days and Wexford, "*did not contain above two hundred United Irishmen.*"[22] The men of Carlow and Kildare were up in arms before the word of the French sailing had even reached Ireland. With little known organisation and no military structure to speak of, they were responding to the shots fired near Dublin.[23]

On Saturday the 25th of May, John Patrickson wrote to Hanover Square to tell the Marquis of Downshire, "*The grand attack was to have been on Sunday, but the apprehension of Lord Edward prevented it. However, last night they began in the whole circle around Dublin.*"[24]

The 1798 Rebellion had begun.

1. Report of a County Meeting of United Irishmen, No date, but must be May 1797, (Lowry Papers, PRONI, D/1494/2/4).

2. John Brims, *Scottish Radicalism and the United Irishmen in The United Irishmen, Republicanism, Radicalism and Rebellion,* ed. David Dickson, Dáire Keogh and Kevin Whelan, Dublin, 1993, pp. 163-165.

3. *Jim Smyth, Freemasonry and the United Irishmen, in The United Irishmen, Republicanism, Radicalism and Rebellion,* ed. D Dickson et al., Dublin, 1993, p. 172, and James Pollock, New York to Downshire, 13th May 1798, (Downshire Papers, D/607/F/167).

4. Lt. General Gerard Lake, Newry, to Thomas Pelham, marked "Private", 16th April 1797, (Transcript of Pelham Papers, PRONI, T/755/4B/361f).

5. A.T.Q. Stewart, The Summer Soldiers, *The 1798 Rebellion in Antrim and Down,* Belfast, 1995, pp. 45-50.

6. Hugh Wheatley, Maybole, Ayrshire, to Edward Cooke, Esq. at Dublin Castle, 8th February 1798, (Rebellion Papers, NAI, 620/29/127).

7. William Getty to James Arbuckle, (enclosed in an Arbuckle letter to Lord Downshire, 18th October 1797, (Downshire Papers, PRONI, D/607/E/335).

8. Humphrey Galbraith, Donaghadee, to the Marquis of Downshire, October

21st, 1797, (Downshire Papers, PRONI, D/607/E/345).

9. *Dictionary of National Biography*, London, 1921.

10. *Northern Star*, 28th April and 1st, 5th May 1797, (the paper's last issue) quoted in Trevor McCavery, *Reformers, Reactionaries and Revolutionaries, Opinion in North Down and the Ards, in the 1790s, Ulster Local Studies*, Vol. 18, No 2, p. 87, and H. Montgomery Hyde, *The Rise of Castlereagh*, London, 1939.

11. Nancy J. Curtin, *The United Irish Organisation in Ulster: 1795-98, in The United Irishmen, Republicanism, Radicalism and Rebellion*, ed. by D Dickson et al., Dublin, 1993, pp. 217-218.

12. Earl Camden to Duke of Portland, 17th June 1797, (PRO London, HO 100/69/397-9).

13. Charles Dickson, *Revolt in the North*, London, 1960, p. 103.

14. *The Press*, 18th November 1797, quoted in Trevor McCavery, pp.88-89.

15. Galbraith to Downshire, October 21st, 1797, (Downshire Papers, PRONI, D/607/E/344).

16. A.T.Q. Stewart, pp. 51-53.

17. Robert Ross in Dublin, 31st March 1798, Lieut. Gen. Gerard Lake, Dublin, 2nd April 1798, both to Downshire, (Downshire Papers, PRONI, D/607/F/119 and D/607/F/127).

18. [John Patrickson], Dublin to Downshire, 12th March 1798, (Downshire Papers, PRONI, D/607/F/90). Earl Annesley could not resist adding in a slightly later letter to Downshire that Sweetman was, "one of the Popish Congress."

19. Court Martial of William McCormick at Newtownards, 21st July 1798, (Rebellion Papers, NAI, 620/2/15/37).

20. Robert Hunter, (Lytton White Papers, PRONI, D/714/2/20A-B).

21. Nicholas Mageean, a number of letters to Cleland between 9th March and 31st May 1798, (Lytton White Papers, PRONI, D/714/2/16, 19, and 21). At the time, Steel Dickson was 52 years of age.

22. Theobald William Tone, Wolfe Tone's son, quoted by Charles Dickson, p. 119.

23. Charles Dickson, pp. 122-123.

24. John Patrickson, Dublin to Downshire, Hanover Sq. 25th May 1798, (Downshire Papers, PRONI, D/607/F/185).

County Down is 'Up'!

Rebellion! foul dishonouring word,
Whose wrongful blight so oft has stained
The holiest cause that tongue or sword
Of mortal ever lost or gained –
How many a spirit born to bless,
Has sunk beneath that withering name,
Whom but a day's – an hour's success,
Had wafted to eternal fame.

Thomas Moore[1]

The Marquis of Downshire had a number of homes. His principal seat was Hillsborough Castle, but when the Rebellion broke out in the north of Ireland he was in his residence at Hanover Square in London. He had little choice but to remain there for the duration. He had intimated to a number of well placed individuals in County Down that he would be glad to hear their news and opinions; and positively insisted that his steward and secretary keep him informed about any affairs that could affect him and his tenants as soon as they happened. Because the bulk of this correspondence still survives, it is an extremely helpful archive for anyone wishing to study the period. Care must be taken with these letters because the writers were so anxious to get the information to his Lordship that they occasionally wrote in too much haste. Later versions sometimes show that a sensational first recording of an event later proved to be somewhat exaggerated or based on a rumour.

That said, the many letters written by two of His Lordship's Hillsborough staff, his Land Steward and his Secretary, Thomas Lane and George Stephenson; by Revenue official Humphrey Galbraith of Groomsport; the Packet Company Secretary Edward Hull of Donaghadee and Land Waiter James McKey of Belfast give some unique first hand impressions of those tumultuous days. Used in combination with each other and with the official records of the day they help weave some local colour into the tapestry of the times. This is particularly true for the unsettled weeks leading up to the outbreak of violence in County Down.

It must always be remembered that although the 1798 Rebellion had a number of very local actions, these were the more overt manifestations of a covert discontent throughout much of Ireland. Anything that happened anywhere on the island was almost immediately known everywhere else. Their own deep-seated prejudices and news of far-off events, such as what was happening in Europe or America, often coloured the judgment of the leaders on both sides and patterns and plans were altered frequently. Nothing was inevitable in the course of affairs at this confused time.

Rebel groupings all over the country might be lying low one day and 'up' the next. The authorities did not know if, where or when the next action would occur. The rebels often did not know either. Stories from Wicklow, Kildare and Wexford had been reaching the north for a week by the beginning of June. The military in Belfast were taking the steps they felt necessary to dampen any ardour in Ulster. Outwardly it appeared they were succeeding.

During the first ten days of June, Downshire received a welter of information. On the 1st of June, James McKey, writing from his home in Belfast, assured Downshire:

> Such a change in Politicks as has appeared in this Town and Neighbourhood within these few days past (since Military Law has been established) is beyond what your Lordship could imagine knowing the people. The stubborn and insolent republican is now become mild and gentle and wishes to put on a red coat in defence of his country.

With the benefit of two centuries of hindsight, it is surprising to a modern reader that a Yeoman officer, who was certain he had his finger on Ulster's pulse, could have formed such an erroneous impression.

Like many others he mistook a few particular impressions for a general trend. McKey, conscious perhaps that he is writing to such an influential magnate, then compounds his error. With a complacency that apparently was shared by the military, he continues:

> Searching for concealed Arms a few were found and the owners severely flogged by the Military, and it has struck such Terror amongst the Republicans that they are ready to do anything to avoid chastisement in that way. I do really think it has a better effect than confining for years in Gaol. Four pieces out of the six Belfast cannon [clearly having been stolen] are given up, and discoveries of guns &c are amaking every day from mitigating the punishment of whipping.[2]

Dean Warburton of Lough Gilly, near Newry, certainly seems to have shared in this optimistic general view. Writing to Under-secretary Edward Cooke at Dublin Castle on 29th of May, he also ascribes some second thoughts to the whole body of Presbyterianism what history was to discover applied only to some:

> The cunning and wary Northerners see that no revolution can be effected without a foreign aid (of which they now despair). The steadiness and loyalty of our militia have damped the hopes and expectations of the disaffected, and I think the Northern Dissenter will now quietly be a spectator of that destructive flame which he himself originally kindled up, and will take no active part in the present attempt.[3]

Cooke immediately wrote to his friend, Wickham, passing on Warburton's views and adding his own explanations for the apparent apathy in the north:

> The quiet of the North is to me unaccountable; but I feel that the Popish tinge in the rebellion, and the treatment of France to Switzerland and America, has really done much, and in addition to the army, the force of Orange yeomanry is really formidable.[4]

From Hillsborough, George Stephenson, who would by then have been aware of the developments in County Antrim, observed what seemed to him to be a dampening of hopes in his own immediate area. With thinly veiled satisfaction he informed the Marquis of Downshire four days later that:

A man has been hanged this morning at Lisburn, taken near Antrim last night with a green cockade, his buttons numbered as to what regiment in Belfast he belonged to, but he would not tell who he was, and was not known. He was well dressed.[5]

The stringent measures still being enforced in County Down were prompted as much from a fear that if the boot were lifted from the beast's neck it would still try to bite. Stephenson's colleague at Hillsborough, Thomas Lane, did not always sing along with him, but on this occasion he seems to be in tune:

Lisburn is dreadfully alarmed from the crowds in the mountains above it... Hanging and flogging have had a fine effect, and some more examples will show the scoundrels what they have to expect.[6]

Richard Annesley, on military duties in Wexford, wrote to Downshire what others were saying to their friends, that, "*You may rely on this war being considered by the Rebels as a religious one. Their priests exhort them, lead them and make them desperate. Some of them have been killed with their vestments on.*"[7]

Downshire may have seen the Earl of Camden's similar assessment to Chief Secretary Pelham. The Viceroy's speculation about the possible effects in Down and Antrim was that:

In the north nothing will keep the rebels quiet but a conviction that where treason has broken out the rebellion is merely Popish; but even with this impression on their minds we cannot be certain that their love of republicanism will not outweigh this inveteracy against Popery.[8]

The rush to highlight the sectarian aspects of the insurrection observed in many contemporary correspondences is sometimes seen as a purely cynical exercise, designed with the Dissenters of Ulster in mind. There probably was a measure of cool calculation employed, but the ingrained arrogance and insularity of the Protestant ascendancy should not be underestimated. Most of this tiny but hugely influential group possessed a casual confidence that their Established Church was wholly right and that all others were wholly wrong. If a sectarian backlash was their own worst fear it would have been politic for

Dublin Castle to encourage such thoughts among their Anglican tenants and perhaps even the less radical Presbyterians too.

The Belfast newspapers were not only carrying the news from Wexford, but embellishing the stories with blood-curdling accounts of mobs of Catholics, led by frenzied priests, picking out Protestants for death or to accept forcible re-baptism to avoid it.[9] Lord Camden was not the only Protestant talking about how this might affect the north.

Although most of his attention was taken up by the events in Antrim, General Nugent was keeping a close eye on Down. He had already taken up Steel Dickson and Robert Hunter along with a number of other United Irish leaders. The steady flow of intelligence from Nicholas Mageean and others kept him well informed about new appointments and planned activities. He ordered more arrests and consulted his maps.

The military had been spread very thinly across County Down in an effort to maintain local visibility. Now, with the threat of forces being assembled, large enough to overwhelm a small barrack or camp, Nugent reconsidered how best to keep the lid on County Down. Apart from a garrison at Downpatrick, he decided to close up all the barracks, to withdraw all troops from the whole of the eastern half of the county and abandon that country to the rebels.[10] His decision was not well received by the hundreds of loyalist families in the small communities of the Ards. They recognised that this withdrawal would be taken by the rebels in that area as the signal to rise.

Nugent realised this too of course, but he knew that by giving up the east of the county he could preserve the west. His limited forces would have enough to do preserving Belfast and holding the line of the Dublin Road through Lisburn, Hillsborough, Dromore, Banbridge and Newry.[11] It is not recorded, but we can imagine that for obvious geographical reasons the Marquis of Downshire greeted this decision more enthusiastically than did Lord Londonderry.

The former would have had to hear the news in London. Now, considering the extent of his up-to-date knowledge of the state of the north, he can hardly have been too startled a few mornings later when he read his mail. Thomas Lane rushed to tell Downshire what was on everyone's lips in Hillsborough:

The Donaghadee Mail of yesterday had scarcely left the place before expresses arrived informing us that the rebels had appeared near Saintfield in great numbers, had drove off numbers of the York Fencibles and begun to fire the houses of the well-disposed inhabitants near there. A large body proceeded on towards Ballynahinch and compelled Captain Magennis's Company of Castlewellan Yeoman to retire here.[12]

James McKey had also put pen to paper in Belfast the instant he had received the news from Saintfield and the other beleaguered outposts:

The Rebels have broken out with uncommon violence in the County of Down. Saintfield, Newtown, Comber and the whole of the country is in their possession and I am sorry to tell you they have drove off every force [that] could be sent and all have retreated, yeomen &c to this town with several detachments from this garrison that was sent out to their relief.

McKey has enough knowledge of the military situation and of tactics to realise the urgent need for more government forces. In addition he is able to point out the difficulties of supplying these in a hurry. He implies that the whole northern part of Down is held by the rebels and that Belfast and Carrickfergus have become the only havens for loyalists, unless they follow the ladies' example and take ship for Scotland.

In short, My Lord, we want force sufficient and we are told here there is seven regiments at Portpatrick ready to come but dare not venture by Donaghadee. Coming by Carrickfergus will add delay and God send that it may not be too long. All we can do here at present is to guard the town until such a thing happens. Every loyal family and every troop has come here from the country in their [the Rebels'] possession. . . . . Our troops here at present are up day and night and I write this longside my horse on guard. Mrs. Hamilton & almost all the females of this town are set out for Scotland by Carrickfergus today, as it is thought this town will be attacked. [13]

Lane, meanwhile, was reassuring his Lordship that all was well. In his letter he commits the same sin as other loyalists were inclined to do when he gives uncritical acceptance to the first optimistic reports coming out of Saintfield. He was so impressed by the military bearing of the Scottish soldiers of the Argyle and Breadalbane Fencible Regiments and the disciplined menace of the horse soldiers that he could not admit the thought that they might be vulnerable. The same day as the fight in Saintfield he puts pen to paper in his home in Belfast to say:

Near twelve last night about 260 of the Breadalbanes reached this place with a small camp of artillery and a squadron of the 24th Dragoons were expected but did not come. And the Breadalbanes had not been here ten minutes before they were ordered to camp with the artillery, and an hour after, the Argyles, 22nd Dragoons and some Yeomen Cavalry arrived here and were joined by the cavalry of this place, proceeding with some pieces of ordnance to Saintfield, where report says they fell in with the Rebels and have slaughtered great numbers.[14]

Some of his troop identifications are incorrect, but, as we shall see, his message to Downshire about the slaughter of Rebels at Saintfield was the victory of optimism over reality.

1. Thomas Moore quoted in frontispiece by Charles Hamilton Teeling, *Sequel to Personal Narrative of the Irish Rebellion of 1798*, London, 1828.

2. James McKey of Mountcollyer to the Marquis of Downshire, Hanover Square, London, 1st June 1798, (Downshire Papers, PRONI, D607/F/192).

3. Dean Warburton, Lough Gilly near Newry, writing to Edward Cooke, 29 June 1798, quoted in W.E.H. Lecky, *A History of Ireland in the Eighteenth Century*, London, 1909, p. 412.

4. Edward Cooke to Wickham June 2nd 1798, quoted in Lecky, p. 412.

5. George Stephenson to Downshire, 8th June 1798, (Downshire Papers, PRONI, D/607/F/208).

6. Thomas Lane to Downshire, 9th June 1798, (Downshire Papers, PRONI, D/607/F/216).

7. Richard Annesley [In Wexford] to Downshire, 9th June 1798, (Downshire Papers, PRONI, D/607/F/215).

8. Lord Camden to Pelham at Dublin Castle, 6th June 1798, (Pelham Papers, quoted by Charles Dickson, *Revolt in the North,* p. 125.

9. Thomas Pakenham, *The Year of Liberty*, London, 1969, p. 224, and Major-General Nugent, Belfast, to Lt. Gen. Lake, 10th June 1798, (Rebellion Papers, NAI, 620/38/121).

10. Thomas Pakenham, *The Year of Liberty*, London, 1969, p. 225.

11. Ibid.

12. Thomas Lane to Downshire, 10th June 1798, (Downshire Papers, PRONI,

D/607/F/221).

13. James McKey, Belfast to Downshire, 10th June 1798, (Downshire Papers, PRONI, D/607/F/219).

14. Thomas Lane to Downshire, (Downshire Papers, PRONI, D/607/F/221).

The Burning of the McKees

And when I mind with how much greediness
We seek the present gain in everything,
Not caring (so our lust we may possess)
What damage to posterity we bring…
What our forefathers planted, we destroy:
Nay, all men's labours, living heretofore,
And all our own, we lavishly employ
To serve our present lusts, and for no more.

George Wither,
A Collection of Emblems, 1635.

Two days earlier than McKey's letter, during the morning of the 8th of June, an observant shepherd or farmer on the high ground of Carrickmannan, a couple of miles north-east of Saintfield might have spotted groups of men making their way down lanes and over fields towards that town from the directions of Ballygowan or Raffrey. These men would later be identified as being from places in the Comber area such as Ballyrickard, Ballycreely, Ballygraffan, Castleavarry, Cherryvalley, Cattogs and the Glass Moss or from townlands between Killinchy and Ballygowan such as Ravarra, Magherascouse, Ballmacashen and Carrickmannan. Men would have been arriving too from around Killynure, Oughley and Lessans to the northwest.[1]

One Lessans resident who does not seem to have been near Saintfield that day was Nicholas Mageean. He had deemed it prudent to keep his head down and stay out of the action during these violent days. He was not to be heard of again until after all the rebellion dust had settled. By then the authorities needed his co-operation if they were to secure the convictions of many senior rebels.

The trickles of men approaching Saintfield that morning swelled to a steady stream which met together at their pre-arranged meeting place on Cow Green at the south end of Saintfield, near where the Belfast road entered the town. Once gathered there, they withdrew to the prominence called Oughley, or Ouley, Hill, two and a half miles north of Saintfield on the road to Belfast.

Not all of these men were committed radicals and republicans, dedicated to a political ideal. Some saw only an opportunity to improve their simple lot in life, either by overthrowing the Dublin parliament and the power of the Castle, or at least by forcing the members of the establishment to review their policies and priorities regarding stringencies like tithes and taxes. Some swore later that they were only there under protest. A few, unfortunately for the impression they were to leave for posterity, had more primitive urges in their hearts.

In marked contrast to what happened in Wexford, the insurrection in Ulster was free from large-scale atrocities; but not totally. Less than a mile from the Cow Green out the road to Lisburn and only a few hundred yards from the Belfast Road that the insurgents would have taken out of Saintfield towards Oughley was a craggy area called Craignasasonagh. This small townland held a number of cottages. One of these was the scene of the only large-scale barbarity in the County Down rebellion. Because of the story's uniqueness and because it is often misrepresented, the whole tale deserves to be told and with as near the full truth as it is possible to get today.

All of the mid-Down rebels would have known of the townland of Craignasasonagh (or sometimes Carricknacessnagh). They knew that there lived in that townland a family called McKee. Hugh McKee and his family were unashamed loyalists in a tight republican area. McKee himself was known to note every expression of disloyalty uttered and every deed of sedition committed in the district. All knew that he then passed this information on to Nicholas Price, the landlord of Saintfield and a pillar of the establishment. In any Ulster context this would, at the very least, make for very strained community relations.

The Presbyterian contempt for McKee and his people was part of a long, nasty and bitter saga in the area. Since 1796, or maybe before, loyalist families such as the McKees, Harpurs and Parkers were in conflict with the radically minded Dissenters of the district. The conflict was bitter enough even to divide the Presbyterians of the area and had gone on for so long that even the disputing factions would have been confused about its exact causes. It rumbled on through 1796, culminating with an attack by over one hundred Saintfield men set on destroying the Harpurs and the Parkers.

This affair had begun in deadly earnest but had dissolved into farce with desertions and confusion. The men had been resolute enough to plan a gathering at Ballyagherty Windmill Hill to the northeast of Saintfield in the middle of Hallowe'en night of October 1796. They intended to make a four or five mile walk through the night to Lisdoonan near Oughley, where the Harpur and Parker families lived and there demonstrate how they felt. They had even thought of ways of dealing with the soldiers who had been put on guard at the loyalists' houses. The men, some armed with guns, some with pikes and others with pitchforks, met up with a party just up the road from Saintfield. This was very near the house of a Jack Sheppard at the crossroads of the Ballygowan road and the road to Lessans. Together they had marched to the fort in Lisdoonan known as the Queen's Forth, where James Williamson told them that he had his tinder box and tobacco pipe and was all prepared to set fire to Harpur's house with them.

James Dougherty, the man who told the Rev. John Cleland this long detailed story, named about forty men, mostly from the Saintfield area. They were under a rough and ready leadership of men who will reappear in the events at Saintfield in the next chapter. These were Richard Frazer, David Thompson, Robert Sinclair, Andrew Orr and two brothers, James and David Shaw. The party even took the trouble to make a detour to the home of William Minnis to warn him to keep his windows and doors shut tight and not to stray out, because his hatred of the two families was so well known that he would be suspected if seen abroad.

These *pro tempore* leaders were taking their time while they waited for their chosen leader to arrive. A local gentleman called John Barnett, or sometimes Laird Barnett, was to head the said party. A few men were sent to Barnett's house to fetch him, but they soon returned with the answer that, "*he could not get, for that he had company with him, the Rev. Mr. Mayne."* At this point a number of men in the group decided that if this was the best that the leadership could do, then they had had enough too and left. Suddenly a man came forward and, *"offered his services and said he had, that day, been at Harpur's and made himself acquainted with the situation of the houses, the strength of the guards of soldiers that protected them and the way in which they guarded and defended them."*

Most of the men appear not to have known their guide, but they determined to follow him anyway. They had proceeded only a little way when they noticed that this self-appointed leader seemed to be missing. After a search around, they realised that he too had deserted them. By now the parties were so tired, confused and fed-up that their resolution dissolved and, rather ignominiously, they decided just to go home.[2]

Nonetheless, the bitterness and the integrity of the hatred were not forgotten. In early 1797 these sentiments raised their ugly heads again. It appears that the Saintfield republicans decided that this was the perfect time to deal with another old foe, Hugh McKee, and with his kinfolk if necessary. Eleven men, who included the Shaw brothers, were charged with making an attack on the McKees' house. They were all from the Saintfield congregation of Presbyterian Minister Thomas Ledlie Birch. He was a well-known United Irishman. Five years earlier he had formed in Saintfield the first Society of United Irishmen in rural Ulster and had been able to boast to Wolfe Tone that he had completely converted his flock.[3] He was later to come to a dubious celebrity after the Battle of Ballynahinch.

Lord Londonderry's agent from Newtownards, the Rev. John Cleland, had been largely instrumental in bringing the charges against these eleven men. At the trial the famous barrister, John Philpot Curran, who had been retained by the defendants, publicly savaged Cleland and this time all eleven men were allowed to go free.

In the courtroom Birch was arrested for treason. The charges later proved to be trumped-up and brought by a loyalist who lived beside him. Although this charge was dismissed, Birch was soon in bother again. Joseph Harpur accused Birch of offering him £50 not to prosecute United Irishmen and of assaulting Harpur's son. On the

6th April 1798, before the charge could be pressed or refuted in court, Harpur was shot at by persons unknown on the Belfast road. There is a common belief that Harpur died in the attack, but he appeared many months later involved in another legal action. The charges had simply been dropped, possibly for lack of corroborative evidence.

Colonel Lucius Barber, who had discovered the Donaghadee Resolutions and the other papers at Alexander's public house, although he was under General Nugent's command, sent a report directly to Castlereagh. He told him that the men responsible were in custody two months later, charged with the shooting of Harpur.[4]

This was the bitter atmosphere prevailing in the greater Saintfield area in the months before the withdrawal of the military. Their departure now left loyalists like McKee and Harpur in a very vulnerable state. When the rebels were called out that momentous June the bitterness still dominated the thoughts in many minds. While other rebel colleagues were intent on fighting the forces of the crown for their political beliefs, a few were bent only on revenge. Once that savoury dish had been eaten, they could join their friends with an enthusiasm to match theirs -- but first things first. They decided it was time to punish a man who they felt had repeatedly wronged them.

The story is a simple one, although beset with confusion. When a large group of insurgents started heading out of Saintfield towards Oughley Hill a number of men left the main party. They would have been well aware that they were very close to the house of the McKee family at Craignasasonagh – and that this was their opportunity to settle old scores. They would have known that Hugh McKee had a good supply of weapons and ammunition in his house, so they took great care not to expose themselves to musket fire. Inside the two-storied house were twelve people, Hugh McKee, his wife, five sons and three daughters (all young adults), a visitor and a servant, John Boles.

It would have been immediately obvious to the McKees why this party of rebels was there. Their arrival may even have been anticipated. The taunting and the shouts of abuse customary on such occasions would quickly have resolved any lingering doubts there may have remained about the intentions of the mob. Through a mixture of fear and their own reciprocal bitterness the McKees may have loosed off some shots, although it is not recorded in any of the depositions if they actually did so. But, suddenly, some of the besiegers gathered up as many combustibles as they could find and started piling them around the house. Their purpose was crystal-clear.

Contrary to popular folk-memory, the McKees' roof was slated, not thatched,[5] and would have been difficult to set on fire without plenty of inflammable materials. Some of the party removed slates from the roof and stuffed the faggots and straw through the gaps in the slates and set light to them. They and the other men then stood by implacably while the house's occupants screamed for mercy. Once the house was well alight the smoke and the flames did their terrible work in a short time. Those inside had the awful choice of running out into certain musket fire or of staying put in what was now a bonfire. In a little while the screaming stopped, leaving only the crackle of the still burning woodwork to disturb the awful silence.

When neighbours later doused the flames after the arsonists had gone away, they found eleven badly burned corpses in the pyre, all members of Hugh McKee's family. According to local tradition they were all buried, along with John Boles, in an unmarked grave in the garden opposite the ruined house.[6] A clutch of eyewitnesses saw this horror. It was not carried out in secret. Masks did not need to be worn. Being identified was not a fear of the culprits. Were they not simply doing the job that their friends wanted done?

But not all their friends wanted this level of retribution. Many rebellious minded people disliked, even hated the McKees, but could not countenance murder. When the heat of the rebellion later settled it was easy to get some of them to tell the magistrates whom and what they had seen. The sworn depositions of these witnesses still survive. Many stories of this atrocity have been handed down for two centuries; many accounts have been written. All of these have left posterity a large number of names.

Some of those named are well known to students of the rebellion, others not. Some later died for the part they played, or that someone said they played. At least one saved his neck by betraying his friends. Like so much in the story of '98, it simultaneously produced the best and the worst of character. Two centuries of folk tales and partial selection of 'facts' have further muddied the waters. Those who would recount the tale have brought so much of their own political or religious baggage to the telling that their objectivity must sometimes be questioned. Oral traditions cannot always be ruled out, but these are sometimes at the mercy of political expediencies or selective memory. The authentic voices of the witnesses, recorded at the time or very soon after, at least have the advantage of being unaltered over two centuries. Whether or not they are the whole truth, they are still the sworn testimonies of God-fearing people who had actually been present.

Four young women, Catherine Quinn, Mary McMaster, Susannah McMaster and Ellen Murry, watched a large group of strange men march up to the McKee house. Catherine swore that the only one she could definitely recognise was Charles Young, presumably because he was local. Two friends of theirs, the sisters Betty and Thora McCall, who lived just across the moss, also saw the men. Betty only recognised two men, although not for certain. They were both Saintfield men. The name of one, she said, was James Shaw, adding crucially that he was, "*dressed in a green jacket,*" and the other was John McKibben, a surgeon, armed with a pistol, "*to the best of her recollection.*"[7]

John Kennedy of Ballyrickard, near Scrabo, saw nothing of the incident at Craignasasonagh. However, his deposition gives some corroboration to Catherine Quinn's statement about Shaw. Kennedy told Cle6land that Shaw was a cotton manufacturer and placed him in the centre of Saintfield later in the day. Shaw had ordered him to stand as sentry outside the back of First Saintfield Presbyterian Church to watch for the approach of the King's Troops. Kennedy testified that, "*Shaw was dressed in a Green Jacket with yellow facings and wore a sword. He appeared to act as an officer.*"[8]

So far we have three candidates for leader-in-charge, with Shaw being the clear favourite. Jean Kearns, Alexander McKee's niece by his wife, has left us a number of names of men she believed to be involved. She identifies McKibben, whom she calls Doctor (although he was probably not a trained physician), and Shaw. Yet again Shaw is, "*on horseback, dressed in a green coat.*" She also mentions David Shaw, Thomas McKeever, James Collins and James Breeze, "*a large able-bodied man.*" Jean Kearns inadvertently tells posterity that not all McKee's neighbours were neighbourly when she includes the line, *"Peggy Thompson called out to the Rebels as they advanced towards McKee's intending to destroy him and them, to show no mercy."*[9]

She indicates another possible leader with the words, *"Saw a man on horseback who appeared to head and command the party and was called Doctor Cord."* This is one of a very few contemporary accounts of this man. Little is known of him, but in Killinchy Parish Churchyard there is a headstone erected to the memory of Dr. James Cord who died on the 23rd of June 1798, hanged after court martial for his part in the rising. Cord (or Chorde, or Choorde), the Killinchy apothecary, had been found guilty, *"on the fullest and clearest evidence [of] encouraging the inhabitants of Killinchy to rebel and with having a command in the insurgent army at Saintfield and Ballynahinch."*[10] It was claimed during his trial that he was the principal insurgent leader at the Battle of Saintfield. This is more than possible considering that it was not until after Saintfield that the better-known players, Munro, Townsend, McCance and Watson made their entrances.

The witnesses appear to agree that it was James Shaw's party of men who set fire to the house. Betty McCall said later she heard it was a fiddler called Orr, who lived somewhere between Saintfield and Killyleagh, who climbed on to McKee's roof and set fire to the house. But this, as a lawyer would say, is hearsay and must be in doubt. However, there is little doubt that the rebel party surrounded McKee's house to prevent any of them escaping.

As the flames were catching hold, a second company of rebels came on the scene. John Boyd of Ravarra led a company of Saintfield pikemen in files two deep to the rear of Hugh McKee's house to support the first party. James Dougherty, the shoemaker from Ballyblack, near Newtownards, swore that Boyd had taken his company there expressly to burn and destroy the McKees and that he had been so ordered by another mysterious figure on horseback who was never identified. Could this be the same mysterious horseman, Dr. Cord, mentioned by Jean Kearns?

Dougherty resented being compelled by the rebels to be there by the threat of, *"a Court Martial as soon as they returned to the Town of Saintfield."* He describes how John Boles escaped from the burning house and made a run for it and was pursued by some of the besiegers. William McGilton caught Boles and stabbed him with his pike.

Dougherty diligently listed as many as he could for their part in this awful episode, but only McKeown's and Miskelly's names appear on other lists:

Samuel Johnston of Tullygirvan	William Dyarmon of Ravarra
James Gorman, Carrickmannan	William Black, Ravarra (Weaver)
William McKeown, Ravarra	William Wallace, Ravarra (Kilnman)
Daniel Murry, Ravarra	Andrew Carson, Ravarra
	(Manservant to Richard Frazer)
Robert Sinclair	Pat Miskelly, Ravarra, (Weaver)[11]

A year later, Charles Young, the man named in Catherine Quinn's deposition, appeared at the Spring Assizes. Faced there with a charge of murder, he turned King's evidence and accused James McNamara, William Shaw, Hugh McMullan and John McKibben of the crime. The informer Nicholas Mageean made a possibly unique appearance before the Judge, Lord Kilwarden and swore that Young was a man not to be credited on his oath. When the truth of Mageean's double-dealing eventually emerged, memories of this description must have made many think of pots describing kettles. A more credible neighbour of the McKee's than Young later charged a number of men with the burning that day. This man was James Gardiner, a man who had been told by John McKibben on the awful day that he "*had a better right to be there than any that were there.*"[12]

Out of the two large parties at the McKee's, Gardiner accused over thirty by name, but only twelve were hanged for their parts in the disgraceful affair. Traditionally this was to balance the number of victims. Of those executed, five were local men, from townlands such as Ravarra and Carricknaveagh. These were William McCaw, William Shaw, Hugh McMullan, James Collins and Thomas McKeever. Seven others, James Breeze, Andrew and James Morrow, Samuel and James Hewitt, Robert Glover and David McKelvey were from townlands in the Killinchy area. Dr. Cord was never charged with any offences at the McKee's.

In passing it is worth mentioning that Gardiner's evidence also named two persons who were present at the McKees'. These men were to feature prominently in the story of '98 during the following few days. These were both Presbyterian Ministers, the Rev. William Adair, of Ballygraffan near Comber, and the young licentiate, the Rev. David Bailie Warden, who came from Ballycastle, near Newtownards and who was a probationer at Killinchy.[13]

Accusations are sometimes made without evidence or proof. After the rebellion was quelled there was certainly pressure put on witnesses of events to make depositions and name names, whether accurate or not. Some deponents may have succumbed, even though swearing their honesty before God. At times the word of a witness was sufficient reason to send an innocent man to the gallows. We do not know if such things happened in this case, but it does seem strange that James Shaw and John McKibben escaped the noose when so many others did not. As was to occur in many cases, the verdicts at the post-rebellion courts-martial were at best a lottery and at worst an indication of a convicted person's connections in the community.

The executions of the twelve who were convicted were carried out nearly a year later. In an unsigned account preserved in the Public Record Office of Northern Ireland is a sad coda to the story. It was written by someone who visited William McCaw, William Shaw and James Breeze in their condemned cells. From the context it is clear that this anonymous man and his two companions, Kenneth McCullough and J.W. Watson, were all clergymen. The account is especially interesting because it shows clearly that the men named in the note, and maybe their accomplices too, were strong in their religious faith, and, although convicted of such awful crimes and facing Eternity on a gallows, they could face death courageously. The transcription has a number of gaps in it, probably because of a delicate and damaged original:

McCullough and Wm. Shaw, Wm. McCaw and J. W. Watson and James Breeze walked hand, in hand...The psalms we sang in walking from the jail to the gallows were 23rd and 24th ... and read the 5th Chapter of Paul's second Epistle to the Corinthians... Then each embraced Each other and desperately took their leave of us all.

…Then they stept up… and Wm. Shaw said he died for his country,…Then Jas. Breeze reached me the Bible and I read the 8th Chapter of Romans…he solemnly declared he never give orders to any Body of men.[14]

1. Post Rebellion Depositions, (Lytton White Papers and Lowry Papers, PRONI, D/714 and D/1494).

2. James Dougherty of Ballyblack giving evidence to Rev. John Cleland, 10th day of February 1800, (Lowry Papers, PRONI, D/1494/2/21, MIC/506 Reel 1).

3. Theobald Wolfe Tone, *The Autobiography of Theobald Wolfe Tone*, 1763-1798, ed. R. Barry O'Brien, London, 1893, Vol. 1, p. 116, quoted in Stewart, p.181.

4. Col. Lucius Barber to Lord Castlereagh, 19th June 1797, (Rebellion Papers, NAI, 620/31/124).

5. James Dougherty's sworn examination, (Lowry Papers, PRONI, D/1494/2/10).

6. W.G.Lyttle, *Betsy Gray, or Hearts of Down*, reprint edition, published by the *Mourne Observer*, Newcastle, 1968, pp. 106-110.

7. Catherine Quinn and Betty McCall's depositions, (Lytton White Papers, PRONI, D/714/3/35).

8. John Kennedy of Ballyrickard's deposition, 16th June 1798, (Lytton White Papers, PRONI, D/714/3/14).

9. Jean Kearns's deposition, (Lowry Papers, PRONI, D/1494/2/20, MIC. 506, Reel 1).

10. Aiken McClelland, in an appendix to W.G.Lyttle, *Betsy Gray, or Hearts of Down*, .p. 178. Cord is sometimes known as Dr. James Choorde, or Coard.

11. Dougherty, (Lowry Papers, PRONI, D/1494/2/10).

12. Jean Kearns's deposition.

13. Aiken McClelland, Appendix, p. 166.

14. Anonymous gaol visitor, (PRONI, T/3042/1a).

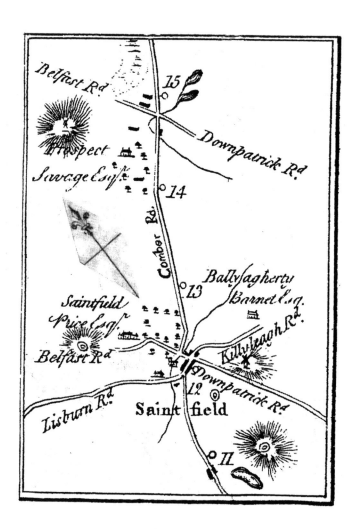

Saintfield

THE ENGAGEMENT
AT
SAINTFIELD

*These are the times that try men's souls. The summer soldier
and the sunshine patriot will, in this crisis, shrink from
the service of their country, but he that stands it now,
deserves the love and thanks of men and women.*

Tom Paine,
Introduction to The Crisis, 1776.

Their business done at Craignasasonagh, John Boyd and his men marched back through Saintfield to the Pound Bridge on the Ballygowan Road. There they met a man called John McGilton of Ballynickle. He seems to have been an older man, but one with experience of military command. He confirmed Boyd in his senior rank. He was seen to, "*put Capt. Boyd in his place at the head of his Company & gave him instructions how to conduct himself in his command.*" Boyd immediately ordered his men to break up the stone bridge in order to hold up the baggage train of the King's troops from the Ards when they came to Saintfield, as come they must. Shortly after this a large company of local rebels, brought by Richard Frazer, arrived in the town and began to deploy in expectation of the troops they knew must arrive from Newtownards.

The sources disagree about who was in overall command in Saintfield. The Rev Thomas Ledlie Birch gives the honour to Frazer, stating that, "*Richard Frazer, Lieutenant-Colonel of the Saintfield regiment, commanded the whole, and greatly signalized himself upon that occasion.*" Birch also indicated his admiration for Frazer by adding that Frazer had, "*suffered not the houses of Price, Clewlow or Curragh to be destroyed,*" contrasting this gentlemanly behaviour with that of the government forces three days later when they burned and plundered their way through the town and its surrounds.[1]

James Dougherty in a deposition taken the very day of the battle at Saintfield insisted that Frazer's men had come under the command of Alexander Hill, another Ravarra man. Over a year later Hill insisted that he was a simple soul who had found himself at Saintfield and that he knew,

> "of no person giving orders at it except a man whom he heard was called Adair, who rode on horseback with a sword in his hand and seemed to have the superior command."

From other eyewitnesses' reports this rider can only have been the Rev. William Adair. He was certainly present at Saintfield and Ballynahinch. John Kennedy of Ballyrickard told Newtownards magistrate James Clealand that he had seen, "*Adair at Saintfield on the same day...with a green belt and a drawn sword.*" Robert Ritchie deposed that he too, "*at Ballynahinch saw Adair on Wednesday, running away from the King's Troops.*"

Hill gave more credit to Adair, swearing that he had, "*ordered the body of men among whom he was to push forward & that he would go back and not leave a man in the town.*" Hill denied all knowledge of any leadership, but James Dougherty in his deposition insisted that, "*he does not know what Rank said Hill held in the Rebel Army but he seemed at this time to take the command of the whole of it.*" The magistrates later chose to believe Hill's denials because they stated that they could not discover enough corroborative evidence to contradict him.[2]

It has always been frustrating to historians that they can have a secure grasp of every officer on the loyalist side and many of the other ranks, because they are so clearly identified in the official reports, whereas trying to come to grips with the rebel leadership is like trying to catch smoke. The insurgent leadership being put in disarray by the sudden call to arms, just when their structures were awry, made for confusion with the early field commands and the obvious dangers of admitting to having held a senior position made many witnesses bashful at the later courts martial.

This combination of confusion and equivocation makes it difficult to be certain about the rebel leadership both at Saintfield on the Saturday and at the action in Newtownards on the Sunday. By way of contrast we know quite a lot about the garrison that Major-General George Nugent had based in the Ards. These were the York Fencibles commanded by Colonel Granville Anson Chetwynd-Stapylton.

This man was the youngest son of a disinherited Anglo-Irish viscount called Chetwynd. He had married an only daughter of the Stapylton family of Yorkshire. In the fashion of the day, he had combined her name with his to perpetuate her family name and, of course, to ensure the inheritance for his children. Chetwynd-Stapylton had been persuaded by the burghers and citizens of York to raise a regiment of the line and become its colonel. The regiment became known as the York Fencible Regiment and was eligible only for home service.

Colonel Stapylton had led the regiment to Ireland some time before the outbreak of rebellion and was not to return them to Yorkshire until four years after it was over. In June 1798 the headquarters of the York Fencibles were in Newtownards. General Nugent reported to Lt-General Lake that Stapylton, like the good officer he was, had observed the chain of command, but had been prepared to use his initiative when his scouts brought more urgent news of the rebels,

"hearing that they were collected at Saintfield, [he] advanced from Newtown Ardes to Cumber, from whence he sent for my orders; but before I could send them to him, he proceeded through Ballygowan nearly to Saintfield."[3]

Stapylton rode that morning from Comber to Saintfield at the head of 270 Yorks, a large number of Newtownards and Comber Yeomanry, both Cavalry and Infantry, two field pieces and an unrecorded host of civilian loyalists who were volunteering with their feet to fight the rebels. Wealthy and prominent citizens from the Ards and Comber area, including some Episcopalian clergymen, had enrolled in the Yeomanry corps of Captains Cleal and and Houghton and many of the civilians had caught the combat fever in time to join the march to Saintfield.

Progress was necessarily slow. A large body of soldiers, with their guns, provisions and accoutrements, usually moves at the speed of the slowest and the roads, although often straight, were narrow. From Newtownards, the troops skirted the southeast slopes of Scrabo Hill and over the easy marching country of Castleavarry and into the narrow streets of Comber.

Having shown the flag in the town centre the Fencibles marched up Comber's steep High Street. Once over the brow of the hill they would have had their first look at the almost arrow-straight road to Ballygowan stretching over the tops of the drumlins of Carnesure and Ballyrush and as far as their eyes could see. This little used road still runs parallel to the modern A21 almost as far as Ballygowan, where it crosses it and trickles, today known as 'The Brae', into the village centre. Like almost every road used by both armies that June, it has been left in modern times to the ghosts of '98.

An exception to this is the road from Ballygowan to Saintfield. Although widened, this is largely the same route as one travels today, except where it approaches near to Saintfield itself. Today a half-mile north of that town, the road from Ballygowan crosses the main A7 Belfast Road. This road from the city was not opened until many years after the rebellion. At this junction in 1798, near the isolated cottage owned by Jack Sheppard, the only road the York Fencibles would have seen here was the lane which went out to the townland of Lessans and then on towards the Castlereagh Hills.

If the advancing troops had their eyes open for a possible attack they may have been aware of the attention they had been receiving along their line of march. The hilly country of County Down lends itself very well to surreptitious observation, especially by those who know the country as their own backyard. Every rebel in Saintfield knew that a small Newtownards force of loyalists was on its way. They would quickly have ascertained how many were in it and probably the names of a number of the yeomen and civilians. The demolition of the bridges was only one of the measures Hill, Adair, Frazer, Boyd and Dr. Cord had taken to greet their visitors.

As Stapylton looked down the road into Saintfield from Sheppard's house, he could see rising in front of him on his right the tree-clad slopes on the eastern side of Mr. Nicholas Price's demesne. Across the road from these trees was a boggy and wooded hollow, which his local spies would have told him was called Doran's Wood. The site has greatly benefited in recent years from careful drainage and is now occupied by Saintfield High School and some modern housing. The main road which now runs past the rear of the school was not there in 1798 of course, so the bad marshy ground continued eastwards until it began to rise again to Ballyagherty Windmill Hill.

Stapylton was too experienced a soldier to advance without due caution. At about half-past four in the afternoon he ordered two cavalrymen to precede the main body and report back. The numerous accounts of the action that day agree that the woods on both sides of the approach road at that moment hid thousands of pikemen and that the ditches and sheughs along the road edge were full of men with charged muskets. Military histories regularly lay emphasis on how desperately difficult it was for officers to prevent even experienced professional soldiers from making careless noises or firing prematurely in such circumstances. Yet incredibly, Stapylton's scouts neither saw nor heard anything. The inescapable conclusion is that these poorly regarded insurgents had learned discipline from someone or somewhere and that among their ranks were some who well knew the business of war. There is no discernible written evidence for it, but this conjures up pictures of days of secret training during the previous months and perhaps even years.

After the dust of battle had settled, Alexander Hill may have had many reasons of his own for modesty about his role at Saintfield, but James Dougherty of Ballyblack in one of his depositions is insistent that Hill deserved the credit for the effectiveness of the rebels' initial attack that day. The clerk who recorded Dougherty's account wrote that Hill had:

sent an orderly Man to the Killinchey Rebels to furnish him with Twenty Rebels armed with guns to be placed in front of said Frazer's Regt. armed with pikes & his orders were for the gun men to cover them in front while the pike men filed off to the right & left & attacked the King's army on their Flanks. [Dougherty] Says the Killinchey Rebels sent word that they could not well spare them on which said Hill said they were cowardly but as there was no time to spare he

issued orders to the Killinchey Men posted about the Windmill of Ballyagherty
to cross over the hollow & attack the King's army in the rere while they would
attack them in front. Says said Hill issued orders to the pike men to rush on the
King's army & not be dismayed at any Men that would fall for as they had not
any discipline they were therefore not to depend on it.[4]

As the Yeoman Cavalry led Stapylton's main force forward, the signal was given and the trap was sprung. On a signal a galling volley of
musket fire cut a swathe through their ranks. A known casualty of this
first murderous fusillade was the Rev. Robert Mortimer, the Rector of
Comber Parish Church, who was killed instantly. He, the Rev. John
Cleland and others, had been enthusiastic civilians in the party and
must have been in the vanguard of Stapylton's force.[5]

Such an unexpected carnage turned the part-time yeomen on their
heels. At the optimum moment, just as the panicked yeomen hit the
front of their own main body that was still advancing, Richard Frazer's
pikemen rushed out of Price's woods at the rear of this body of soldiers
and where the baggage wagons were. A man, McKinstry, said by some
to have been leading the charge, was perhaps the first rebel to die in
the action.

Sergeant Levick (or Lewick) and a party of Fencibles were cut off
from the main body and the wagons and surrounded by another party
of pikemen from Doran's Wood. Levick later wrote:

> As we were going across a bog we were followed by a party...When they came
> up to us they told us to lay down our arms or we should all be dead men instant-
> ly. They took us to a house and took all our arms from us. They then took us
> toward their camp. . . and said we should be well treated until such time as they
> heard of the army using their prisoners ill, then we should suffer the same fate,[6]

Stapylton's men were in danger of being skewered with pikes if they
could not get themselves off the road. All the initiative was with the
rebels at this point. John Carson of Cherryvalley proudly held aloft
their colours, a piece of green on a graip shaft.[7]

The hand-to-hand fighting was wild and fierce. Sword and empty
musket were of little use against rows of thrusting pikes. The cavalry
and artillery, usually the scourges of pike battalions, could hardly turn

in the narrow roadway and when they broke through the hedges, the trees and bushes restricted their movements.

Ensign Michael Sparks, who was in charge of Stapylton's ordnance, put his impressions of their difficult situation down on paper some time afterwards:

> The ground the rebels had chosen was the most advantageous that could be imagined, so much so, that I could not, during a great part of the Action, bring either of my two guns to bear on the right, and was obliged to remain idle, exposed to an heavy fire for some minutes.[8]

Stapylton realised that he would not be able to deploy his field pieces until he could separate the opposing forces. The rebels, of course, had other ideas. They did not consider that withdrawing and assembling a distance away to become targets for canister and grape shot was in their best interests. So the bloody combat continued for some time at close quarters.[9]

A local minister spoke to one of the York Fencibles shortly after the battle. This soldier reported that one of his colleagues, a Frenchman who had fought many battles in France, had told him that:

> for danger and desperation this skirmish exceeded anything he had ever before witnessed. The soldiers were driven into disorder and every man had to fight his way in the best manner he could in opposition to the charged pike and other weapons to which he had not been accustomed.[10]

Stapylton finally managed to force his way up the slope into Price's demesne, from where his big guns could fire more effectively. The gun crews fired many shots at the rebels but the gunfire was not nearly so effective as it would have been in more open country. To some degree it made up for his inferiority of numbers and for a while preserved a noisy equilibrium, but the Colonel was very aware of the danger of being encircled. Ensign Sparks seems to have been alert to this possibility too:

> At length a strong column of rebels advanced on our left, [i.e. from Doran's Wood] attempting to turn our flank and surround us. I waited until they came so close that I must make sure work, and then poured on them a heavy fire of Canister shot, which soon put that column to flight with dreadful slaughter. At

that instant their party on the right made a desperate attack on our ranks where I was with the guns, and also on our baggage, and then it was that D[ea]r James and Lieut. Unite fell.

Stapylton also had to watch many of his men die. A sensitive officer always regrets any deaths on the battlefield, but the loss of fellow officers with whom he has mixed every day and who have been close friends hurts the most. Lieutenant William Hawe Unite and sixteen-year-old Ensign James Sparks, who appears to have been a close relative of the above William, were Yorkshiremen who had been with the Fencibles for some time. Their loss was bad enough, but that of a third officer must have struck Colonel Stapylton to the very heart.

His cousin, Captain William Chetwynd, son of the Rev. John Chetwynd of Cork, had been killed in the first hail of metal. One local tradition tells that a farmer called Daniel Mellin from Tonaghmore had seen Chetwynd rallying his men in the confusion and had put a musket ball through him, although another version maintains that it was a random shot.[11]

Stapylton could see that his force was badly outnumbered and the day was going against them. There were moments of hotly contested action when hopes were raised, but there were just too many rebels pouring out of the woods. His only hope of salvation was to be reinforced from Nugent's reserves.

Nugent's report of the battle to General Lake agrees that it was impossible for Stapylton to turn the tables on the insurgents with his limited force. The colonel knew that with enough troops he could carry the day, but Nugent, back in Belfast, had to think of the bigger picture. He tells Lake that Stapylton,

"remained some time on the ground and sent to me for Reinforcements, but it being late in the Evening, and the Safety of this Town not to be hazarded, I ordered him to retreat to Cumber."[12]

The loyalist *Belfast Newsletter*, like most of the frightened non-combatants in the city, had heard from returning soldiers only what it wanted to hear. The June 12th edition of the newspaper confines Stapylton's losses to 20 King's men. In the same paper it states that the rebels lost, "*upwards of 500 men, among whom were several of their lead-*

ers." These officers, went on the Newsletter, were dressed in, "*green jackets, turned up with white vest, buckskin breeches, half-boots, hats with white cock-neck feathers and green cockades.*"[13]

Humphrey Galbraith, the revenue officer at Groomsport, was another who did not have the benefit of Nugent's report when he wrote a letter three days later. Whilst other gentlefolk were flying to safety in Scotland, he had galloped to Belfast and found lodgings. From his bolt hole he exulted to his friend Edward Hull, who had escaped from Donaghadee to Stranraer, about the, "*splendid victory gained by Colonel Stapleton and the Yorks at Saintfield.*" He relays to Hull that some Donaghadee men were among the Yeomanry casualties, "*Tom Merry, Bob Lin, the saddler, and some others of the Yeomen were killed.*" He then compounds his mistaken belief of a great victory with a story he has heard about an officer who was a mutual acquaintance, "*Palmer proved himself and has got a nickname in the regiment for his gallantry. His whole cry was, 'Pepper away, fine fun boys!*'"[14]

After the battle, Stapylton, perhaps in Comber, was completing the details of a bad day and compiling the real casualty lists. There were large numbers of wounded, including the seriously injured Lieutenant Edensor. Worse, the loyal forces had lost, in addition to the three Fencible officers, two drummers, five sergeants, forty-two soldiers, five of the Newtown Yeoman Cavalry, two of the Infantry and four volunteers (two of whom were the Rev. Robert Mortimer and his nephew).

This accords well with figures Galbraith later sent to his friend David Ker at Stranraer, "*Capt. Chetwyn, Lieuts. Sparks & Unit, Edensor wounded, 37 men killd. & a few wounded. Of the Cavalry, poor Tom Merry & Lin the Saddler & many others.*" Galbraith adds the detail that Captain Houghton had had both of his Horses in turn shot under him and been forced to march home on foot.[15]

Stapylton had been forced to leave his dead behind him along with the slain rebels on the field at Saintfield. Local tradition says that the majority of these Yeomen and Fencibles were buried without grave markings in a mass grave at the back end of Saintfield's First Presbyterian Church graveyard. To this day this small area is known as York Island. This patch is beside the bridge over the little Saintfield River, just across the road from Colonel Price's gate-lodge. Although all the surrounding land has been drained and built on, York Island has remained boggy, tree-lined and wonderfully evocative of that day of Saturday, 9th of June 1798.

The dead rebels had all been buried by the time the large band of their fellows from the Ards arrived at Saintfield two days later on the Monday. As they passed the gate-lodge they saw the dead Fencibles being interred.[16] All of the corpses had been found on the field after the battle. They had been stripped and looted, as was the way of war. They even recognised the Reverend Mortimer's milk-white body, still propped awkwardly against a gate.

James McKey of Belfast, writing to Lord Downshire as soon as he heard the full news, expressed his feelings about the loyalist deaths, especially that of Mortimer and hoped soon to be in a position to exact some measure of revenge on the rebels:

> My heart was like to burst with grief today at seeing Mrs. Mortimer and her nine children, who these murderers were the means of robbing of a husband, a father, and their only support…Tomorrow I hope in God that I might get a shot at [the rebels] as it would gratify me to take the lives of these fellows [more] than anything I ever met.[17]

The numbers of rebel dead are unknown, as are the identifiable sites of most of their graves. There are many people living today in mid or north Down who will give an enquirer the names of some of those who fought and died at Saintfield, but after two hundred years these are difficult to verify. Many of them did find a resting place, mostly unmarked, in First Presbyterian churchyard and indeed there are still two simple grave markers beside York Island. These were James McEwan of Ballycreely and John Lowry from Killinchy. It is thought that the rebels were buried closer than they might have wished to the bodies of the Fencibles. It was also far enough indeed from their homes, but they do lie with their comrades-in-arms, near the site of what they would have regarded as a great victory.

A student of the battle who visits the parish church of Comber will see just inside the main door there a handsome memorial to the York Fencible officers who fell that day. The tablet reads:

In Memory of Captain WILLIAM CHETWYND
Lieutenant WILLIAM HAWE UNITE
and Ensign JAMES SPARKS
late of the York Fencible Infantry who fell bravely
fighting for their King and Glorious Constitution
In an engagement near Saintfield With the rebels
On the 9th day of June, 1798
Their brother officers Impressed with the deepest sorrow and with the highest
sense of their courage and manly virtues have erected This Monument.

The sculptor has made interesting use of the word 'engagement' for what happened at Saintfield. The Fencibles could hardly have called the action a victory since they had been forced to retreat to Comber. They would certainly not have admitted to a defeat, especially by a motley crowd of rebels; and the eventual victory of Nugent's main force at the Battle of Ballynahinch gave the loyalists an excuse to describe the earlier action in Saintfield as a tactical skirmish, or the classic and non-committal 'engagement'.[18] However the men who were making their way to their new camp at Creevy Rocks just outside Saintfield were well aware that they had been left in possession of the field of battle and had watched their enemy's retreat. These United Irishmen were in little doubt about who were the victors of Saintfield.

Chetwynd-Stapylton's woes were not over. Not long after he reached Comber, word was brought to him that the insurgents had already taken Newtownards and that his own plans to invest it were now lost. His only remaining alternative was to take his tired and defeated men to join Nugent's main army in Belfast.

1. Rev T L Birch, *A letter from an Irish emigrant to his friend in the United States giving an account of the commotions of the United Irishmen and Orange Societies, and of several battles and military executions, Philadelphia,* 1799, quoted in Aiken McClelland, *History of Saintfield and district,* Saintfield, 1971.

2. Depositions sworn at Newtownards by: Robert Ritchie, 16th July 1798, (Lytton White Papers, PRONI, D/714/3/15), James Dougherty of Ballyblack, Saturday the 9th Day of June 1798, (Lowry Papers, PRONI, D/1494/2/10),

Alexander Hill, September 27th 1799 (Lytton White Papers, PRONI, D/714/3/45), and John Kennedy of Ballyrickard, 16th Day of June 1798, (Lytton White Papers, PRONI, D/714/3/14).

3. Major-General George Nugent, Belfast, to Lt. Gen. Lake, June 10th 1798, (Rebellion Papers, NAI, 620/38/121).

4. James Dougherty of Ballyblack, in examination at Newtownards, 9th Day of June 1798, (Lowry Papers, PRONI, D/1494/2/10).

5. James Arbuckle from Dublin, to Patrick Heron, normally of Kirroughtrie, Scotland, 12th June 1798, (Transcripts of Heron Papers, PRONI, T/3162/1/5).

6. Sergeant Levick of the Yorkshire Fencible Infantry at the Court Martial of John McClery in Downpatrick, 31st July 1798, Charles Dickson, *Revolt in the North: Antrim and Down* in 1798, Dublin and London, 1960, quoting (Rebellion Papers, NAI, No code no. given).

7. John Kennedy of Ballyrickard in Examination before James Clealand at Newtownards, 16th June 1798, (Lytton White Papers, PRONI, D/714/3/14).

8. Ensign Michael Sparks, printed in Robert M. Young, *Historical Notices of Old Belfast and its Vicinity,* Belfast, 1896, quoted in Stewart, *The Summer Soldiers, The 1798 Rebellion in Antrim and Down*, Belfast, 1995.

9. Charles Dickson, *Revolt in the North: Antrim and Down in 1798,* Dublin and London, 1960, and A.T.Q. Stewart.

10. The Rev. Samuel Edgar of Ballykine, near Ballynahinch, in the *Belfast Magazine,* Vol. 1, No. VI, 1 July 1825, quoted in Dickson and Stewart.

11. Aiken McClelland, in an appendix to W.G.Lyttle, *Betsy Gray, or Hearts of Down,* p. 175.

12. Nugent to Lake, June 10th 1798, (Rebellion Papers, NAI, 620/38/121).

13. *Belfast Newsletter*, 12th June 1798.

14. Humphrey Galbraith at Mr. Fuller's, Belfast to Edward Hull at Stranraer, June 13th 1798, (Downshire Papers, PRONI, D/607/F/235).

15. Humphrey Galbraith at Belfast to D Ker at Stranraer, 11th June 1798, (Dobbs Papers, PRONI, D/2651/2/143).

16. Anonymous eyewitness, quoted in W. McComb, *McComb's Guide to Belfast,* Belfast, 1861, p. 128.

17. James McKey, Belfast to Downshire, 11th June 1798, (Downshire Papers, PRONI, D/607/F/222).

18. Charles Dickson, pp. 141-143, and A.T.Q. Stewart, pp. 183-188.

Insurrection in the Ards

Soldiers of the ploughshare,
as well as soldiers of the sword.

John Ruskin,
Unto This Last, Essay No. 3.

Carefully kept in the National Archives of Ireland in Bishop Street in Dublin, among many thousands of public and private papers, is a document considered indispensable to anyone researching the activities of the United Irishmen at Newtownards, Saintfield and Ballynahinch in the sunshine patriot days of early June 1798.

It is described by its writer as, *"a Narrative of the Principal Proceedings of the Republican Army of the County of Down during the late Insurrection."* It tells of events from just before the breaking out of insurrection in County Down up to the eve of the Battle of Ballynahinch. The document comprises a few sheets of apparently contemporary rag paper. The paper has been so diligently and frequently examined and pored over throughout the last two centuries that it is in an extremely delicate condition. From its appearance it is clear that at some time in its long life, the pages have been torn into pieces and later rejoined. The writing is still remarkably legible even though today the paper is only held together with loosely sewn thread.

The apparent author is an otherwise completely unknown William Fox, whose putative signature appears twice on the document. An examination of this account discloses a great amount of detail about the involvement of the men of the Ards in the affairs of June 1798. The document is a very valuable primary source, describing as it does the actions of a rebel leader during the few days leading up to the

Battle of Ballynahinch, and is usually accepted as the authentic voice of its author.

However a more careful examination of the format of the document raises a number of questions. The paper is not dated, but seems to have been written in the early years of the Nineteenth Century. The writer first boasts that he was, "*a good Deal concerned in the Affair of the Insurrection,*" and then immediately retreats into a modest disclaimer, "*I hope no Person will charge me with Egotism if I must frequently introduce my own Actions to your Attention.*"

Throughout the document the writer is very careful, through the use of initials and aliases, not to incriminate any of the principals who might have escaped detection and punishment. A few years ago it was discovered that the most misleading alias in the document is that of the writer himself. In recent years it has been demonstrated that the true identity of the author was David Bailie Warden.[1] We have already encountered this young licentiate and schoolteacher during his journeys around north Down in the early months of 1798. Warden was born and raised in Ballycastle near Greyabbey, just over the back wall of the Mount Stewart estate.

He was an intelligent lad marked out early as a perfect candidate for the church. He had begun his Presbyterian clerical training as a pupil of Rev. James Porter of Greyabbey.[2] At a meeting of the Presbytery of Bangor at Steel Dickson's old church at Glastry on Tuesday 2nd February 1797 it was minuted that David Bailie Warden had received his licence to preach the gospel.[3] He preached his first sermon on 11th June 1797 at Belfast. By the summer of 1798 he had accepted a call from the Presbyterian Church at Killinchy, just a short boat trip across Strangford Lough away from both his home at Ballycastle and Porter's church at Greyabbey.

Warden himself, as we have seen, was an enthusiastic member of the United Irish movement in the Ards. He well knew what was going on in the months before the insurrection and seems to have been one of the first to be 'up' in the Ards. In the paper which he called his Narrative, but which he never owned, nor claimed to be autobiographical, he places William Fox in a central role all through the gathering of the men of the Ards, their attacks on the town of Newtownards and their march through Saintfield to Ballynahinch.

For many years the story of William Fox was taken at face value and, although he was unknown, his account accepted as totally true. It was assumed that there must have been a William Fox, or that it was a cover-name for a known rebel. Somehow, because it has now been demonstrated that the hand that wrote the first person account was that of David Bailie Warden, some chroniclers have taken it as read that the first person perspective must have been Warden's own, even though there is no record that he ever claimed that it was.

Undoubtedly there are those who have accepted the William Fox account without question and then spent much of their time fitting other pieces of evidence around it. They have been able to accept the discovery of the account's authorship by David Bailie Warden – one of the central characters in the drama and someone who could, just possibly, have been the leader of the men of the Ards.

However a comparison of dates and places suggests strongly that Warden in fact may have written his account of the journey of the men of the Ards to Ballynahinch, but with a fictitious hero. Some will find this difficult to accept, even though it is entirely plausible. Of course, some so-far-undiscovered evidence may some day come to light to disprove this hypothesis and it may transpire that Warden was the true hero. But, if the story of 1798 in the Ards can accommodate the faction of *Betsy Gray and the Hearts of Down* without hurting the reality, it can surely tolerate what appears to be Warden's fancy.

The document itself is certainly no fake. Its very condition would convince anyone of its great age and genuineness and it is a short step from that to accepting all of its details as genuine too. Warden did not set out to tell an untrue story and we do know that he was present most of the time. However, it is certainly arguable that what Warden probably did when he began his attempt on a history of the rebellion, was to attempt to make his account of the rebellion more interesting to his readers by enhancing the truth. He could do this by having the story told by a modest hero who was able to play an otherwise impossibly ubiquitous role in the activities of the Ardsmen.

In his Narrative he tells the story from the point of view of the imaginary William Fox. In reading it, we must remember that it is the character Fox who claims the central role in the Ards, not the author. Warden himself does appear to have been a great enthusiast and even advocate for the insurrection and he did have a fairly senior position in the Down Society. However, all other evidence points to his involvement being at a level somewhat below that of a senior colonel. Significantly, he is not named in any of the court martial depositions or eyewitness accounts as a senior commander or colonel of the Ards rebels either before or during the insurrection.

We can be fairly sure that Fox is entirely imaginary, because nowhere in the comprehensive lists of rebels, such as those court-martialled afterwards, the depositions taken at the time of these courts martial, the records of prisoners, nor in the *Black Book of the North*, does the name, William Fox, appear. This storytelling device of having a central hero or champion allows Warden's account to have, at a number of widespread locations, the immediacy of the first person.

Warden did not attempt to write his narrative until much later, after years which saw him being imprisoned for a period, having his licence to preach withdrawn, then being compelled to emigrate to America never to return and later becoming a highly successful career diplomat.

Warden never forgot the man who had given him his first training. Forty-six years after James Porter's execution and his own escape from the noose, Warden sent his old notebook to Porter's son. It contained the comments he recorded at Porter's lectures on natural and experimental philosophy all those years before. James Porter Junior was proud to write in his own family history in 1844, "*A curious little book containing an abstract of these lectures, taken at the time by D.B. Warden, the U.S. Consul at Paris, is now in my possession, having been sent to me by Mr. Warden a short time ago.*"[4]

In his William Fox chronicle Warden has him address the Men of Down and insist that even in those later years, "*My Heart and my Thoughts cannot be separated from your Interest and your Sufferings,*" and is confident that they, "*still retain that bold Independence of Thought, that manly Possession of Principle, which characterises the brave Republican.*"

Warden states his opinion that, because of the arrests of inspirational leaders and the poor quality of some of their replacements, "*the Insurrection commenced in confusion,*" and the rebel forces were, "*in no better Order than a mere Country Mob.*"

Although he is critical of the leaders in general, he is more generous about the individuals he mentions. In the time-honoured fashion used by many writers before him, Warden introduces his hero Fox to the story as an eager young man who finds himself caught up in fiery events and whose steel is tempered by that furnace. His previously unrecognised leadership qualities surface and he quickly finds himself very close to the Down county leadership of the United Irishmen. When referring to these men he rarely uses actual names, usually describing them as Gentlemen with whom he is very friendly.

Since the narrative was written some years later in America and some time after the event, Warden's coyness about identities seems overly cautious. A number of years into the nineteenth century some degree of protection for those old rebels still living in Ireland might have been required, but it is frustrating to a modern reader always having to guess every time which of the possible leaders he might mean.

He has William Fox begin his Narrative on Sunday, the 3rd of June 1798 by disclosing that one of the Gentlemen, whom he knew well, allowed him that day to see a secret Express, which said that, "*the Colonels of United Irishmen in the County of Antrim were averse to Action, but that the Defenders were 5,000, all ready for Action, [and] asked if our County had put itself into a State of Readiness and were answered in the Affirmative.*"

The close friend who had received this message was undoubtedly a senior officer in the United Irishmen and one who was well known to Warden. This man may well have been the Rev. James Porter.

We will see later that Porter and his family claimed that he was not involved in the insurrection itself. Nonetheless, at a Colonels' Meeting of the United Irishmen in Saintfield on 23rd March, Porter was reported to have been appointed to a senior position in the County organisation.[5] He was also said to have been present at a Meeting of the Colonels of County Down at Saintfield on Thursday, the 31st of May, along with Jas. Clokey of Ballynahinch, representing eight

Regiments, George Sinclair of Ravarra, all three of them described as Brigadier-Generals, James Hamilton of Moneyrea, John McMaster of Donaghadee (deputising for Francis Falloon), the Rev. Mr. Miles of Moneyrea, James Townsend and nine other Colonels and Majors.[6]

Warden would not have been able to comment on this meeting with any authority in his Narrative because he was not there. We know that on that very day he was at a Committee Meeting for the northern half of the County in Newtownards. An anonymous letter to the Rev. John Cleland flattered Londonderry's agent by telling him this meeting had agreed,

> "from the danger that might occur from meting in a town such as Newtonards whear such a man as Mr Cleland resided as Magestrate and no dute [doubt] might have spies under him that it would be wise to adguen [adjourn] to Greaby."

This letter was most likely from a casual informer, supplementing the steady stream of information that Nicholas Mageean was supplying on a regular basis to Cleland. The writer appears to be under the impression that Mageean stayed in Newtownards to pass on the news from the other meetings, but Mageean as we know was actually at Saintfield. The anonymous correspondent states that the principal figures at the Greyabbey meeting were Warden, who is described as tutor to Mr. Hughes's family and Andrew Bryson, of the Cottown.

The probationer took a key role at Greyabbey. The informer adds that Mageean, pleading an apprehension for his safety, *give the Reports to Warran [Warden] for to deliver to them in Greaby and hee himself wated in Newton Ards and sent them to Greaby as they came.*[7]

There seems a strong possibility that Porter, like many others, was enthusiastic for the cause right up to the actual breaking out of hostilities, but that for whatever reasons of his own, possibly despair caused by the confusion Warden highlights, he stayed at home from the Friday, 8th June.

In Warden's Narrative, Fox and his gentleman friend, having studied the message from Antrim, concoct a plan to go to that town to discover their most recent designs. The Narrative later states that this plan, *"failed through the Absence of another Gentleman, without whose*

Consent I could not officially attend the Antrim Meeting." This gentleman was most probably the Rev. Dr. William Steel Dickson, who had
been made Adjutant-General for County Down on 12th May 1798 at
a Colonels' Meeting at Harrison's Public House in Dromore.[8]

Two days later, according to Warden's account, on Tuesday, 5th June,
Fox went to Nicholas Mageean in Saintfield. Yet again Warden has
Fox in company with an anonymous companion and the pair then go
on to Ballynahinch to meet Steel Dickson. The following afternoon
Warden places the two men once again with Mageean in Saintfield.
On this occasion Mageean told them that he had only just received a
special message brought by John Hughes of Belfast. This was to the
men of Down inviting them, *"to rise, adding that by 12 o'clock the next
day (Thursday) the County Antrim would be in Arms,"* and that they
would attack the town of Antrim.

Warden then has Fox assure readers that he,

> had previously been informed of the Resignation of the Antrim Adjutant-General
> [Simms], and of the consequent Disorgan-isation of that County – the news of
> McGean gave me Hopes that Affairs had been better managed, and that all
> might yet do better. I therefore turned to Saintfield and enquired at a certain
> Gentleman [Dickson?] there if he had received the News from Belfast, who told
> me he had – I then asked him if he would act according to the express Request,
> and being answered that he would, I next enquired what would be the most
> proper for me to do and was directed by him to go to ---------- and order the
> Colonel of that Regiment to put it into Motion as soon as possible.

Fox rather self-importantly says that he approved of the Plan and so
immediately proceeded as he was ordered.

Many contemporary documents survive which describe the events
of these same few days. Reading them tells us that Warden was most
certainly aware of what did actually happen, but that he has employed
some poetic licence in his Narrative. His account is quite detailed,
even though there are deliberate gaps in it, but much of the narrative
carries the stamp of authenticity only possible from an eyewitness or a
close confidant. But it can only be read in conjunction with the huge
number of other surviving letters and reports.

One of such papers was written on Wednesday 6th June, probably by the informer, Nicholas Mageean. This note was apparently

penned in haste for the information of Nicholas Price of Saintfield, Lord Castlereagh, Lord Londonderry and the Rev. John Cleland. The last named was the most probable recipient, although he would always have passed on any such news to the others immediately.[9] When one compares Mageean's letters with the Warden/Fox account, one is struck by the similarities between them and the almost identical details of the activities they describe. However one crucial difference is that Mageean names two entirely different individuals as being the principals involved. He tells of John Hughes, stationer from Belfast, the day before, carrying a message from Henry Joy McCracken, meeting two men, "*the Revd. Mr. [John] Miles, a Probationer of Moneyrea & teaches a school & James Townsend, Probationer, & tutor in the Revd. Porter's.*"

Like Warden, at that time Miles and Townsend can only have been in their early twenties. It is known that Miles received his licence to preach the gospel on 7th February 1797, five days after Warden.[10] Townsend may have preceded both of them by a number of months, but the records for the four years up to February 1797 are missing from the Bangor Synod records. This has caused some writers to claim that Townsend was never a church minister, even though he is often described as such in more contemporary papers, such as Mageean's, above. He is also described in later evidence as wearing clerical black when he departed from Greyabbey.

James Townsend and John Miles, were both well-known United Irishmen and, in fact are included on a list of Presbyterian ministers implicated in the rebellion.[11] Interestingly, this list also gives the name of one of the other implicated ministers as David Bailie Warden. The famous *Black Book of the North*,[12] which gives another list of 189 names (117 of them from County Down) of people involved in the north in 1798, also includes Townsend, Miles and Warden, plus all the other rebels mentioned above.

It would appear that in 1798 neither Miles nor Townsend had yet received a call to a congregation of his own. As Mageean states, the former seems to have been assisting at Moneyrea and the later tutoring James Porter's children in Greyabbey.

Both Townsend and Miles were named as being present at the above-mentioned 31st of May Meeting of the County Down Colonels at Saintfield. The message Hughes had brought to the meeting from McCracken was for Steel Dickson. It told him, fairly peremptorily, "*that the Co. Antrim were ready for action & for him to put the Co. Down in motion & that if he would not they would find a Man that would.*"

Later on that Wednesday, according to Mageean's note, at about half past five in the afternoon, a man called Owen Leslie had brought him a second express from McCracken, Hughes and David Thompson saying that, "*the County Antrim intended seizing on the Magistrates assembled in Antrim at the Sessions, for Hostages as a beginning to their rising & desiring N. Mageean to carry their message to Dr. Dickson.*"

Mageean soon found out that the last instruction was already impossible. The two young men, Townsend and Miles, had suddenly arrived at his house at six o'clock with the awful news that Lord Annesley's Castlewellan Yeomanry had made Dr. Dickson a prisoner in Ballynahinch at about 9 o'clock the previous evening. The two probationers had actually met with Dickson, a man they both knew well and admired. He had told them how important it was for the Down command to be re-established, but also to await the news from the proposed Provincial Executive Meeting at Ballymena on the Friday 8th June.

Dickson had been taken up very soon after this encounter and marched to Goldie's camp at Blaris near Lisburn on Wednesday the 6th June. Townsend and Miles, who had either witnessed the arrest, or heard about almost immediately, fled the scene. They had then called at James Tannahill's near the Spa Well and secondly at James Clokey's. Both of these were well-known United men, highly respected within the movement, but Miles and Townsend, incredibly, when one considers their youth, had rejected them as leaders. They actually stated that Clokey was, "*not a warm enough man in the cause,*" to even consider for Adjutant-General. This may have been a good decision, because on Thursday 7th June James Clokey along with a number of others, possibly including Tannahill, were taken up on the orders of General Goldie and put, "*in close confinement in the Camp.*"[13] This can only have been Blaris.

Ignorant of this future development, Townsend and Miles had already decided, "*that the Revd. Mr. Porter should take the command.*"

Townsend *"went express to Porter for that purpose taking Killinchey in his way meaning to warn them."* Miles went to his home ground of Moneyrea to warn his own people.

In Mageean's message to the authorities the reason he gives for Townsend's going to visit Porter by way of Killinchy was to warn the rebels there, *"by calling on the Revd. Mr. Warden."* There are two important and clear implications here. One is that Warden had some close connection with the Killinchy rebels, perhaps even a rank of some importance with them, and the other, of course, is that Warden, in fact, had been at home in Killinchy during these crucial hours.

Mageean's writings are not to be entirely trusted, but his message of 6th June does exist and was written years before Warden wrote his Narrative. As a paid informer, Mageean would have been anxious to implicate anyone he thought was active in the rebel cause and would have included any names or deeds that might prove useful to the authorities. This message to Cleland reads like Mageean has just received the sensational news that the long expected rising is to be immediate and that he wishes to inform the authorities as soon and as accurately as he can who is centrally involved. It shows that at this early date Warden was already knowledgeable of what was going on amongst the rebels, but probably not yet very actively involved.

It seems certain that Warden himself took a busier part when the rebellion did break out, but with a less senior position than he gives to Fox in those affairs. Warden would have known that some men rode, as he describes Fox and his companion doing, to Donaghadee and Bangor, rounding up support. In the days following he probably did witness what he describes at Newtownards, Saintfield and Ballynahinch and may even have carried out some of the actions himself, even though he gives all of the credit to William Fox.

There is an interesting entry in the Minute Book of the Bangor Presbytery for that May. At a thinly attended meeting the Revs. Callwell, William Sinclair of Newtownards and James Porter of Greyabbey recognised that the Rev. James Knox was the properly appointed minister of Donaghadee Meeting House. Mr. Knox was unable to perform his pastoral duties that summer, so a roster of supply preachers was drawn up for that short period. In view of what was ahead of them all, it is interesting that these men were James Hull, David Bailie Warden, John Miles, James Porter, William Sinclair and Dr Steel Dickson.[14] Whatever his actual involvement, Warden must have reflected on the irony that only two or three weeks before 'Pike Sunday' he had agreed to serve as supply preacher at Donaghadee.[15]

If Warden was not the leader in charge of the Ardsmen, then who was? None of the eyewitnesses disagree with the essentials of his version, but when their accounts ascribe responsibility for certain actions, they all give different names to the leaders. Just as at Saintfield, it is very difficult to establish who really was in charge during these first few confused hours. In the terrible days just after the rebellion was crushed many of those who had played leading roles were understandably careful about admitting it, or were in hiding, or were already dead.

In the immediate aftermath depositions were taken from dozens of rebels who had been taken up, but who were not regarded as sufficiently important to execute. In the Ards area the deposition hearings were conducted in the main by the two Cleland brothers, the Rev. John, with whom we are well-acquainted, and his brother, James, the Yeomanry Captain, who always seems to have spelt his name, Clealand. Those who made such depositions invariably claimed to have been coerced into joining the rebels. They often added a story of how the point of a pike had been presented to them with the choice of carrying it to Saintfield by its blunt end or of having to deal with its sharp end. For instance, James McPhee of Drumawhey swore that Samuel Burrowes, in company with several armed men, had, *"seized him by the breast with his left hand and presented a pike to his breast and told the deponent to turn out or else he would destroy deponent and his property."*[16]

When asked to name their leaders the deponents usually did so, but with such a level of disagreement that one can only choose quite arbitrarily between the different versions. Either that Sunday morning and afternoon between Bangor and Newtownards there was utter confusion, or the witnesses made a deliberate attempt to portray just that.

A tailor from Newtownards called Hugh Montgomery made a voluntary oath to James Clealand about another Newtownards man called John Byers. This man, he said, *"wore a shoulder belt with a sword by his side and was called sergeant,*" and had given him a gun on Sunday, 10th June and taken him to Scrabo Hill and later had led many men through Comber to Saintfield and Ballynahinch.[17]

Alex. Halliday of Bangor, a weaver,[18] and Jas. Petty, a labourer from Carnalea[19], agree with each other that, "*Jas. Francis of Bangor appeared to have the command of the party,*" although Halliday also says Archibald Martin gave a number of orders, possibly as a subordinate officer. Another candidate for the position of leader in charge of the Newtownards/Bangor rebels, at least at the time of their recruitment, must be a stonemason from Conlig called Archibald Wilson.

James Robinson, a flax hackler, who lived in the nearby townland of Rathgill, declared under oath that a stout genteel man, whom he does not name, "*told him if he would go and tell Archie Wilson of Conlig to tell the people to rise, to give them a fair chance for their lives he would let him go.*"[20] Robinson then admits that he, "*armed with a bayonet on a pole,*" went off in company with a number of men, including his friend, William Clark, Junior, a labourer from Conlig. Archie Wilson acted as Captain and took them to Conlig mountain and thence to Newtownards and up on to Scrabo Hill. Later, Robinson was one of the lucky ones who escaped from the action at Ballynahinch and managed to make his way home to Rathgill unharmed.

William Clark totally supports his friend's story and adds some more detail. He made oath that he, "*saw Archibald Wilson act as Captain and George Hamilton and John Allen act, as he believes, as inferior officers or sergeants.*"[21]

Many of those accused of being leaders eventually went unpunished, or had lesser punishments, but at least three Bangor men suffered the supreme penalty. James Dunlop, who was a carpenter, was accused by a number of Bangor boatmen, James McBlain, George Sloper, Andrew Newton and others, of being in charge of men and swivel guns at both Saintfield and Ballynahinch. So overwhelming was the evidence that the court summarily sentenced Dunlop to immediate hanging.[22]

Archibald Wilson in the years since 1798 has become something of a folk hero in the Conlig area, but Clark throws out a hint that Archibald was not the only determined member of his family. In his deposition he makes the intriguing declaration that, "*he was ordered to join the Rebels by Archibald Wilson's sister, Betty Wilson.*"[23] We can only imagine that encounter.

There is no record of the later life of Betty Wilson, but it is certain that Archibald was caught soon after the rising, tried and hanged. What is less certain is the location of the gallows. A persistent story describes Wilson, after swearing his innocence at his trial and going to his execution on his bare knees, singing psalms and being hanged at Bangor Pier along with James Dunlop and a third man named Robert Robinson.

According to the *Belfast Newsletter*, after being court-martialled and found guilty of rebellion and treason Wilson was hanged at Conlig.[24] In a third version an eye witness states that the execution was carried out at Newtownards. Sergt. Hamer, supported by Sergt. Thomas Beckett, both of Capt. Barber's troop of Lancashire Light Dragoons, swore on 30th June 1798 that:

> Captain [Archibald] Wilson of the Rebel Army of the County Down was Hang'd at N.Townards on Tuesday the 26th June 1798, and after he had been hanged for the Space of Eight Minutes, he was took down and his head cut off By one of the Lanc[ashi]re. Light Dragoons, and left upon the Spot, Sticking upon the Point of one of there own Inverted Spikes.[25]

When his family at last recovered possession of Wilson's earthly remains, they were treated with more respect. In Bangor Abbey graveyard a headstone was erected to Wilson's memory. The stone was crowned with leaves, a hammer and an axe. Below this the sculptor, and we can easily imagine he was a former colleague of Archie's, chiseled, with more attention to his poetry than to his spelling:

> Here lieth the body of Archibel Wilson of Conlig who departed this life June the 26 in anno 1798, æg 26 yr.

> Morn not, deer frends, tho' I'm no more
> Tho' I was martred, your eyes before
> I am not dead, but do sleep hear
> And yet once more I will appear.

That is when time will be no more
When thel be judged who falsly sore[swore]
And them that judged will judged be
Whether just or onjust, then thel see.

Purpere, dere frends, for that grate day
When death dis sumance you away
I will await you all with due care
In heven with joy to meet you there.[26]

It appears that confusion ruled in north Down and the Ards in those
first few days, with the leadership mostly coming from the loudest
voices. It was to be a little while before some chain of command was
organised among the hundreds of men milling around between Bangor
and Newtownards. This was on Pike Sunday, as it later came to be
called from the forests of those weapons on view all over the county
that day.

In another part of the Ards many had been 'up' for somewhat
longer. When word had arrived on the Saturday evening that the men
of Saintfield and Killinchy had risen Edward Hull of Donaghadee,
Secretary of the Packet Company, had written to the Marquis of
Downshire stating that the rebels of Donaghadee had been mobilised
the moment the detachment of the York Fencibles had been with-
drawn from that port to Comber and Newtownards.

The military that had been garrisoning the smaller towns had been
ordered to replace the troops who had been recalled to Belfast:

On the breaking out of the disturbances at Antrim, the York Fencibles at
Newtownards were ordered to Belfast to replace the Monaghan Regiment, all
the outposts of the Regiment were ordered in and Donaghadee with the rest - of
course the town was left without any Protection whatsoever. It was evident that
the People were determin'd on Insurrection for some days before which oblig'd
all the loyal inhabitants of the town to join the Military and about thirty of them
did sit up for three or four nights.

Within hours the Donaghadee rebels had taken over the harbour
and the large whinstone Customs House that closed off Donaghadee's
Parade at Kelly's Steps and were soon masters of the town. It would
appear that the fast sailing cutters of the Packet service, with their

important swivel guns, had been withdrawn just in time and taken to Scotland on Major-General Nugent's orders.

These Packets were now under the direction of Lord Ranelagh of the *Doris* and for the duration of hostilities and a number of weeks after, would be operating between Portpatrick and Carrickfergus.[27] The last sailing of a Packet from Donaghadee had taken as many refugees as it could carry:

> All the Revenue and Post-Office Officers, and their official papers, and all the loyal inhabitants, were ordered on board one of the Packets on Saturday evening. Their embarkation was covered by a cutter ordered there by Lord Ranelagh for that purpose, and few of the respectable inhabitants remained.[28]

These gentlefolk of the district and pillars of the loyal establishment, must have been in terror for their lives. Humphrey Galbraith complained to his friend Hull:

> It was lucky I got a chaise on Friday and terrible not to let me know that the [Packet] cutter was ordered there to take us all on board, which I never heard till Col. Stapleton told me in Newtownards, and desired me to push on to Belfast while the communication continued open, which it has never been since.[29]

The road to Belfast was closed soon after this. General Nugent was able to write to Lord Viscount Castlereagh on Saturday 9th June from Belfast that he would send all messages in future through Carrickfergus because Donaghadee had been, "*abandoned as an unsafe port for the Packets to frequent and for the Mails to pass to at present.*"[30]

The loyal citizens who could afford a boat of any kind, saw their only escape route as the short sea passage to Portpatrick and that if they wished to avoid being made prisoners of the insurgents, as many others were, then their journey had better be soon. When the status quo was overturned, it happened very quickly. The Rev. Francis Hutcheson, Rector of Donaghadee, Bishop Pottinger of Down and sixty others paid a Guinea a head for passage to Cumberland on a returning collier. The Hutcheson and Pottinger families then journeyed to Carlisle, there to await developments. In a letter to David Ker of Portavo, Hutcheson complained that such was the hurry to escape with his wife and their five children, that he was stuck in England without a single servant.[31] Ker was wealthy enough to secure rooms later at the Head Inn in Stranraer.

Edward Hull was among the huge gathering of wealthy refugees in Stranraer too. As soon as he could, he sent a letter to the Marquis of Downshire giving him many details:

> Our time was so short we could bring nothing but our Cloaths – Mr Smith, Mr Getty, Mr Dobson Russell and a number others with Familys and about thirty Loyal Inhabitants with their familys embark'd [for Stranraer]. They were latterly oblig'd to fight off their retreat as the Insurgents were embodied the moment the Military left Donaghadee. The present situation of affairs there is this, Every Man has been oblig'd to join the rebels on pain of death. Mr Nevin was dragg'd out of bed and a Pike presented to him either to make use of, or to submit to be put to death. He is in their custody as well as a great many others.

This letter concludes with a postscript which left the Marquis in no doubt that Hull was laying the blame exactly where every northern loyalist was laying it:

> P.S. Many Regiments are said to be on their march here for Ireland. If three or four had been in the North more than were there all I think wou'd have remain'd quiet, but withdrawing the Troops was the signal for Insurrection.[32]

The rebels rarely wrote down their thoughts or actions, or if they did they later destroyed them, so we usually know of these only from the writings of others. The latter require careful reading, especially where the writer is predisposed to an unkind interpretation of rebel behaviour. The *Belfast Newsletter*, hardly neutral, a week after the quelling of the insurrection had this to say about the rebels in the days when they had possessed Donaghadee:

> We have been able to collect the following particulars of the conduct of the insurgents at Donaghadee:- Early on Sunday morning the 10th instant the Rebels entered Donaghadee, and were joined by some of the lower orders of that town. A few houses of the well-affected were broke into, and wine and spirits taken out, by which many got intoxicated; they then compelled some peacable inhabitants, by threatening them with instant death and destruction of property, to join them, and marched them to their camp at Ballynahinch.[33]

Could this apparent disorder be the reason why horsemen had to be sent to Donaghadee to exhort them to join the fight at Newtownards and Ballynahinch, or has the newspaper story been submitted by a Galbraith or a Hull who wished to demonise the rebels and their supporters? There are certainly inaccuracies in the story; the most obvious being that Donaghadee had actually been in rebel hands since the Friday, or before, and remained so until many days after Nugent's forces could re-establish control following their victory at Ballynahinch. It does seem probable that a number of Donaghadee men did go to Newtownards and Scrabo and that a large detachment was present at Ballynahinch. It also seems likely that many remained in their town, exulting in the heady undreamt-of atmosphere of being in control of the harbour, the town and its people, even if they did realise that it might only be for a few short days.

1. David Bailie Warden, A Narrative of the Principal Proceedings of the Republican Army of the County of Down during the late Insurrection (Rebellion Papers, NAI, 620/4/41). As A.T. Q. Stewart, (*The Summer Soldiers*, Belfast, 1995) points out in his Notes, p. 271, this document was for a long time assumed to have been written by the William Fox whose apparent signature heads the paper, but is now known to be the work of David Bailie Warden. The Home Office papers 100/86, "Warden's Narrative" in the Public Record Office have persuaded R. B. McDowell, (Ireland in the Age of Imperialism and Revolution, 1760 -1801, Oxford, 1979), and Stewart, that the author can only have been David Bailie Warden.

2. James Porter Junior, unpublished paper written in 1844 in America (Porter MSS, PRONI, D/3579/2), Porter Jun. says that he, "Shall follow pretty closely the short account of my father's life and fate drawn up by my brother, Alexander, for the use and request of D. B. Warden, a pupil of my father, and who, at one time, contemplated publishing a history of the United Irishmen of 1798."

3. Minutes of the Presbytery of Bangor meeting, held at Glastry on Tuesday 2nd February 1797, (PRONI, D/1759/1D/15).

4. James Porter Junior, an account of James Porter's life, (Porter Manuscripts, PRONI, D/3579/2).

5. Evidence sworn before Rev. John Cleland, Lord Londonderry's agent in

Newtownards. (Lytton White Papers, PRONI, D/714/2/16).

6. This is an unsigned, undated report from a government informer to Dublin Castle. It was probably written by Nicholas Mageean, who was present at the 31st May Meeting. (Rebellion Papers, NAI, 620/54/30). It is supported in its detail by a note dated June 2nd 1798, but not signed. (Lytton White Papers, PRONI, D/714/2/23). This may be Mageean sending the same information to Cleland and thence naturally to Londonderry and Nicholas Price.

7. Anonymous report [but possibly from the devious Mageean himself] to Rev. John Cleland, (Lytton White Papers, PRONI, D/714/2/19).

8. Evidence sworn before Rev. John Cleland, (Lytton White Papers, PRONI, D/714/2/21).

9. This letter is to be found in a collection of letters and depositions about the rebellion, (Lowry Papers, PRONI, D/1494/2/24N).

10. Minutes of the Synod of Ulster Presbytery of Bangor, Tuesday, 7th February 1797, (PRONI, D/1759/1D/15 MIC/637/4).

11. Charles Dickson, Revolt in the North, London 1960, Appendix XXIV. This list also gives details that Townsend subsequently went to America and that Miles was licensed on 5th September 1797. Although Dickson recognises the involvement of Warden in the County Down affairs, he mistakenly names William Fox as the author of what is now known as the Warden Narrative.

12. The Black Book of the North, (McCance Papers, PRONI, D/272/1).

13. George Stephenson at Hillsborough to the Marquis of Downshire at Hanover Square, London, (Downshire Papers, PRONI, D/607/F/208).

14. Minutes of the Presbytery of Bangor meeting, held at Donaghadee on Tuesday 1st May 1798, (PRONI, D/1759/1D/15).

15. Minutes of the Presbytery of Bangor meeting, held at Donaghadee on Tuesday 1st May 1798, (PRONI, D/1759/1D/15).

16. Samuel Burrowes, (Lytton White Papers, PRONI, D/714/3/10).

17. Evidence sworn on 8th November 1798 before James Clealand, Justice of the Peace, Captain of the Newtownards Yeomanry and brother of Rev. John Cleland. (Lytton White Papers, PRONI, D/714/3/39).

18. Alex. Halliday, (Lytton White Papers, PRONI, D/714/3/29).

19. James Petty, sworn before James Clealand, 22nd July 1798. (Lytton White Papers, PRONI, D/714/3/19).

20. James Robinson, sworn before Rev. John Cleland, 19th June 1798. (Lytton White Papers, PRONI, D/714/3/6).

21. William Clark Jnr., sworn before James Clealand at Newtownards, 10th July 1798. (Lytton White Papers, PRONI, D/714/3/13).

22. Court Martial of James Dunlop, 6th July 1798, (Rebellion Papers, NAI, 620/2/15/20).

23. William Clark Jnr., sworn before James Clealand at Newtownards, 10th July 1798. (Lytton White Papers, PRONI, D/714/3/13).

24. *Belfast Newsletter*, edition of Friday, June 29,1798, "Tuesday last Archibald Wilson, mason, was executed at Conlig, between Newtownards and Bangor, having been found guilty by court martial of rebellion and treason."

25. Sergeant James Hamer, contemporarily transcribed copy of Hamer's evidence, countersigned by Sergeant Thos. Hyde, Lancashire Light Dragoons, and endorsed by Captain James Clealand, N.T.ards Yeomanry Infantry, (PRONI, T/2286/1). On the back of the document are a number of scribbled notes and figures, the most legible of which is the declaration, "Success to the King and Constitution of Great Britian and Ireland and to Every loyal Subject."

26. Richard Clarke, Gravestone Inscriptions, Volume 17, Bangor Abbey Graveyard.

27. Edward Hull at Stranraer to the Marquis of Downshire, (Downshire Papers, PRONI, D/607/F/224), and Major-General George Nugent, Belfast, to Lt. Gen. Lake, June 10th 1798, (Rebellion Papers, NAI, 620/38/121).

28. *Belfast Newsletter*, edition of June 18, 1798.

29. Humphrey Galbraith to Edward Hull at Stranraer, (Downshire Papers, PRONI, D/607/F/235).

30. Maj. Gen. Nugent to Lord Castlereagh, (Rebellion Papers, NAI, 620/38/98).

31. Rev Francis Hutcheson at Carlisle to David Ker at Stranraer, 15th June 1798, (Dobbs Papers, PRONI, D/2651/2/146).

32. Edward Hull to Downshire, 11th June 1798, (Downshire Papers, PRONI, D/607/F/224).

33. *Belfast Newsletter*, edition of June 22, 1798.

The Attack on Newtownards

Was none who would be foremost
To lead such dire attack;
But those behind cried, "Forward!"
And those before cried, "Back!"

1st Baron Macauley, Lays Of Ancient Rome,
Horatius At The Bridge. 1842.

The rebels had known for weeks that if and when insurrection broke out, the strategy was for the men of Down to take control of the Packet port of Donaghadee and to take possession of the key towns of Newtownards, Saintfield, Downpatrick and Ballynahinch. They were then to join up with the men of Antrim across the River Lagan at Lisburn. For those who came from the north part of Down this meant that Newtownards must be captured and occupied. David Bailie Warden claims in his Narrative that the plan was William Fox's, but even if we accept that this was not the case, we still do not know for certain who did formulate the attack.

Warden certainly puts much on Fox's young shoulders. Unencumbered by modesty the author continues his first person narrative. We read that on Thursday, 7th June, he reconnoitered the town of Newtownards, settled his approach and fixed his communications, "*having either personally, or by Expresses, given Orders to the different Corps who were to compose my Division.*" Fatigued by his efforts, and having learned that all the Principal Officers had been arrested, he "*resolved to carry the Point with my own Division and accordingly proceeded to Scrabo Hill, which I had fixed for my Place of Rendezvous.*"

He continues, "*After having waited there in the Fields until 1 o'clock in the Morning, I had the further Mortification of finding not a single Person attending,*" and that he could, "*also easily perceive by the unusual light kept up in N'Ards that the Garrison was alarmed and upon its Guard.*"

Warden soon has Fox verifying his suspicions as fact, and stating, "*that Colonel Stapylton had compleat Information of the intended Attack and was prepared to receive us.*" This anecdote has a ring of truth about it, not to mention the necessary hindsight, and more than likely describes fairly well what actually did happen. Scrabo Hill was a suitable eminence for assembly and the launch of an onslaught on Newtownards; other witnesses certainly recall a sluggishness about the early movements of the Ards rebels. It is most likely that they hid on their whinny hilltop and watched Staplyton's troop movements for the following three days.

A few miles away from Newtownards, early on Saturday evening, the 9th of June, a small boat crossed Strangford Lough and put into Kircubbin. It carried the sensational news that the men of Killinchy were up. Hugh Loughlin of nearby Ballygraffan immediately set out across the Ards Peninsula to alert his friends in the nearby parishes. It is not recorded if he was one of many messengers in a co-ordinated call-out. We only know that Loughlin met with William Wallace somewhere near Ballywalter and gave him the momentous news. He advised Wallace to return to his home at Ballyferris and, "to be ready."[1] It is not hard to imagine numbers of men riding to all parts of that country to spread the word.

This middle Ards country was a stronghold both of Dissent and republicanism. No record or roll of names exists of United Irishman membership in the peninsula, but within those few square miles were the homes of not only the Rev. James Porter of Greyabbey, but also two more young Presbyterian probationers, the Rev. Archibald Warwick, at Kircubbin, and the Rev. Robert Gowdy of Dunover. These three, and many others, would not have known it, but they did not have long to live.

The chosen Adjutant-General of the County Down rebel forces up to three days before the rebellion, and the man whom Henry Joy McCracken and the Ulster Provincial Directory had instructed to call out that county, was the Rev. Dr. William Steel Dickson. It is well known that he was pastor in Portaferry in 1798, but the Presbyterian Church at Glastry is where he had started his County Down ministry. Loughlin's ride would have taken him past most, or all, of the churches and manses of the above-named clergymen.

Saturday evening was the call to arms. Men from the country lying to the south of Ballywalter seem mostly to have gone to join their cousins in the Upper Ards in what culminated in the attack on Portaferry Market House. Those from Ballywalter village and the townlands to the west and north either crossed Strangford Lough to join their Killinchy colleagues at Saintfield, or they chose, or were ordered, to make their way up the western side of the peninsula and join the Ardsmen on Scrabo or Movilla Hill.

With so many colonels now incarcerated, the few men with leadership qualities were trying to establish a pecking order. By Saturday express riders were soon sent to the towns of Bangor and Donaghadee and the surrounding countryside. They were to tell whomever they met, that the men of Killinchy were up; that they should gather whatever weapons they could; bid their families farewell and make their way to Movilla Burying Ground. On their march there they should collect as many men and weapons as they could from the surrounding villages and farms. The leaders then prepared for an attack on Newtownards. They would capture and garrison the Market House and then go on to support their brothers in arms at Saintfield.

The capture of this central building in Newtownards was of great strategic importance to the insurgents. In the absence of a castle or some other stronghold in the town the Market House was the nearest thing to its bastion. It was always going to be regarded as a symbol of authority and strength. The Market House in Newtownards was relatively new, having been completed in 1776. In that year the famous tourist, Arthur Young, praised Lord Londonderry's father, Alexander Stewart, because he had erected, "a very handsome Market House and laid out a square round it."[2] In 1798 the imposing bulk of the Market House stood at the north end of a square which had narrow streets entering it from north and south, and at three of its four corners.

In the early morning of Saturday the 9th of June, Captain Fowler of the York Fencibles learned of the thousands of rebels gathering on the hills round Newtownards. He quickly occupied the Market House. He had been left behind with twenty men in the town because he was unwell, but he and his men could recognise their duty. Between Saturday and Sunday they must have watched the street openings on the corners of the square like cats watching mouse-holes.

In the hours around midnight, large bodies of Bangor and Donaghadee men, supplemented by others from the Ards Peninsula, had already reached Newtownards, or were rapidly catching up with those who had. Once again there was an apparent confusion of command, with a number of men being given the credit or blame for it by later deponents anxious to save their own skins. This confusion had been exacerbated by the sudden arrest of Steel Dickson, and was also in part caused by the great size of the total party and the large area over which the small groups ranged.

Except for Captain John Byers, the previous day's recruiting sergeants seem to have stood aside for other men as they gathered at Movilla Cemetery. A number of different names were given in evidence at Courts Martial later. These included Archibald Martin, Archibald Wilson, James Francis, James Dunlop, Andrew Russell of Ballycroghan, William Davidson, both Andrew and David Bryson, Edward Rogers, James McKittrick, Rev. James Hull, Dr. James Jackson, Captain of the Guard Jig Fullerton of Newtownards, General Neville Taylor of Craigboy and others.[3] Some or all of these probably had some superior rank and may have been identified as leaders by witnesses who only had a limited grasp of the activities in their immediate vicinity.

Most of those named as leaders probably commanded squads or platoons, but Doctor Jackson seems to have been a senior officer of the Newtownards men until they came under Munro's command on Monday the 11th of June. The precise details of how many came from each place, where they met up and exactly how they came to the edge of Newtownards is unknown to us today.

We do know that the leaders were wise enough to consider the more boring, but essential, logistics for moving such a large body of men. They would have to be fed, possibly for a long number of days, and order would have to be preserved, not only on the field of battle, but on the march too. A number of the survivors later admitted under oath, usually in the presence of one of the Clelands, that they had taken food or other useful items from a variety of sources on the journey. But, just as at Saintfield, when the details of their requisitioning is contrasted with the stories of the undisciplined pillaging of many of the troops and yeomanry, one is struck by the good behaviour and basic decency of the rebels.

On Movilla hill, as the leaders watched the brightening sky of the early dawn eclipse the glimmers of the lighthouse brazier on the Copeland Islands, the time was judged right for the attack on Newtownards.

The attack was necessary for a number of reasons. The rebels knew that if things did not go too well at Saintfield, many hundreds of their fellows would be forced to return home the way they had gone, and a garrison in Newtownards waiting for their scattered retreat would be fatal to them. Linked to this was the desire to hold the town themselves. The Donaghadee men were probably bragging how they were now the masters in their town and those from Bangor were no doubt matching them boast for boast. Another, and more immediately important reason for capturing the Market House, was that if successful their largely unarmed forces would be able to take possession of any arms and ammunition that might be found there.

Scouts had brought encouraging news about the military situation. They had observed that, like all the outlying towns in the area, Newtownards had been abandoned by its main force. The rebel command would have seen Colonel Chetwynd Stapylton take the York Fencibles, the great majority of the Newtownards Yeomanry Cavalry and Infantry, a number of civilians and clergymen, with the support of two six-pounder guns, to Saintfield the day before. He had left the defence of Newtownards to Fowler's few York Fencibles, some yeomanry and an unknown number of local volunteers.

As always in such circumstances, opinion was divided about the next step. Some of the rebels were determined to attack the town, while others would just as soon have filtered back to their homes before being missed. The balance of opinion to attack was swung by the late arrival of 300 armed reinforcements. Warden's account tells us that the entire body was immediately, "*divided into two Divisions of equal Number, the one was to march into the Town by North Street and the other down Movila Street*". They were to meet at the Market House. These were the only feasible approaches that would achieve surprise and coincident onslaughts from two directions.

A Corporal of the York Fencible Infantry a fortnight later swore before God that, "*he was stationed in the Market House of Newtownards and about 3 o'clock in the Morning he saw a large body of armed men march down North Street in the said town.*" This Corporal William Sparks, who possibly was related to the two Ensigns who were at Saintfield the previous day:

> saw Saml. Rankin of Newtown Ards marching in the front of the party with a drawn sword in his hand, the sword appeared to be a broad troop sword, appearing to have command of the Rebels."[4]

In Belfast the following day Humphrey Galbraith had heard, possibly from the daily Bulletin, that, "*150 pikemen marched into N'Ards 4 deep at half past 3 in the morning.*"[5]

The approach of the rebels down North Street must have been difficult. Apart from any moonlight, they could only have used the flare of torches outside the Market House and an occasional light at a window as their guides. They must have been extremely apprehensive, if not terrified. Every cautious step they took exposed them more to the light of the torches, yet they knew their professional opponents were formed up and ready behind these lights.

They would have been able to see the open archway through the middle of the Market House and must have dreaded the anticipated welcome of an enfilade of musket balls and canister up North Street. Some may have spoken the age-old grace of the soldier or sailor in such circumstances, "For what we are about to receive, Oh Lord deliver us." They must also have prayed that their colleagues would indeed arrive simultaneously to double the force and to divide the defenders' fire.

The synchronising of watches for joint attacks is a fairly modern concept. The two forces, with nothing to keep time but counting their racing pulses, lost their co-ordination. The Movilla/High Street party was late, and the advantage of two attacks from opposite directions was lost. Rankin and William Davidson of Greenwell Street, Newtownards had formed a line before the Market House and commenced their attack. In the fashion of a professional soldier describing an attack by civilians, Sparks dismissed this unsuccessful assault with, "*In a short time the Rebels were dispersed by the fire from the troops.*"

In his letter to Edward Hull on the 13th of June, Humphrey Galbraith is more expansive. He is able to give some more details about the action and its casualties than he had two days earlier, and to give credit or blame where he believed it lay:

> On Sunday morning last at half past three 150 pikemen marched down North Street into Newtownards and Sergeant Noble was there with twenty men as a guard for the baggage and Packet shot [originally intended for Donaghadee]. He threw his little party into the Market House and shot six and wounded one, put them to flight, kept the field of battle, took eight pikes, broke and destroyed them and he would have killed sixty instead of six only for Captain Fowler who would not let the men fire as they advanced, till they were in the square…The men killed on Sunday at Newtownards are James Kain of Ballyferris, John Morrison of Ballywalter, two sons of David Maxwell of Ballywalter, one son of Stewart, a blacksmith of Ballywalter and another wounded, Andrew Adams of Ballywalter, killed, one sergeant and one man of the Yorks killed.[6]

This letter must have embarrassed Hull a little when he read it. Two days before, on the 11th, he had written to Lord Downshire in London to apprise him of events in his homeland and had relayed the worst of the rumours before the facts were known. Hull had unfortunately passed on a much more pleasing but very inflated version to his Lordship:

> Newtownards was attack'd on the night of the 9th Instant previous to the departure of the Troops from thence. The Insurgents were repuls'd with the loss of Five Hundred men, but the York Fencibles lost Three Officers kill'd, Two Wounded and One Hundred Men.[7]

Warden who, like his alter ego Fox, may well have been in the party approaching the Square from the east and possibly had some part of the command, tells us that as soon as they heard the sounds of musket fire this party was ordered to advance on the double. They were just approaching the corner of High Street and the Market Square when they were, "*almost overturned by the other Division who had thrown down their Arms and fled.*" The men who had just come down High Street immediately turned on their heels and the two groups fled headlong. This ignominious flight did not slow down until the frightened hordes reached the graveyard on the top of Movilla Hill a good mile away. There the officers were able to restore some order to their forces and take stock.

The sight of men and boys being killed and wounded by the musket fire of the defenders in this unsuccessful attack had made a strong emotional impact on the rebels, unused as they were to such horrific sights. They tended to the wounded as best they could and buried some of those who had died from their wounds in unmarked graves that cannot now be identified.

Often a rebel's family took this uncontroversial course either to prevent any later harassment or perhaps to avoid any contention within the family. A few families did carry their loved ones' bodies home for burial and subsequently proclaimed their involvement proudly on their tombstones. A walk round Whitechurch Cemetery near Ballywalter will discover headstones of a few who fell before Newtownards Market House that morning. One man was given the simplest of epitaphs,

> JAMES KAIN, who was killed at
> Newtownards on the 10th day
> of June 1798 aged 47 years.

Near Kain's baldly stated memorial is another large stone, this one now lying on its back. For the historian it carries a more useful message, and in addition gives an echo of the tribute to Archibald Wilson at Bangor:

> This stone was erected in memory of Hugh and David Maxwell of Ballywalter whose bodies are here interr'd. They fell in an attack made on the town of Newtownards the 10th of June 1798.

> Lo, Erin's genius hov'ring o'er the tomb
> With mournful eye surveys the hallow'd sod
> Where sleeps her bravest sons in earth's dark womb.
> Tears fall, hope whispers, "Cease, they dwell with God."[8]

The rest of that Pike Sunday the officers at Movilla drilled their panicked troops until they were in a sufficient state of discipline to march them to Conlig. There they were to consolidate and supplement their band with more reinforcements from the towns of Bangor, Donaghadee, Killinchy and Killyleagh. Musgrave, in one of the first histories of the Down rebellion, relates that at this time some of the party on Conlig Hill were sent back to Bangor to attempt to entice more men to join them. During their recruitment drive these rebels broke into Robert Ward's house and plundered it for arms. This building was situated a few yards away from where the present North Down Borough Council offices stand. This latter Bangor Castle was built in 1852 by the son of Robert Ward to replace the older structure.

At Ward's house the rebels braved a lecture from the Rev. James Hamilton Clewlow, Rector of Bangor, an ardent loyalist. Some of the men refused to listen, but another group considered what the clergyman had said and went to him with a plea for him to go to General Nugent and obtain a protection for them. Three weeks later in the *Belfast Newsletter*, a "Mr. Clewlow of Bangor" offered a, "*proportionable Reward*" for the recovery of, "*14 Sergeant's Swords, 18 Drummer's Swords, and 2 large brass blunderbusses, with other Arms, the property of the Hon. Robert Ward -- The Swords were cut and thrust blades, with black handles, made by Gill.*"[9]

Telling the story of these Bangor men, Musgrave then says that they ran into two young Presbyterian Ministers. One was the ubiquitous James Townsend and the other a Rev. James Hull, from Ballyvarnet, near Rathgael. As we will see later, Hull and Townsend were there for another, and very specific, purpose, but they took time to deal with the looters. The two young clerics, "*abused them as cowards and traitors to their cause, compelled them to re-assume their arms, and marched them to a hill called Scrabo, near Newtown.*" The loyalist historian, Musgrave, adds that these lawless men did not learn any lesson. When they reached Saintfield, he claims, they once again displayed what he called their true colours by taking, "*possession of the houses of Messrs. Price and Clewlow, which they plundered.*"[10] The latter gentleman would have been the Rev. James Clewlow, Rector of Saintfield and the son of James Hamilton Clewlow. Details are unknown about any damage at

Clewlow's, but the rebels are still remembered in Saintfield for empty-ing Nicholas Price's wine cellar, slaughtering some of his finest beef cattle and inexplicably breaking the legs off a superb sideboard.

By all accounts James Townsend seems to have been an exceptional young man, gifted with natural leadership and, as many of the primary sources tell us, someone who was in close proximity to the decision-making in north Down. Both Townsend and Miles were talking to Steel Dickson on Wednesday, 6th June when he was arrested and had almost immediately dismissed any claims that either James Tannahill or James Clokey could take command. They had taken it on themselves to approach James Porter about taking command, and to inform Bailie Warden of what was now happening. Although one or both may have been present during the Saturday attack on Newtownards and the sub-sequent flight, the names of neither Townsend nor Miles can be found in the confusion of later depositions. Townsend is soon placed close to the action once the Sunday's better attempts at organization start to become evident. He is identified by such a weight of evidence of lead-ership from this point on that the strong possibility that it was really he who was the true inspiration for Warden's hero figure, William Fox, becomes compelling.

There will be some who choose to dismiss the large body of evidence that supports this contention and who are welded to the belief that Warden's account is autobiographical fact, even though unsupported by any corroboration, simply because the 'Fox Account', now known to have been written by Warden, is such a revered document. The real value of the Warden account is its authentic voice of a participant. All who are interested in the story of the rebellion in Down in 1798 are indebted for the many eyewitness details of affairs it contains. However when Warden describes his hero, Fox, going through, "*several Stages of Promotion*," until the evening he was chosen, "*Chief of the combined Ards Brigade*" it would seem from the balance of evidence that in reality he is talking about James Townsend.

Definitive evidence cannot be found for this, but it seems very likely from the various court martial depositions and other comments made by leading figures in the rebel hierarchy. Townsend appears to have assumed more and more of the command of the whole Ards contingent, gradually being recognised by all as their colonel-in-chief. At his court martial after Ballynahinch Henry Munro swore that it had only been at the insistence of James Townsend that he had taken command of the Down rebels. If Munro's claim was then, or is now, to have any credence, it must be recognized that Townsend was a very senior figure indeed. Dr Jackson, James Hull, John Miles and others seem to have been content to serve as his subordinate officers. The evidence points to Townsend being in overall command of the combined men of the Ards from their gathering on Movilla Hill until they met up with Munro near Saintfield, and subordinate only to Munro until ultimate defeat.

James Hull too played a large part in the activities of the Ards men during this time. He was the son of a well known, and well-respected Bangor minister. In early 1792 he had been appointed by the Bangor Presbytery to be the "constant supplier", or full-time, but unordained, minister at Donaghadee Meeting House. There seems to have been some unexplained trouble about this appointment, but the missing entries to the Synod minute book between 1793 and February 1797 cannot shed their light on the matter. The Rev James Porter was some-how embroiled in it, but it is not recorded why. There is no indication of how it was resolved, but Hull never did accept the call.[11]

James Townsend still had to get his men through the town of Newtownards and on to Comber. On the Monday morning on Conlig Hill, after cheering the late arrivals from the surrounding countryside and jeering some of the more discouraged members of their force as they slunk off to their cottages and farms, the majority were again prepared to face the guns in Newtownards. When they cautiously approached the Market House this second time they were amazed to find that it had been evacuated, and this time the town was taken without opposition.

The small garrison defending Newtownards had in fact been with-drawn on Sunday while the rebels had been restoring their spirits and scouring the country for men and arms. The Yeomen had marched from Newtownards over the Great Road that took them over the drumlins down through Dundonald and into Belfast. We know a little about this march because Mrs. Mattie McTier of Cabin Hill wrote to her brother, Dr. William Drennan, in Dublin a week later:

> …Sunday afternoon eight soldiers, a woman and child, were sent to me, and by Major Fox on horseback, desired to make their quarters good…I gave them good ale, though they prayed for water, being just off their march from Newtown, where they had been fighting all day, I pitied them much. Two were wounded.[12]

Neither Mattie McTier nor Major Fox realised at this meeting that five weeks later this officer would have the awful duty of overseeing the hanging of Henry Joy McCracken in Belfast's Cornmarket.

In addition to the psychological boost the capture of Newtownards Market House gave the insurgents, it also gave them some much-needed weapons. What they found in the Market House, and the good quality of the loot taken from other sources, added greatly to their arms. Galbraith commiserated to Edward Hull that, "*Poor Major Blewitt left all his baggage behind at Newtown, when he went to battle.*"[13] In other letters we discover that Major Blewitt also had had to contend with getting his wife to Scotland. Although he was probably not the only army officer to do so, he also had to go without sleep through Saturday, Sunday and Monday nights.[14]

On the Monday morning the Newtownards United men were now encouraged and re-motivated by being masters of their town. They had received the news that their fellow-rebels were now in control in Bangor, Donaghadee, Comber and Saintfield. These men of the Ards and north Down only needed some rest before they set out to join their fellow rebels at Saintfield. Accordingly they were marched to Scrabo where they would have both a good outlook over the flat farmland stretching away to Comber, and a strongpoint for defence if the Fencibles should return their way. Their grasp of what had been happening in Saintfield was improved by the arrival among them of a number of men who had been in the action there.

Warden encapsulates their mood when he describes the express arriving from Saintfield urging the immediate help of the Ardsmen. He describes how the men, "*having prepared their Minds to rest, began to complain loudly of being disappointed, and some Companies refused to march altogether and began to talk of returning Home.*"

The difficult task of moving large numbers of reluctant men took some time and it was 11 o'clock before the rearguard marched off the hill. In the night they met up with even more Bangor men in Comber. They had with them six three-pounder swivel guns requisitioned from the revenue cutters stationed at Bangor.

It is often said that the provider of these swivels was James Scott of Ballymaconnell, near Bangor, and that he brought a contingent of Holywood men with him. However the sworn testimonies of eyewitnesses suggest that the man responsible for the guns is more likely to have been the Rev. James Hull. As we have seen, James Townsend had gone with Hull into Bangor, but had left his colleague to manage the progress of the slower guns while he hurried back to Scrabo where he was needed.

James McBlain, a boatman from Bangor, who admitted that he was escaping back home at the time, met James Hull, "*who was armed with a pistol or two,*" and some common farm cars, on which, McBlain says, were nine swivels. These were small cannons, often carried by boats such as those of the Packet Service between Donaghadee and Portpatrick, or by revenue or coastguard cutters. They were not mounted on trucks like larger cannon, but on swivel posts fixed to the ships' structure. They could fire small iron round-shot about the size of apples or canister. They were necessary weapons for the small boats that used them, although the guns were mainly used with blank cartridges for signalling. At sea the prospect of facing even the small shot they fired could often deter an attack by anything smaller than a frigate or a man o' war.

James Hull told McBlain and others to keep guard on these precious weapons and to push them to Newtownards. Alexander Halliday, a Bangor weaver, claimed that he too was under the same command. He stated that earlier he had seen, "*the Revd. James Hull at Bangor on Sunday night on horseback saying he was going for the cannons.*"[15] Halliday added to his deposition a story typical of the dark humour often found amongst Ulstermen. He stated that Hull, "*On his way into Bangor from Newtownards on Sunday night met John Campbell of Bangor, a Master of a Vessel, who gave him a white handkerchief and advised him to carry it.*"[16]

Warden, in his Narrative, talks repeatedly about Fox's young friend who, like Fox himself, had a seniority in the rebel ranks. He discreetly refers to this friend as Mr. H. His choice of nom de guerre gives some support to the assertions of McBlain and Halliday that the officer who provided the swivels was James Hull. By describing their actions exactly they also give some sustenance to the contention that Fox and his Mr. H. were actually Townsend and Hull:

> When arrived in Comber we were joined by a Detachment from Bangor under the Command of Mr. H: with some Swivels and then the whole Body began to march off together where we arrived [at Saintfield] about Sunrise.[17]

Hance Wilson of Ballygrainey, near Six Road Ends, a member of the Ballymaconnell Company, saw James Hull at Ballynahinch. According to Wilson's account, Hull *"had the appearance of a senior officer, riding around on horseback and carrying a sword."*[18]

Townsend and Hull led the men of the Ards out of Newtown, along the same roads followed by Colonel Stapylton two days earlier. Some hours later, the men had marched through Comber and Ballygowan without opposition and reached Saintfield in the early hours of Monday morning. When they arrived at Saintfield, the leaders of the men who had won the Battle of Saintfield had come to meet them. They received the new arrivals with kindness and respect, but said that there were no arrangements made for meals or sleeping accommodation. This can hardly have pleased the men, most of them not having slept for two nights, and having marched much of Sunday and Sunday night. The best they could arrange was to sleep for four hours that Monday morning in the open street in Saintfield.

1. Wm. Wallace of Ballyferris, (Lytton White Papers, PRONI, D/714/3/18), 17th Day of June 1798 at Newtownards.

2. Arthur Young, *A Tour in Ireland*, Cambridge, 1777, p. 47, and Trevor McCavery, *Newtown, A History of Newtownards*, Belfast, 1994, p. 88. This Market House, which still graces Conway Square, was designed to take the commercial centre away from the older market place overseen by the Plantation Mercat Cross at the junctions of High Street, Movilla Street and Greenwell

Street. The new square itself was named after Stewart's daughter-in-law, Lady Sarah Frances Seymour-Conway, the first wife of Lord Londonderry, and was to be a focus for the cardinal thoroughfares, North, South, East and West Streets. The Market House was originally meant to be at the centre of a much bigger square than the one seen today, but even before the Market House had been completed a narrow Frances Street was entering the square just at its rear. Almost immediately the northeast corner of the square was being in-filled with townhouses. (Humphrey Galbraith, from Belfast, to David Ker in Stranraer, 11th June 1798, (Dobbs Papers, PRONI, D/2651/2/143). The square would later be given even greater focus by widening and lengthening Frances Street to the east, and the cutting of a totally new street to the west through many of the town's gardens and houses in an effort to improve the journey through Newtownards for traffic on its way to and from the Packet Boat terminal of Donaghadee. The western of these, "fine new boulevards," would be dated for all time by being given the name of the Prince Regent. But the opening of this street was to be nearly twenty years into the Nineteenth Century.

3. A number of witnesses quoted in (Lytton White Papers, PRONI, D/714/3/6-39, Lowry Papers, PRONI, D/1494/2/4/98 - D/2/24R and Humphrey Galbraith, Downshire Papers, PRONI, D/607/F/235).

4. Corporal William Sparks, York Fencible Light Infantry, (Lytton White Papers, PRONI, D/714/3/38). Sparks 's deposition states quite clearly that the insurgents came down North Street at, "about three o'clock in the Morning."

5. Galbraith to Ker, 11th June 1798, (Dobbs Papers, PRONI, D/2651/2/143).

6. Galbraith to Hull, (Downshire Papers, PRONI, D/607/F/235).

7. Edward Hull to Downshire, (Downshire Papers, PRONI, D/607/F/224).

8. Gravestone inscriptions copied in Whitechurch Graveyard in the spring of 1998.

9. *Belfast Newsletter*, edition of Friday, July 6th 1798.

10. Sir Richard Musgrave, *Memoirs of the Different Rebellions in Ireland*, Dublin, 1801, p. 555.

11. Minutes of the Synod of Ulster Presbytery of Bangor, (PRONI, D/1759/1D/15 MIC/637/4).

12. Mrs. M McTier at Belfast to Dr Wm Drennan in Dublin, Wednesday, Postmarked June 20 1798, (Drennan Papers, PRONI, D/591/718).

13. Galbraith to Hull, (Downshire Papers, PRONI, D/607/F/235).

14. Galbraith & Rev Francis Hutcheson, both to David Ker in Stranraer, 11th and 15th June 1798, (Dobbs Papers, PRONI, D/2651/2/143 and 146).

15. James McBlain, Depositions of some Bangor men, (Lowry Papers, PRONI,

D/1494/2/16, p. 11), and Alexander Halliday, (Lytton White Papers, PRONI, D/714/3/29).

16. Alexander Halliday's Deposition, (Lytton White Papers, PRONI, D/714/3/29).

17. David Bailie Warden, (Rebellion Papers, NAI, 620/4/41).

18. Hance Wilson of Ballygrainey, (Lowry Papers, PRONI, D/1494/2/16. p. 13.

The Rebellion in the Upper Ards

Let us then, be up and doing,
With a heart for any fate;

H.W. Longfellow, (1807 – 1882)
A Psalm Of Life.

On the morning of Pike Sunday, 10th June 1798, at almost the same time that their Lower Ards comrades were attacking Newtownards Market House, a party of rebels recruited from the Upper Ards area were making a similar assault on the Market House in Portaferry. Captain Charles Matthews Esq. of Inishargie House had been detailed by Major-General Nugent to defend the town of Portaferry. Just like Fowler in Newtownards, Matthews had chosen the Market House because it was a strong stone building with a commanding position in the square and, as in most Ulster towns, it was the nearest thing to a defensible stronghold. It had been designed a few years earlier as a focus for fair-day trading, but it was to perform a more strategic function that June day. It would give Captain Matthews and his Portaferry Yeomanry an unrivalled range of vision for any approach and a wide field of fire in the event of an armed attack.

Matthews would have guessed that the rebels' intentions were to take and hold the town of Portaferry. He would also have expected numbers of rebels to cross the narrows to Strangford and raise the men of the Lecale country. The county town of Downpatrick was only three hours march away, through country where there were known to be large numbers of Defenders and United Irishmen waiting to join this rebel army.

Captain Matthews, an experienced officer, knew that the rebel force could not bypass his makeshift fortress and leave him in command of the town behind them, so he made his preparations for withstanding their inevitable attack. He sent a messenger to Colonel Stapylton in Newtownards asking for some help, and began to convert Portaferry Market House into a fort.

Market houses of the day almost invariably had their ground floors left open for a comforting draught of fresh air during livestock dealing, but which could serve as a shelter on wet days. A tactic that had already been used a few days earlier for attacking such buildings in County Antrim assaults was for the attackers to pack the open ground floor with combustibles and then smoke or burn out the defending garrison from the upper floors. It would appear that Matthews had heard of this because he had taken the precaution of blocking up the archways of Portaferry Market House with masonry before he installed his men and matériel.

The rebel plan was to assemble on the edge of town where the present-day road from Cloughey meets Anne Street. At this point there was a choice of routes into the market square. Once gathered, the rebels divided their force into a number of parties who then took these different roads. Some went off down the hill and turned left into Church Street, while others went straight down High Street. They were aware that the defending garrison was well armed with muskets and that the Yeomen could fire up these two principal streets, and down Ferry Street and Castle Street towards the Narrows at their foot.

The group attacking Portaferry Market House is sometimes portrayed as an ignorant and motley mob of pitchfork-waving peasants. However, eyewitnesses observed that when they reached the edge of the Square they "*scattered and went into different houses in the Square and fired on the Market House through the windows.*"[1] This use of buildings as cover sounds much more like an urban attack straight out of a modern guerrilla's military manual than a quasi-mediæval onslaught.

Like many stories of these confused days there are different versions about what met the rebels in Portaferry Square. There is a tradition, repeated in many written works, which says that the Yeomanry was helped a great deal by the cannon fire from a ship anchored near the quayside.[2] One cannot dismiss such stories, but a careful examination of the layout of Portaferry's town centre does raise serious doubts about the effectiveness of any such support.

There certainly was such an armed vessel in the Narrows, the 400-ton revenue cutter *Buckingham*, under the command of Captain Hopkins. It would have been armed with some swivel guns. The little three-pound balls fired by such a weapon would not have carried much menace for infantry hiding in houses and in doorways to the north of the Square. Even if the guns were charged with canisters of half-inch shot, they would not have annoyed the rebels very much from the quayside.

On the seaward side of the square an Orange Hall stands on the flat-topped crag where the fish market used to be held. Even if there were no buildings on this crag in 1798, or between it and the shore, the topography is such that only the roof of the Market House would have been visible from just offshore. The only corridor for effective artillery fire could have been up Ferry Street, however, there is such a curve and gradient on this street that any gunner firing from three hundred yards away would have found it well nigh impossible to hit anything in the square except perhaps the slates of the Market House. From the water the buildings on Ferry Street blocked out almost the whole view of the Square. A howitzer or mortar might have fired over the intervening land and buildings, but such a heavy weapon could not have been mounted on a ship as small as a cutter. The only task Hopkins's guns could have performed from their swivel posts on board the *Buckingham* would have been to remind the insurgents that they were there by serving them with an occasional blast of canister if any were foolish enough to try to escape down Ferry Street.

If Captain Hopkins's guns spoke that day a much more likely use of them can be found in another source. This account agrees that the *Buckingham* did anchor at the quayside, but that its swivels were swayed up on to the quay during Saturday. They were then hauled manually up the hill to the Square. Matthews would probably have accepted any type of ammunition, but surely used canister if he could get it. He deployed his small artillery on either side of the Market House ready to welcome the rebels whom he expected on Sunday morning.[3]

An edition of the *Belfast Newsletter* three weeks later carried a short account of some rebels who had escaped to England (dealt with elsewhere), which has an interesting footnote that creates another choice for the historian. This states that the *Dykes* of Maryport lent her gun carriages to the Yeomen of Portaferry for their two cannons. Certainly mobile gun carriages lending confusion to the rebel forces by deploying from strategically better locations sounds more than plausible. This might be where the story of the revenue cutter swivels originated.[4] One wonders if this is the same coal boat that had been used by the rebels some weeks before for smuggling arms into the peninsula.

The defending troops in the Market House, safe from being burnt out and secure behind their thick stone walls, were well able to keep up a disciplined musket fire to keep the rebels at bay. Had the Portaferry insurgents possessed some artillery to support their attack, they might have evened up the odds, but without such destructive weapons they were almost powerless. Their undoubted courage, however misguided, was not enough. Eventually and inexorably the steady fire led to their repulsion and defeat. The word went through the rebel forces to withdraw.

It is not known if they had a contingency plan for withdrawal, or whether they made the decision on their way north, but they were soon headed for Inishargie, in the middle part of the Ards Peninsula. They left behind in Portaferry a similar number of casualties as their Lower Ards colleagues had done in Newtown.[5] The retirement of the defeated rebels to Inishargie is sometimes considered to have been an ignominious retreat, but it was really more of a tactical withdrawal. Some of the Portaferry rebels may have attempted to join the men of the Lower Ards at Scrabo, now that their plans to take Downpatrick were thwarted. We do not know whether any succeeded in catching up in time to join in the fighting at Ballynahinch on the following Wednesday morning.

Captain Matthews himself probably did not realise that the rebels had actually won at least two small but potent psychological victories. Two of his Yeomanry had already deserted to the rebels.[6] It may even have been their suggestion that took the Portaferry rebels to Inishargie House. They certainly displayed a sense of mischief in their choice of a new camp at the residence of their recent enemy.

On their way to Inishargie the main party had wended their way out of Portaferry, possibly by the Mountain Road through Abbacy, or else straight past Lough Cowey. Either way they would soon have passed the Deer Park walls on their right and the impressive height of Ardkeen fort on their left. They doubtless considered the latter if they should be in search of a strong point to defend. But they continued their march unopposed, crossing over the Salt Water Bridge, and then taking the right fork through Rubane, to catch their scouts and the quicker men at Inishargie House.

Soon after the rebels had left the town, the Yeomanry received orders from General Nugent to leave Portaferry. This evacuation of the forces had been done in all the other north County Down towns such as Killyleagh, Newtownards, Comber, Bangor, Donaghadee, and by extension the surrounding countryside too. Effectively the whole area and its inhabitants had been abandoned in order to consolidate the forces in the provincial capital of Belfast and the county town of Downpatrick. Matthews's force of Portaferry Yeomanry was ordered to cross the Narrows to Strangford and thence march south through the Lecale to join the other troops in Downpatrick.[7]

It has always seemed strange that the rebels who had attacked the Portaferry Market House so passionately on Pike Sunday never came back to the town to occupy it after its desertion by the Yeomanry. If they had all gone to Scrabo and thence to Ballynahinch this would be understandable, but we know that large numbers of armed insurgents were milling around the Upper Ards area for some days after they left Portaferry and that occasional forays were made back to the town during that time, yet no concerted attack was ever made after the first one.

John Dalzell of Abbacy and Portaferry men John Dorrian, William McMullen, Joseph McGibbony and Robert McCreery are all mentioned by witnesses as having some authority over bands of men in the Upper Ards for some days. The numbers varied during this time, but sometimes there would have been as many as two hundred.

The reason men entered and left the ranks was the alternation of coercion and desertion. John Dumigan, a labourer of Ballyminnis, swore before James Clealand a few weeks later, that on Tuesday morning the 12th of June he had been:

> forced away by threats of John Dalzell of Abbacy to join the Rebels about a quarter of a mile from Portaferry. There were about 40 or 50 of them together at that time but they increased as they came along until they came to Ardkeen Deer Park walls and there they were put into ranks three deep by Robt. McCleery of Portaferry. McCleery was armed with a bayonet.

Dumigan tells how McCreery led the party to Inishargie House where they halted. There, he says with a discernable hint of envy, *"John Beck, near Portaferry, Patrick Murray, Jas. Stewart of Portaferry, James Lyons of Portaferry made a pretense of going to look for pike shafts through the wood and left the party and escaped home"*.[8]

Pat Braniff of Portaferry lends credence to this testimony, if words sworn by a devout man before his God require any. He tells of John Dalzell's return to Portaferry, *"The Yeomanry went over to Strangford and on Tuesday morning Dalzell came into town and told the people whoever did not join him should be destroyed."*

Braniff says McGibbony led him and the other conscripts to the Deer Park walls and on to Inishargie:

> Robt. McCreery, Esq. of Portaferry took command of the party and put them into ranks three deep and marched them to Inishargie and after coming there the party lay down on the grass to rest and on hearing the cannons firing a consternation took place in the party and rumour prevailed that a party of the King's Troops was coming from N'Ards, whereupon some of the party ran and took up their weapons.[9]

Robert McCreery probably never did reach Ballynahinch and seems to have seen little action, and he survived those perilous days. He died with his memories 39 years later, a man of 81 years, and was buried at Ballyphilip Graveyard in Portaferry.[10]

It is known that Dalzell, Dorrian and McMullen managed to get themselves to the Isle of Man, and may indeed have lived the remainders of their lives there. An excise officer by the name of William Harvey insisted that on the day after the attack on Portaferry Market House he had been caught by rebels and taken to Inishargie Camp. There, he says, the men in command were the three mentioned above. General Nugent had clearly been made aware of these men, because he later fumed that the Manx Lieutenant-Governor had, "*liberated without any notice whatever 27 prisoners who had taken shelter there, amongst whom were McMullan, Dorrian and Dalzielle.*"[11]

The militant action in and around Portaferry had little impact on the Down part of the insurrection, and yet it produced much of the subsequent legal controversy. The three Presbyterian ministers who were famously court-martialled later were charged with having been involved in the activities in the Upper Ards Peninsula theatre of the rebellion. The Rev. James Porter of Greyabbey was accused of stopping King's messengers on the road through his village, the Rev. Robert Gowdy with having had a command at Inishargie and the Rev. Archibald Warwick of being with the rebels at Inishargie and of having pistols. In spite of all the sworn deposition evidence, and indeed even in the absence of any damning evidence against them, all were hanged.

As we have seen earlier, Porter was almost certainly a very active United Irishman in the years before the movement took the giant step into armed revolt. But he probably took no significant part in the action; and the charges against the two Probationers, Gowdy and Warwick were, at the very least, vague and confused.

It becomes apparent that in the reign-of-terror days after the rebellion an éminence grise was able to make use of the legal processes in order to avenge some undocumented, and possibly imagined, wrongs. However the actions in the Upper Ards might have been viewed by the different factions at the time, there is little small likelihood these three clergymen were the instigators of the attack on Portaferry or even the most senior United men at Inishargie.

This property is about twelve miles from Portaferry, roughly in the middle of the Ards peninsula. Situated about a mile inland from

Nuns' Quarter, Inishargie House was conveniently near what was then known as the great road to Newtownards. It was the obvious route round the north end of Strangford Lough, although a better way from Portaferry to Belfast was across the Narrows and through Killyleagh and Comber. It is obvious that the quickest means for the rebels to join up with Munro would have been to cross these Narrows and then through the Lecale, to Ballynahinch. For Portaferry men, finding the necessary boats would have presented little difficulty.

Trevor McCavery relates that some of these men commandeered a coal boat, which surely can only have been the *Dykes*, and would have taken it and a group of insurgents to Strangford had it not been for Captain Hopkins threatening through a megaphone that he would blow them out of the water if they did not return to shore. This use of the Revenue cutter was probably more effective doing this than it could have been in bombarding them on the Sunday.

There is no documentary evidence that any men from Portaferry ever reached Ballynahinch. So confused were the times that we shall probably never know for sure, but some men from the 'low country' possibly did manage to join up with their fellow rebels somewhere between the hills of Scrabo and Ednavaddy.

In his Narrative, written many years later, the Rev. William Steel Dickson tells the harrowing story of what his wife and family suffered immediately after the attack on Portaferry. Before the Yeomanry left there, Mrs Dickson left the family cottage beside the road to Ballytrustan and walked into the town. There she had applied to Captain Matthews for protection as far as Donaghadee. Matthews would have had little idea whether the Packets or any other boats were operating. He would only give her a handwritten passport to protect her as far as Donaghadee. The eldest Dickson son was serving as a Surgeon in the Royal Navy, so it was left to the fifteen-year-old second son to act as escort to his mother and sisters. He saw them safely to Donaghadee, which they found was still in rebel hands.

The next day Dickson's son tried to return to Portaferry, but the boy's difficulties were only beginning. On the road some rebels stopped him, and his horses and cars were confiscated. He was then taken to the rebel camp at Inishargie and thence to Newtownards. The boy managed to escape and quickly made his way to Portaferry. This time he was arrested by some Yeomen, who by that time must once again have been in control at Portaferry. Once recognized, he was immediately confined in Downpatrick Gaol for a fortnight.

After this frightening experience, the cold Earl Annesley of Castlewellan interrogated the young lad. Because he would not give up any information about rebel leaders, young Dickson was cruelly told, "*You cannot hurt your father now -- he was hanged in Belfast yesterday.*"

Luckily for the boy, he did not have long to grieve over this misinformation. By chance, the fair-minded Colonel Stapylton was present at the enquiry. Instantly he intervened, telling the magistrates that the boy had answered their questions truthfully, and added, "*Don't be alarmed, my child – you have nothing to fear – your father is alive and well.*" This effectively ended the boy's interrogation and ensured that he was immediately released on parole.

As with other rebel-occupied areas, there is no record of Inishargie House, like the other 'big' houses in the Peninsula, being sacked. Essential foods and equipment was often confiscated, or "requisitioned". Dickson claims in his Narrative that such requisitioning of foodstuffs was not only being carried out by rebels. Some Yeomen took three cows, three horses and "*a dozen of nice sheep*" from his little farm just outside Portaferry. The beasts were not all butchered, but by the time they were returned to his house, they had suffered so much that they were almost worthless.

Steel Dickson was proud that his congregation members and their neighbours had not touched his house, even though violently urged to do so by his sworn enemy, Colonel Edward Trotter Savage of the town. In his Narrative, Dickson exacts some revenge on this gentleman, saying, with an anger that was understandable if not very charitable, that he was only a savage by character, and that:

> His father's name was not Savage; and even his mother could not, as was said, give him that of his father, with any certainty, unless she had been a Ventriloquist.[12]

1. Pat Braniff of Portaferry, Examination before James Clealand at Newtownards, 2nd August1798, (Lytton White Papers, PRONI, D/714/3/25). On this same paper John Gordon tells almost the very same story.

2. Charles Dickson *Revolt in the North*, London, 1960, p. 145, and A.T.Q. Stewart, *The Summer Soldiers*, Belfast, 1995, p. 190.

3. Trevor McCavery, "*A system of terror is completely established*"; *the 1798 Rebellion in north Down and the Ards* in 1798, *Rebellion in County Down*, Eds., Myrtle Hill, Brian Turner, Kenneth Dawson, Newtownards, 1998. McCavery is quoting from G F Savage-Armstrong, (ed.) *A genealogical history of the Savage family in Ulster being a revision and enlargement of certain chapters of the "The Savages of the Ards"*, London, 1906, pp.361 ff.

4. *Belfast Newsletter*, 3rd July 1798.

5. A.T. Q. Stewart, pp190-191.

6. George Stephenson, Lieutenant of the Hillsborough Yeomanry, writing to his patron, the Marquis of Downshire, (Downshire Papers, PRONI, D/607/F/226.

7. Major-General George Nugent, Belfast, to Lt. Gen. Lake, June 10th 1798, (Rebellion Papers, NAI, 620/38/121).

8. John Dumigan of Ballyminnis, Portaferry, Examination before James Clealand at Newtownards, 2nd August1798, (Lytton White Papers, PRONI, D/714/3/25).

9. Pat Braniff of Portaferry, Examination before James Clealand at Newtownards, 2nd August1798, (Lytton White Papers, PRONI, D/714/3/25).

10. McCleery Headstone Inscription in Ballyphilip Churchyard, "*Robert McCleery, son of William and Agnes, died 1837 ag. 81*".

11. Charles Dickson Revolt in the North, London, 1960, p. 147.

12. Rev. William Steel Dickson, D.D., *A Narrative of the confinement and exile of William Steel Dickson, D.D.*, Dublin, 1812.

Waiting for Nugent

From camp to camp, through the foul womb of night,
The hum of either army stilly sounds,
That the fixed sentinels almost receive
The secret whispers of each other's watch.

William Shakespeare,
Henry V, Act 4, Chorus, Line 1.

Anyone following the main A21 road from Saintfield to Ballynahinch today will see, on their left, about a mile out of Saintfield, a very narrow way called the Drumnaconnell Road. This was the road along which the rebels marched to Ballynahinch. A few hundred paces down this narrow road and on the left is a whin-covered, craggy hill almost 500 feet high. It is called the Creevy Rocks. Here the victors of Saintfield had spent the Sunday basking in the joy of it. Some of them had been resting and drilling at Creevy Rocks since the Saturday evening, their ranks gradually being augmented with parties arriving from all over north Down. On Monday the 11th, the Ards men arrived from Scrabo to join forces with the bulk of the rebel army on this hill.

Like all warriors since the dawn of time they whiled away the hours telling each other stories of their brave deeds and their fortitude under fire. Many had been joined there by their friends and families. An observer at the time described, "*a motley crowd of men and boys, women and children,*" enjoying a few precious hours in the early summer sun.

The first junior officers arriving there had gravitated to each other with one overriding concern on their minds. Not only had they lost Steel Dickson, but Clokey and most of the Down colonels had been taken too.[1] They had come through victoriously at Saintfield but now they sought an undisputed leader.

They needed someone with a knowledge of military tactics and an air of authority; a man who would inspire the farmers, fishermen and flax workers of Down to victory. That this matter taxed the minds of more than those at Creevy Rocks is suggested by Young,[2] who says that on Saturday night, 9th June, an unnamed Belfast lawyer, who was legal adviser to the Provincial leadership of the Society of United Irishmen, had a man in mind. He, *"called on Harry Munro at the latter's residence in Market Square, Lisburn,"* to press him to take command in Down. Young later places Munro at Ednavaddy Hill in Lord Moira's estate, dressed for duty, in full uniform of green jacket, turned up with yellow, white vest, buckskin breeches, half boots and a hat with white feathers and a green cockade.

All other evidence insists, with some justification, that Munro's acceptance of the marshal's baton had more spontaneity than this and that it happened somewhat earlier, at Creevy Rocks, rather than later at Ednavaddy Hill. Charles Dickson wrote that years afterwards Jemmy Hope insisted that Munro was, *"appointed by acclamation to the chief command,"*[3] while A. T. Q. Stewart offers the words of Munro's sister-in-law that he had acted, *"more from impulse than reflection."*[4]

Henry Munro, a linen merchant from Lisburn, is variously described as a charming, striking and handsome fellow, even, *"of outstanding bodily strength and activity."*[5] There are many stories of Munro's impressive physical prowess, such as that he could leap across the locks on the Lagan Canal, or vault two horses standing side by side.[6] One must make allowance for the possibility of some degree of legend making after the event, but one can easily recognise the hero in Harry Munro.

He had an air of authority about him which was noted wherever he went. To the men assembled on Creevy Rocks he must have seemed the answer to a prayer, especially to those officers who knew the importance of an overall commander who would maintain a concerted plan in the face of so many opinions and so little discipline. Those with the necessary knowledge, authority and experience in the organisation were all taken up, while the enthusiasts who would have eagerly taken their places were either tactically ignorant, too young or else clearly not up to the task.

A few years earlier Munro had been a highly regarded sergeant in the Volunteers. When his former colleagues explained to those who did not know him that he had a sound practical knowledge of military strategies and tactics, the acclamation at Creevy Rocks was almost inevitable. Henry Munro's surname is sometimes found spelt as Munroe, Monroe, or Monro, but this account will use the first given, except in direct quotations, since this is the one most usually found, and would appear to be the form he himself used.

He was proud of his direct line of descent from Robert Munro, 15th Baron of Foulis. A descendant of this laird, General Robert Munro, came to Ireland in 1642 during the Nine Years War, and was later defeated by Owen Roe O'Neill at the Battle of Benburb in June 1646. There is also a tenuous link with the men of the Ards, one with even a tinge of irony. Robert Munro settled in Ireland and eventually married well. His wife was the widow of the Second Viscount Montgomery of the Great Ards who brought as a dowry some good County Down townlands. General Robert Munro's brother, Daniel, also came into enough good lands to be regarded as a gentleman. He was the great, great grandfather of Harry Munro of Lisburn.

Munro was born in 1758 and in his youth he served his time as an apprentice in the linen trade. Although he devoted much of his time and energy from 1778 onwards to the cause of the Volunteers, he worked hard too at his business, and twenty years later he had become a fairly wealthy agent buying and selling linen webs. He was a member of his local Freemasons' Lodge and, unusually for a United Irishman, a staunch Episcopalian.

Munro's name is not recorded on informers' lists as being present at County or Provincial Meetings of the United Irishmen, but he had signed the oath. Dickson quotes Latimer as saying that in 1795 Munro was converted to the cause the day the authorities flogged a fellow member of his Lisburn Masonic lodge, a man called Hood. Munro's journeys round the Lagan valley and mid-Down would have given him a perfect cover for making secret contacts and attending clandestine meetings. This does not prove his involvement of course, nor any seniority, but everything known about his life and character suggests sympathy with the beliefs of the United Irishmen and an agreement with their objectives. These, added to the qualities of leadership recognised at Creevy Rocks, warrants the confident use of the expression, "Cometh the hour, cometh the man."

Munro's military experience had taught him the importance of discipline and a strong chain of command. He would have known some of the officers in charge at Creevy Rocks and so he had little argument when he expressed his wish that the men were to be put through some organised drill exercises and weapon training, both to help make the waiting easier and to inculcate some measure of unchallenged discipline into his troops. We can imagine that this mostly Dissenter army, by now grown quite large, found an unquestioning obedience to any authority hard to take, after many Sundays absorbing the Presbyterian beliefs about hierarchy and freedom of thought interspersing a lifetime putting these beliefs into practice. That an Episcopalian such as Munro seems to have convinced them of the need for it is indeed a tribute to the quality of the man.

Munro knew that, sooner rather that later, he was going to have to face a large army on the field of battle. It was not inevitable that this should have been at Ballynahinch. The insurgent army might have chosen Saintfield as their stronghold and dared Nugent to come to them. They might have gone through mid-Down to Rathfriland, where they knew there was a large measure of support waiting for them. They might then have pressed on through Newry and on to Dublin, inviting Nugent to pursue them.

Thomas Lane wrote from Hillsborough to inform Lord Downshire a few days after the battle in Ballynahinch that the rebels had been planning to cross mid-Down to Hillsborough and the Dublin Road, "*I am busy with Sharland in taking examination, by which it appears had not the army attacked them when they did Monro intended to have marched here the next night.*"[7]

Wherever the confrontation might come, Munro knew his men must be as ready as he could make them in the short time they must surely have. Munro's officers already knew the value such measures were to those recruits who were totally untrained. They split the men into smaller platoons and companies under some of his junior officers, and marched and counter-marched them all day in the summer-dry fields near Creevy Lough until they could wheel, turn or advance on a word of command.

Six weeks later, on the 17th of July 1798 the *Belfast Newsletter* carried the story of the hanging of Richard Vincent for, "*drilling men at Creevy Rocks,*" with the unsympathetic comment that, "*he died hardened!*"[8] According to a note of July 1798 found among Cleland's depositions, this Vincent was hanged on the evidence of a William Parker, who appears to have been a yeoman and may have been one of the Saintfield family of that name. It is not a sworn testimony but has every appearance and ring of authenticity.

Parker claimed he had been, "*taken prisoner during the Rebellion by Saml. Johnston and another man called Dick Vincent.*" These two had marched him to the Board Mill where their companies were marshalled. They then took him to Saintfield to hang him. These accusations, added to the charge of drilling men at Creevy Lough, ensured Vincent's conviction. Parker's account, although it damned Vincent, excused him from the last chapter of his horror story. Parker implies that at a drumhead court-martial in Saintfield the rebels reprieved him, but that Johnston, acting alone, had immediately, "*marched him to the Leveroge marsh to hang him there for a sign to the Orangemen.*"[9] Mercifully for him, but unfortunately for Vincent, Parker was discovered and rescued.

Two others were hanged with Vincent at Lisburn. As was so often the case, the occasion produced poignancy, dignity and even a little black humour. A young man, who had no outward appearance of militancy, was stopped by Militiamen and taken to Lisburn. He had raised their suspicions by stuffing a piece of paper in his mouth and eating it. In Lisburn he refused to give his name or say where he had come from or where he was bound. In frustration a soldier knocked off the man's hat. Fatally for him, inside the hat was a green cockade. Within half an hour he was hanged. Some time later it was discovered that Henry Joy McCracken had sent a man called Crabbe with a message to alert the United Irishmen in the south that the rebellion had begun. It was assumed that the man who ate the dispatch was Crabbe.[10]

Tom Armstrong was picked up by the soldiers near Lisburn. He too had a cockade in the lining of his hat. Once again this little piece of circumstantial evidence was sufficient for the drumhead court. Armstrong was offered a pardon if he informed on other leaders. His wife entreated him to take the offer for the sake of their two children and her. Witnesses reported that after some agonised moments, Armstrong drew himself to his full height and replied:

> No, Mary, I will not save my life on such terms. Were I to do so, great numbers of wives would be left widows, and many children deprived of their chief protectors. I will leave only one widow and two children, and the God of the widow and the fatherless will take charge of them.[11]

The Ards contingent had all joined the throng at Creevy Rocks on the Monday afternoon. The numbers continued to grow all that day as latecomers continued to arrive. There was a smaller group of rebels occupying Oughley Hill, about three miles to the north of Creevy Rocks. At both camps the atmosphere was not all stern-faced determination. As at Ednavaddy later in the week, there was laughter and fun amongst the seriousness, and because the first hundreds had arrived on the Sabbath there had been time to worship God and ask for His sustenance.

One of the most enduring stories of those days tells of the preaching of the Rev. Thomas Ledlie Birch at Creevy Rocks on Pike Sunday. Unfortunately, although many witnesses report seeing him in the camp that day, only one source says that he actually preached a sermon there.[12] It gives Birch's text as Ezekiel, Chapter 9, Verse 1, "*Cause them that have charge over the city to draw near, even every man with his destroying weapon in his hand.*" The minister then, according to this one paper, addressed his open-air congregation with the words:

> Men of Down are gathered here today, being the Sabbath of the Lord God, to pray and fight for the liberty of this kingdom of Ireland. We have grasped the pike and musket and fight for the right against might; to drive the bloodhounds of King George the German King beyond the seas. This is Ireland, we are Irish, and we shall be free.

It would be easy to dismiss this story as one of the many romantic fictions attached to the Rebellion story in subsequent years. But anyone who knows the Ulster character and who can empathise with this large assembly of hard-wrought Presbyterians will harbour no doubts of their need for some pastoral care and support. Birch and the other clergymen present may have dealt with this unusual challenge to their ministry by circulating among their people with a few words of comfort here and a moment's prayer there. They may even have organised a service of more traditional congregated worship. We may never know the details, but, without the presence of a chaplain at Creevy Rocks, and later at Ednavaddy Hill, the field officers would undoubtedly have been seeing more desertions from the rebel ranks, and a much-depleted force with which to face General Nugent wherever they should meet him.

In the streets of Ballynahinch on the morning of Saturday, the 9th of June, there had been no signs of impending battle. There was certainly a palpable tension in the air, but there were not many people on the streets. Those few who had ventured out spoke in twos and threes in hushed voices. Rumours abounded. Some of the stories carried to the town would prove true, others would be exaggerations, and some were probably outright lies. Strange faces were suspect. People minded their business and spoke only to those they could trust. They knew only too well that the rebels were gathering in numbers in Saintfield, in anticipation of a battle against Stapylton's army. Later in the day when they heard the cannons roar from those six miles away, the Ballynahinch folk would all hear them as if they were in the next field. In a few days they would discover that the citizens of Belfast, twenty miles away, had heard that gunfire too.

The Rev. Samuel Edgar, Seceding Presbyterian Minister in Ballynahinch, was very aware of the tension on the streets of Ballynahinch that morning. He describes how the uneasy calm was abruptly shattered by the arrival of Captain Magennis's Company of Lord Annesley's Castlewellan Yeomanry in the main street.[13]

The inhabitants of Ballynahinch were not overly pleased to see the Yeomanry, but what really incensed them was the sight of a shackled prisoner with them.

We know from the same letter that told of the arrests of Clokey and others in Ballynahinch that, under the direction of General Goldie, a rebel had been:

> hanged this morning at Lisburn, taken near Antrim last night with a green cockade, his buttons numbered as to what regiment in Belfast he belonged to, but he would not tell who he was, and was not known. He was well dressed.[14]

The people of Ballynahinch would have heard this story. There is no indication if the prisoner dragged into Ballynahinch town centre was actually known to the bystanders, but the sight of yet another victim was too much for their taut nerves. Almost as suddenly as the yeomen had arrived, a spontaneous attack was made upon them. In defence the soldiers raised their muskets and fired over the heads of the crowd. One of the local shopkeepers, who had joined in the scuffle, was hit by a musket ball and killed instantly. He was Richard Cordner and his tombstone can still be seen in Magheradrool Churchyard.[15] There is no indication if the shot was aimed or a stray, but the gathered crowds were so angry that the yeomanry was forced to withdraw from the town without their prisoner.

There was no celebration of victory among the Ballynahinch folk over this business. The fatality and the dread of the retaliatory action they could expect saw to that. According to Edgar, scores fled their houses, "*in terrifying apprehensions that the military were on the road to burn the town.*" He paints a vivid and evocative picture of how the countryside was in turmoil about that eventuality, and this even before the events in Saintfield that same day were properly known:

> The countryside was all in motion. Some hesitated what side to join. Some decided to join neither, but were much perplexed in devising means of safety from the soldiers and the people. Goods and furniture were carried to places of concealment. Some left the neighbourhood, and the better to cover their departure from a scene of disturbance, and to escape in safety, summoned the people, as they themselves retreated from the theatre of action, to turn out and repair to the camp.[16]

The people of Ballynahinch were wise to expect the troops, even if they could not yet have known that Lieutenant-Colonel George Stewart, at the head of about 800 men was already on his way. While the men of the Ards had been fighting and occupying Newtownards and Portaferry, Lt-Col. Stewart had marched from Belfast to Blaris Camp. There he had taken command of the Argyle Fencibles and up to a half battalion of General Goldie's Dragoons from Lisburn and Hillsborough.

This force arrived in Ballynahinch at four o'clock on Sunday morning. They had been dispatched by Major-General Nugent to quell any disorder in those parts as soon as the news was received from Magennis and Lord Annesley. In his official report, Nugent gives us a very detailed roll of the detachments sent under Stewart's command:

> I have sent Lt. Col. Stewart, (Ass't Quarter Mast' Gen'l) with the Argyle Fencibles, a Field Piece and 30 Dragoons to Ballynahinch, to endeavour, if possible, to throw himself into Downpatrick with those Reinforcements and to take sole command there till further orders. The garrison [at Downpatrick] consists of 100 of the York Fencibles, 30 of the 22nd Dragoons, the Kilmore and Seaforde Yeomanry, the Inch and Down Yeomanry and probably the Ballyculter Corps with all the Orangemen to be collected in the neighbourhood. Some of those Corps have not received their Arms or Ammunition, but I hope the surrendered Arms will serve the Purpose 'till I can convey a supply from hence to them.[17]

Lord Downshire's man, George Stephenson, a Lieutenant with the 3rd Iveagh Yeomanry from Hillsborough, gives an additional local flavour to the make-up of this force:

> The force consists of 320 Argyles, 140 Mr. Forde's yeomen, 70 22nd Light Dragoons, 20 Makefield's cavalry, 16 Lisburne ditto, 24 Waringstown ditto and 57 Hillsborough ditto. [627 men] and 120 York Fencibles [Captain Mussenden sent 17 of the troop after them] and force-marched them to Ballynahinch.[18]

Had Stewart remained in Ballynahinch, the next few days would undoubtedly have been different. However, we know that Nugent had already voiced his concern about the county town of Downpatrick. He sent a second express to Stewart, telling him to march east and secure Downpatrick.

They were to be joined there by the Portaferry Yeomanry, who had retreated to the Lecale after abandoning their hometown and crossing the Strangford narrows. Local horsemen probably did keep Munro informed about these manœuvres, considering that Creevy Rocks was only a twenty minute ride from Ballynahinch. He must now have realised that the town of Ballynahinch had been left without defence.

According to Warden's Narrative, William Fox and his friend, Mr. Wm. H. were the first into Ballynahinch:

> At first light General Munro ordered the whole Army to march forward about a Mile towards Ballynahinch. We there halted and, having ordered Mr. Wm. H and me to proceed forward with two Brigades to dislodge the Enemy from Ballynahinch, we accordingly began our March and arrived at the Place about one o'clock, which we found had been evacuated the day before. We took quiet Possession of the Town.[19]

A. T. Q. Stewart and Charles Dickson are in agreement that this task was in fact given to James Townsend, the probationer minister from the Newtownards attack, and the man who had led the men of Ards to Creevy Rocks. Munro clearly had sent Townsend on this reconnaissance, probably accompanied with his Ardsmen. On their way into Ballynahinch they met no opposition from the garrison Stewart had left behind.[20] But this was not the first advance party into Ballynahinch. In fact an earlier company had gone into that town and taken possession of it, but with much more heat than the later cool and quiet arrival of Townsend's company. The second party simply swelled the number of insurgents in effective control of the town.

During the night Lieutenant-Colonel George Stewart had received word at Blaris about the movements of the first group of rebels to enter Ballynahinch. At four o'clock on the morning of the 11th he reported to his commanding officer that about 700 rebels had already overcome and imprisoned the small Yeomanry garrison in Ballynahinch and were now in possession of the town.

Stewart had force-marched his cavalry towards Ballynahinch; this had taken them well ahead of his artillery and infantry. Although this separation of forces limited his options, he decided the best action was to drive in quickly with the dragoons. Hearing of his approach, many of the rebels fled in large groups back towards their strength near Creevy Rocks. About seventy of them, possibly having been cut off from their fellows, dashed for safety into the woods at the front of Lord Moira's demesne at Montalto. When faced with cavalry, infantrymen would often run for the trees if their pike-ranks were broken, but on this occasion the ones who fled straight towards Munro's host turned out to have made the better choice.

Much of the woodland on the opposite side of Dromore Street from Montalto's gates is still there behind the houses and shops. That morning the rebels who ran in there knew that trees would always offer some cover and protection from the Dragoons' sabre slashes that they knew would destroy them in an instant. Stewart simply ordered his horsemen to surround the plantation until the slower infantry could arrive. Unrealised at the time, what followed was something of a small-scale rehearsal of what was to happen in almost exactly the same place two days later.

As soon as they arrived the Argyle Fencibles were ordered to march through the trees in close order, inexorably pushing the rebels down to the Ballynahinch River. The rebels had the choice of fighting at close quarters against professional, well-trained footsoldiers amongst these trees, or of running before them. Those who stayed may briefly have had the better of it, because those who cut and ran were like rabbits before vicious dogs when they came out to face the cavalry in the open killing ground.

In a letter to his Marquis, Stephenson disagrees slightly with the detail of Nugent's official report, but not with the sentiment of it as he adds some personal detail:

> We left [Blaris] at one and went to Ballynahinch where some of the rebels had been the day before and that night, but on our approach they ran in all directions. They were pursued, and 25 or thereabouts, all that could be found, killed. They had the day before taken seven of Lord Annesley's Yeomen and when we came up they were preparing to hang them. Parties were sent out on all the roads but particularly on that towards Saintfield. Two prisoners made and brought in who were the very men that were to hang the yeomen. They were tried and one of them hanged directly. Something appearing favourable to the other he was conveyed here a prisoner.[21]

Only about twenty or so rebels who had remained in the woods managed to escape by running through the houses and vegetable gardens. The remainder were slaughtered. The yeomen prisoners must have considered themselves the luckiest of men when they realised that they were again free. Stewart sent patrols after the fleeing rebels, but with little expectancy of catching many. His real motive was better reconnaissance. What he most needed was a good grasp of the local topography and knowledge of just what forces were in his vicinity.

Before he could do anything more than choose a strong point from which to command the town, Stewart again received orders from Nugent to proceed the ten miles to Downpatrick and secure that town. It is amazing that Stewart's party did not meet Townsend's men as they approached Ballynahinch from Creevy Rocks, because Stewart's line of march was out the Downpatrick Road via the townland of Ballylone. A very short time after his force had passed there, Townsend's party arrived at the same junction where the road from Saintfield met the Downpatrick Road at Ballylone. Although it is not recorded, it is possible that Townsend, by then in full knowledge of the morning's work in the town, hid his men some distance up the Saintfield Road until Stewart's rearguard was well out of sight and sound. He was then able to march into Ballynahinch unopposed.

At the Court Martial of Henry Munro a week later, a letter from the rebel general to "Citizen Townsend", who surely must now have been his second-in-command, was produced as evidence against Munro. We must assume that it was written and carried to Ballynahinch some time between Townsend's arrival there and that of Munro. The rebel commander acknowledged it as being in his writing, and it helped damn him. Strangely it seems to have had little effect on the punishment of the Rev. James Townsend. In full it reads:

WORTHY CITIZENS,

We have had some small reinforcements, say 300 men; I hear your's is much more. I hope the Defenders have rallied to you. Send me express. I send you some ball cartridges. You must press for provisions as we do. I will send you some more today, and anything that can be got here.
Munro.

Tuesday Morning.

The citizens are all in choice spirits longing for action. Health and Respect.[22]

When Stewart left Ballynahinch he made excellent time to Downpatrick, bringing his guns and men through what was then very boggy country to arrive at his destination by seven o'clock that evening. The troops secured Downpatrick, set out their piquets and made camp.

"If you're marching, you're not fighting!" is the age-old comfort of the infantryman, but better still is that rare experience in a war situation of having neither to march nor fight. Stewart's troops had the whole evening and night before their Colonel received his new orders commanding him to return to meet Nugent's army. Nugent could not be certain where they might meet Munro's army for their inevitable battle. It now looked most likely that it would be Saintfield or Ballynahinch, or somewhere else in the drumlin-strewn valley of the Ballynahinch River.[23]

On the morning of Tuesday, the 12th of June, after Townsend had quit Creevy Rocks, Munro heard the news that Stewart had left Ballynahinch for Downpatrick. The message was probably brought to him by a member of Townsend's detachment, and which was in reality a reconnoitering party. Munro's recognised knowledge of military tactics would then have made him ascertain that Stewart's march was neither a feint nor a diversion. Once he was certain that the way was clear, he sent a horseman to summon the men at Oughley and ordered the main part of his army to march into Ballynahinch.

This order to the rebel forces prompted one of their number to part with a letter he had been holding for some hours. This message from a son to his father is the only surviving letter written by a County Down rebel in the field. It is therefore the nearest we shall ever get to the thoughts going through the minds of those young, or not so young, men who had found themselves in such a turmoil of excitement on one hand and trepidation on the other. It may not be totally representative of every one of the insurgents, but is certainly worth quoting:

June 1798 Saintfield

Dear Father
I am afraid you will be troubled about me, but I hope you need not with God's
[help]. I hope there is no danger. We marched to Conlig and then to Scraba
and from these such without meeting any of the enemy. Our army is about
5000 commanded by General Monro. A part of the men went to By.hinch today
and the soldiers ran Before ours got near them. We are well Treated here and
the men in good heart. There was 48 Yeomen and soldiers killed here Saturday
and 9 of the others. I intend to be home as soon as possible.
Yrs,

John Patton
Ballybogilbo
Grayabbey[24]

Munro's main body, just like the advance detachments before them, would have had to travel the Drumnaconnell Road towards Ballynahinch. It is quite straight and therefore the shortest distance between the two points. Unlike a traditional twisting Irish road circling round the drumlins, this road is more in the style of a Roman road. Today it still goes over the hills rather than round them, and runs to a point about half a mile out of Ballynahinch centre where it meets the Crossgar Road at Ballylone, very near Windmill Hill. When Munro's men reached there, Townsend's party was waiting for them.

Because this old highway has long been superseded by the newer road and has been largely ignored by developers, it is still able to evoke the spirit of the men of '98 marching to their fate. A walker can almost hear the singing of the men and the shouts of encouragement from supporters at their doorsteps; men left behind through age or infirmity to protect their cottage hearths. We can even see the marching men eyeing the houses they passed by, wondering if they concealed a troop of the King's soldiers. They must have had thoughts whether a strange silence indicated an abandoned property or perhaps a loyal family hiding from the largest crowd of armed men they had ever seen.

When Munro climbed to the summit of Windmill Hill, he could see for miles in every direction. The dark masses of Donard, Commedagh and Bearnagh could just be seen over the drumlin tops fifteen miles to the south; Slieve Croob was clearer, looming blackly only five or six miles to the south-west. If they squinted really hard, to the north they could just about see Oughley Hill and Creevy Rocks. Perhaps most importantly they could easily see Ednavaddy Hill less than a mile away to the west.

The town of Ballynahinch and its river lay between the two hills, Windmill and Ednavaddy. Munro discussed the lie of the land with his colonels and decided to make his main camp on Ednavaddy. It stood to the north-west of the town, a 400-foot prominence in Lord Moira's demesne. He immediately sent out messengers seeking as much reinforcement as could be found. For a variety of reasons, not always clear, the response was disappointing. Many of the men from Ballynahinch had already run away to the hills of Slieve Croob. A local observer, whom this account will shortly meet more fully, suggested that, "*many of them had embarked with as much show of ardour, and as much profession of courage as their neighbours,*" but when, "*the frowning front of war presented its terrors,*" they had melted away rather than risk their lives for the cause."[25]

There was known to be a large body of militant men, Defenders and United Irishmen, gathering in the Rathfriland area. They did not even travel north to Ednavaddy. They later claimed that they were so confident of a victory over the troops there that they preferred to wait for the subsequent march on Dublin after the successful outcome they anticipated at Ballynahinch.[26]

One man, who did find his way to Ballynahinch, and home again after the battle, was William Brunty of Drumballyroney, an unimportant rebel foot soldier. Later in his life he left his rebel beliefs behind and accepted the more loyalist line of his brother, Patrick. Patrick had gone off to St. John's College, Cambridge, had gentrified his name and been ordained. He had then accepted the Hawarth parsonage in Yorkshire. There he eventually sired four children who achieved varying measures of fame as writers. Their names were Charlotte, Emily, Anne and Branwell.[27]

Other writers agree about the absence of south Downers and local men at Ballynahinch. Unlike at Saintfield, Munro's army on Ednavaddy was made up mostly of men from the north-east of the county. An almost contemporary writing of 1803 colourfully stated,

"The rebels came out of the eastern part of the county as the plague of locusts came in Egypt."[28]

It has often been stated that there was no Roman Catholic involvement in the Down actions in 1798. In fact, Lord Downshire's Land Agent, Thomas Lane, praised the Marquis's Catholic tenants, boasting a few days after the rebellion that, *"The cloven-footed Presbyterians employed all their emissaries, aided by a Catholic or two, to prevail on the Romans in Upper Iveagh to join them, but they failed."*[29]

Rather confusingly for some, it is recorded elsewhere that there were at least 450 Catholic Citizen Soldiers, led by Captain Hugh Jennings, on the rebel side at Ballynahinch, and Roger Magennis's Corps of Catholic Yeomanry on the loyalist side. The latter were noted as being active in the destruction of the advance rebel detachment during the slaughter on the banks of the Ballynahinch River in the early morning of Tuesday 12th June.[30]

We know quite a lot about the rebel camp on Ednavaddy Hill from contemporary observers. One of these was the twelve-year-old boy called James Thomson, the witness who had been so critical of some of his Ballynahinch neighbours. He had watched the rebel army march through Ballynahinch and make their way through the lower slopes of Lord Moira's Montalto estate to make camp on the northern side of the hill. Thomson's uncle was Lord Moira's gardener, so the boy would probably have known the layout of the estate quite well. The south and east sides of Ednavaddy Hill today are heavily wooded, probably more so than two hundred years ago. To the north and west the hill is still a grassy slope where one can easily imagine thousands of rebels and their friends disporting themselves in the warm summer sunshine.

The *Belfast Magazine* published Thomson's riveting description of what he saw at Ednavaddy Hill a quarter of a century later. He must have taken notes at the time, so vivid are his descriptions and so much do they carry the ring of truth. A persuasive reason for giving his account the credence it has always received is the combination of the young Thomson's eager intelligence and the professional reporting skill he developed in his subsequent career as one of the nineteenth century's foremost academics.

Reason tells us that James Thomson's great career as a mathematician would at least in part have been due to him being both naturally gifted at observing and recording with precision. His word pictures of the hours at Ednavaddy certainly tell us much about the people who were there; that they were not just armed rebels, but ordinary citizens too. Thomson was keen to use the opportunity to examine the camp as closely as he could:

> At my very particular and urgent request I was allowed to satisfy my curiosity by accompanying them; as I was so young a boy, as to be secure against detention and danger.

Once on the hill, he toured the site taking in the various scenes with an avidity and curiosity that no intelligent lad in such circumstances could contain. What he saw made a life-long impression on him. Anyone who has seen huge summer crowds at modern all-day events such as a warm Easter Monday at Tollymore or Saul, motor-cycle races at Dundrod or the North-West, or a Twelfth of July gathering, will have a good idea what the top of Ednavaddy Hill must have been like that summer's day of respite.

Some groups would be rowdy, perhaps buoyed up with a little fortitude brought along in a stone bottle for that purpose. Others would be alone or in groups with their God. Many would have wrapped themselves in the bosoms of their families. There would have been men honing the edges on their bayonets and pike heads, some maybe talking, some maybe singing a melancholy rebel song. Time would have weighed heavily on their minds in the calm before the storm they all knew was coming.

These men, and their women, were there for the gravest of purposes. If God granted them success against Nugent's forces, who knew where their next steps might lead? They were very conscious of the significance of the moment. Their belief in the tenets of the United Irishmen had been strong enough to make them leave their homes and hearths a day or two before. What they wished for their homeland overrode all their other concerns and fears. They had armed themselves and walked to Ballynahinch cloaked in their commitment to the cause and loyalty to their fellows. Fear might yet drive them to desert, but if their courage held, the next day they believed they would strike a blow for equality and Ireland's freedom. It is unlikely they made any more arguments about the principles they were fighting for. These were seeped in their bones where they did not need more airing.

In the way of warriors, most of them probably talked little about tactics or fighting on the morrow. The prospect was too awful for that. "Mind out for the childer, Mary," or, "Now, you go to my brother if you need help," would have been more the tone of the conversations. William McComb, in his *Guide to Belfast*, published the personal narrative of an anonymous observer, who may have come from Ballywalter or Greyabbey. This man had participated in the affairs since the attack on Newtownards Market House. He had seen enough of the horrors of war to show him that he and his companions were not headed for success and glory as he had imagined. He had suffered, "*the mortification of seeing numbers of the most active propagators of the Union stealing homeward, and leaving the poor fellows whom they had seduced exposed to all the danger.*" He told McComb's readers what his brother had said to him the day before the battle, "*We must all die early in the morning. If I be killed first, search my pockets and take what money you can find, and endeavour to save your life by flight. If you reach home alive tell my wife how I fell.*"[31]

The youthful Thomson, however, enjoyed the sights that greeted him on the Hill:

> The eye was presented with a mixed and motley multitude: some walking about; others stretched listlessly on the green turf along the field; a considerable number sheltering themselves from the scorching rays of a burning sun under the shade of the trees with which the field was skirted.

He was amazed at the number of females there were, "*females whose breasts beat as high in patriotic ardour as those of their husbands, their sweethearts and their brothers,*" Many, he says, were servants. Most of the women were on the hill on errands similar to his own, but he does state that:

> two or three of them remained on the field during the battle, submitting to their share of its labours and dangers and performing as valiant deeds as the men.

Thomson does not record it, but several of the females he saw there must have walked many miles after the men from the Ards districts. The dearth of local men on the hill would have ensured the absence of the married women of Ballynahinch, although one could easily imagine some of the local children finding excuses like Thomson to go up the hill and see these strange armed strangers. We can also easily be convinced of the presence of some excited young ladies finding reasons to mix with the thousands of warlike men who had so suddenly arrived on their doorstep.

Thomson was in no doubt that everyone there that day had chosen to appear for the duration in their, "Sunday clothes," even though, as was shown at Saintfield on the previous Saturday, most of the rebels owned so little that, given the chance, they would take any garments or footwear they could get. The fighting men wore no uniforms, but the majority of them had about their persons something green to proclaim their allegiance. It might have been a ribbon of that colour, but mostly it was a sprig or small branch, usually laurel. Many wore badges or devices made by relatives. These might have been a harp entwined with shamrocks, but without the crown; or a lion and unicorn shown falling down; or the Cap of Liberty, perhaps with Croppy slogans on it.

The women of Ballynahinch were asked to provide food for the insurgents. There was some objection, but not much, because all were happy to do something to help, with, "*the females, the old men and the boys, who alone remained at home, in general wishing full success to the cause providing that success could be achieved without personal danger to sons, husbands and brothers.*" Oaten cakes, wheaten bread, casks of butter, jugs of milk, sides of bacon, salted beef and, appropriately for this mid-Down drumlin landscape, baskets of eggs, began to be carried into the camp by the boys and young women of the town at around one o'clock that Tuesday.

Their provisions received and properly recorded, the visitors were then shown round the camp. The leaders, with their green or yellow belts, were pointed out, and the weapons displayed, and their uses explained. There were a number of muskets, some with bayonets on their muzzles, and the swivels from Bangor. A number of men had poor quality swords or pitchforks to arm themselves, but by far the most common weapon was the pike, that "truly formidable instrument."

We are accustomed to think of pikes as simple and unvarying poles with points. But the appellation covered everything from a long stick with an old bayonet tied to its tip, to a carefully crafted weapon. They were usually home-made, being just ash poles with steel or iron heads. Thomson carefully explains their differences in design and use, just as some of the rebels must have done for him that day. He explains that pikes:

> had generally wooden shafts seven or eight feet long with sharpened heads of steel of different forms and commonly ten or twelve inches in length. Some of these heads consisted simply of one longitudinal piece; but others had another piece crossing this and forming a sort of hook, which were thought likely to be of use in dragging horsemen from their seats, or cutting the bridles of their horses.[32]

A few hours after Thomson's visit to Ednavaddy, a messenger came to Munro with a newly printed paper. General Nugent, at five o'clock that very evening, had issued a Proclamation, *"That ruthless manifesto, which should have roused the tame and nerved the feeble, chilled the ardour of some, whose firmness had not hitherto been suspected."*[33] More importantly it gave many men, already in Ednavaddy Camp, second thoughts about being there, and maybe first thoughts about getting away at the earliest opportunity. The Proclamation read:

Belfast, 11th June 1798, 5 pm.

Major-General Nugent commanding his Majesty's forces in the North of Ireland, being desirous of sparing the effusion of human blood, and the total devastation of the County of Down, is pleased to, and does hereby, extend to the Insurgents in said County the same terms of submission and atonement that have been so eagerly and gratefully accepted by many of their equally deluded neighbours in the County of Antrim, to wit:

That if those unfortunate persons who, by the arts of selfish and designing people, have been seduced from the allegiance to their true and lawful sovereign, his Majesty King George the Third, to become Rebels and Traitors to their country, will return to their duty as faithful and peaceable subjects, and to their respective houses and occupations, the General positively and surely engages to them that no one whatever in the County ... shall be molested, or their property injured, and that, as a proof of their return to loyalty and good government, they must in the course of twenty-four hours after the date of this proclamation (making allowance for more distant parts of the county) liberate all the loyal persons of every description now in their custody, and send them to their respective places of abode, and that they also depute some person to receive all their arms and offensive weapons of every denomination, with the ammunition belonging thereto, who shall be sent to the General to where they are to be deposited; and that they also deliver up the principal persons who have been most active in instigating or compelling them to engage in their late wicked practices.

Should the above injunctions not be complied with within the time specified, Major-General Nugent will proceed to set fire to the towns of Killinchy, Killyleagh, Ballynahinch, Saintfield, and every cottage and farmhouse in the vicinity of these four places, carry off the stock and cattle, and put everyone to the sword who may be found in arms.[34]

The proclamation was circulated everywhere, but especially over the region of disaffection around Ballynahinch. On Ednavaddy Hill it was generally received with ribald amusement. However its last clause later gave a number of reluctant or dissembling rebels the excuse to disclaim their own involvement in the uprising by naming and blaming others, and possibly offered some of the more active rebels the chance to plead a less enthusiastic involvement. Nugent had backed up his warning with some dire threats. If his instructions were not complied with within his time limits, all armed men or women, whether on the battlefield or not, would be put to the sword; their livestock would be forfeit and carried off; and their cottages or farmhouses burnt to the ground. It was emphasised that the warning was not intended to apply to individuals or their families only.

In the face of such draconian promises it is not surprising that a number of those assembled on Ednavaddy Hill decided that discretion was the better part of valour and marched or slunk away. What is surprising, however, is that thousands held to their principles and clove to their friends in the full knowledge of what they could expect if they were not successful in the imminent battle. It is not known which came first, but on the same day that Nugent issued his Proclamation, Munro defiantly issued his own. It was later produced at his Court

Martial, and has one benefit over Nugent's in that it is extremely short:

GENERAL MUNRO' S PROCLAMATION TO HIS ARMY
AND THE INHABITANTS OF THE CO. DOWN

Not to pay any Rent to disaffected Landlords, as such Rent is confiscated to the use of the National Liberty War.

Head-Quarters, Ballynahinch, 12th June, 1798.[35]

Nothing now would prevent the drama being concluded the way everyone had always known it would end.

1. George Stephenson, Hillsborough, 8th June 1798, to the Marquis of Downshire, at Hanover Square. London, (Downshire Papers, PRONI, D/607/F/208). Stephenson was a Lieutenant in the 3rd Lower Iveagh Troop of Yeoman Cavalry. He writes that, "David Armstrong, Clokey and Carlisle of Ballynahinch were taken up again yesterday." [He also mentions Beattie, Ormsby, Captain Cowan and his brother, Lieutenant Cowan, and that they are all in close confinement at Blaris Camp.]

2. Robert M. Young, Ulster in '98, Episodes and Anecdotes, Belfast 1893, p. 78.

3. Charles Dickson, *Revolt in the North: Antrim and Down in 1798*, Dublin and London, 1960, p. 200.

4. A. T. Q. Stewart, *The Summer Soldiers, The 1798 Rebellion in Antrim and Down*, Belfast, 1995, p. 206.

5. Charles Dickson, p. 119.

6. Robert M. Young, p. 84.

7. Thomas Lane, Hillsborough to Downshire in London, 17th June 1798, (Downshire Papers, PRONI, D/607/F/245).

8. Charles Dickson, p. 148, and *Belfast Newsletter*, 17th July 1798.

9. Wm. Parker in unsigned note, July/ August 1798, (Lytton White Papers, PRONI, D/714/3/31).

10. Rev. Dr. R.J. Bryce MSS., quoted in Robert M. Young, p. 80.

11. Robert M. Young, pp. 80-81.

12. A. T. Q. Stewart, p. 206, quoting Aiken McClelland, 'Thomas Ledlie Birch, United Irishman', *Proceedings of the Belfast Natural History and Philosophical Society*, 2nd series, vol. 7 (1963), pp.24-35. According to McClelland, the actual paper was owned by Mr. Colin Johnston Robb, of Magheratimpany, whose great-grandfather, James Robb, had been a Yeomanry officer at Ballynahinch, and whose great-grand-uncle, James's brother, had been a rebel.

13. Thomas Lane to Downshire at Hanover Square, 10th June 1798, (Downshire Papers, PRONI, D/607/F/221). Lane states that a large body of rebels, after driving the York Fencibles out of Saintfield, had proceeded on towards Ballynahinch and compelled Captain Magennis's Company of Castlewellan Yeoman to retire to Hillsborough.

14. Stephenson, Hillsborough, 8th June 1798, to Downshire, (Downshire Papers, PRONI, D/607/F/208).

15. Richard Cordner headstone in Magheradroll Churchyard, Inscription, "*Here lieth the body of Richard Cordner of Ballynahinch who departed this life June 9th 1798 aged 48 years.*"

16. Rev. Samuel Edgar, quoted in A. T. Q. Stewart, *The Summer Soldiers*, pp. 186, 207-208.

17. Major-General Nugent's official report to Lieutenant-General Lake, sent 10th June 1798, (Rebellion Papers, NAI, 620/38/121).

18. George Stephenson, Hillsborough to Downshire, 12th June 1798, (Downshire Papers, PRONI, D/607/F/226).

19. David Bailie Warden, A Narrative of the Principal Proceedings of the Republican Army of the County of Down during the late Insurrection to the Men of Down. (Rebellion Papers, NAI, 620/4/41).

20. A. T. Q. Stewart, p. 209.

21. *Ibid.*

22. *Belfast Newsletter*, Tuesday, June 18th 1798.

23. Major-General Nugent's Official Report of the Battle of Ballynahinch to Lieutenant-General Lake, Belfast, June 13th, 1798, (Rebellion Papers, NAI, 620/38/137) and George Stephenson, Lieutenant of the 3rd Lower Iveagh Troop of Yeoman Cavalry, writing to his patron, the Marquis of Downshire, (Downshire Papers, PRONI, D/607/F/226).

24. John Patton, a young man who was at Scrabo and Ballynahinch, (McCance Papers, PRONI, D272/73/31).

25. James Thomson (1786-1849) in *The Belfast Magazine*, 1825, Vol. I, No. I.

26. Nancy J. Curtin, *The United Irish Organisation in Ulster: 1795-98*, in *The United Irishmen, Republicanism, Radicalism and Rebellion*, ed. David Dickson, Daire Keogh and Kevin Whelan, Dublin, 1993, p. 219.

27. Juliet Barker, *The Brontës*, London, 1994, quoted in Stewart, pp. 209 and 263.

28. John Moore Johnston of Rockvale, Ballynahinch, quoted in the appendix to W.G.Lyttle, *Betsy Gray and the Hearts of Down*, Newcastle, 1968.

29. Thomas Lane to Lord Downshire at Hanover Square, 24th June 1798, (Downshire Papers, PRONI, D/607/F/272).

30. W.G.Lyttle, *Betsy Gray and the Hearts of Down,* Newcastle, 1968, Aiken McClelland, in the appendix.

31. Anonymous witness quoted by McComb in *Guide to Belfast*, Belfast 1861. The man who spoke these words claimed that he had met up with a party of Ardsmen at Ballyboley, where the road from Ballywalter meets a road from Greyabbey. He also mentioned that he had at the time been married a month.

32. James Thomson (1786-1849) in *The Belfast Magazine*, 1825, Vol. I, No. I. Thomson went on from Ballynahinch to be Professor of Mathematics at Glasgow University. His more famous son was Lord Kelvin, whose statue stands outside the Ulster Museum.

33. Charles Hamilton Teeling, *Personal Narrative of the Irish Rebellion of 1798*, London, 1828, p. 26.

34. Major-General Nugent's Proclamation, dated Belfast, 11th June, 1798, 5.pm, quoted in full from W. G. Lyttle, *Betsy Gray, or the Hearts of Down*, Bangor, 1888, originally published in the columns of the North Down Herald, and reprinted in book form at least eight times since then, the most recent by the *Mourne Observer*, Newcastle, 1968.

35. *Belfast Newsletter*, Tuesday June 18th, 1798.

Nugent's March to Ballynahinch

But hark! My pulse, like a soft drum
Beats my approach, tells thee I come;
And, slow howe'er my marches be,
I shall at last sit down by thee.

Henry King, An Exequy, 1657.

A t around nine o'clock on the morning of Tuesday, 12th of June, Major-General George Nugent and the forces he had assembled in Belfast left that place in full panoply of war. By intention they were so impressive that eyewitnesses said they had never seen their like. Lord Downshire's regular correspondent, Humphrey Galbraith, described the sight for his Lordship. He wrote that Nugent had:

> marched out yesterday morning at ten with such a sight as I never saw; an army, whose line of march extended for upwards of three miles, horse, foot and artillery, with howitzers, pioneers, miners, sappers, entrenching tools &c.[1]

James McKey wrote to Lord Downshire that he was champing at the bit with the Belfast Yeoman Cavalry, who were being held in reserve.[2] This company had been put under the temporary command of General Thomas Goldie, who had been sent from Blaris with a portion of the Breadalbane Fencibles, "*with orders to prevent the inhabitants of Belfast from rising in the absence of the troops*".[3] McKey reckoned no one had ever seen such troops:

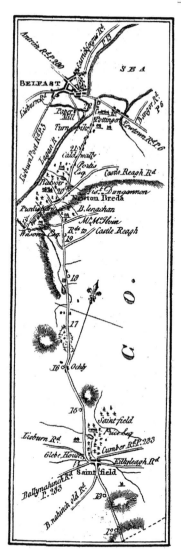

Nugent's March Route

General Nugent with about one Thousand of as fine Troops as the world ever produced, with six pieces of Cannon and General Barber, Marched from this Town at 10 o'clock this morning to meet the rebels as it was pretty well known they would not submit.[4]

These fine troops included the Monaghan Militia, the Fife Fencibles, 60 armed cavalrymen of the 22nd Light Dragoons, and Barber's cannon and two howitzers. The last named pieces of ordnance were short, heavy guns, a bit like mortars, which fired shells at higher trajectories than cannon. They were particularly destructive when used with exploding canisters filled with grapeshot, used against infantrymen hiding in woods or out of sight behind hilltops or houses.

Nugent's route was over the River Lagan by the Long Bridge, and up the County Down side of the river, through Lagan Village, the open country of Ballynafeigh and Newtownbreda and thence to Carryduff. At this point, Nugent detached Colonel Stapylton with a force of men to shut off the way home for any fleeing Ardsmen. In his official report to Lake he stated that he had:

ordered Col. Staplyton with the York Fencibles, 100 of the Monaghan Militia, 40 of the 22nd Dragoons and one Field Piece to take Post at Cumber to cut off the retreat of the rebels to the Ardes if they had stood at their Camp near Saintfield.[5]

220

Because Nugent did not send his Report to Lake until the 13th of June, he was able to tell his superior that he had heard from Stapylton, "*that he had cut off and destroyed a great number of them endeavouring to make their escape that way.*"

It is clear from his Report that Nugent, at the point where Stapylton left him, was not yet sure exactly where the rebel host was. They may have stood at Saintfield or may have gone elsewhere. He had no choice but to proceed to Saintfield and find out.

Like those followed by the rebels on their way from Newtownards to Ballynahinch, the road from Carryduff to Saintfield in those days was not the one we know today. Halfway between the A7 to Saintfield and the A24 to Ballynahinch is the now rarely used Killynure Road. This runs directly south-east, right over the top of Oughley Hill. The Killynure road then skirts the west side of Saintfield House demesne to enter the town from the west. As they crossed the summit of Oughley Hill Nugent's men must have remarked on the signs that it had until recently been a rebel camp, although it was now completely deserted. He does not record it, but a local tradition claims that his host was fired upon from the vicinity of the Oughley standing stone, causing it to fall on its side.

Because of the cumbrous character of artillery, the march had been conducted at a steady, rather than a brisk pace. Apart from the Lagan there are no rivers between Belfast and Saintfield to slow the advance of infantry or cavalry, but artillery pieces are baulked by all but the smallest streams. Nugent told Lake that, "*On our approach to Saintfield I found the enemy had destroyed several of the Bridges which occasioned a considerable delay.*"[6] Nugent would not have known it at the time, but one month later three men, Robert Boyd, John Fulton and William Marshall Snr. were to be convicted of breaking down Killynure Bridge to prevent the artillery from crossing the stream there. They were sentenced to transportation. Marshall's son, also William, was acquitted.[7]

Nugent soon had his opportunity to show by example the extent of his determination, and perhaps something of his frustration:

> I halted a short time at Saintfield to obtain information and finding that all the Inhabitants in and about this place had quitted their houses, and most of them had joined the Rebels, I ordered the Town of Saintfield to be burnt.[8]

Understandably, this drastic action soon produced the information that the rebels had all decamped for Ballynahinch, and Nugent immediately followed them there. He sent out scouting parties to search for signs of rebel sympathy along the route. Any hint at all of such fellow-feeling was to be taken as a sign of disregard of the proclamation, and a good reason to burn down the guilty parties' homes. His line of march was marked by Thomson, *"with a small glass,"* from Annaghmore Hill near his home at Spamount:

> As we continued our look-out from the hill, the approach of the party from Belfast was in a short time announced by the smoke and flames of the farm-houses, which they set on fire indiscriminately on their march from Saintfield to Ballynahinch.[9]

Nugent followed the same route from Saintfield as Munro had done. When he had almost reached Ballynahinch, he found a large detachment of five or six hundred rebels defending Windmill Hill. These men were under the command of Samuel McCance. Munro had earlier made him a First Lieutenant and Thomas Watson a Second Lieutenant, while they were at Creevy Rocks. McCance's men had been sent to the windmill.[10] Nugent could not skirt round this force. He had to reduce their makeshift fortress before he could proceed. He established that Lieutenant Colonel Stewart had already returned from Downpatrick, and had reached Ballynahinch some two hours before him. In fact it had been the unexpected arrival of Stewart's forces that had sent Thomson and all the other non-combatants off Ednavaddy and back to their homes.

Nugent resolved upon a frontal attack on Windmill Hill. He formed his troops into two sides of a right angle with Stewart's men to guard his flanks. The multihued troops who had accompanied Stewart from Blaris to Ballynahinch, Downpatrick and back to Ballynahinch again, had now been supplemented with 100 York Fencibles and some Yeomanry Infantry from Downpatrick.

They formed up on the left of Nugent's Monaghan Militia and made a fierce onslaught on the rebels on the hill. In the face of concerted attack, McCance was still so certain of the strength of his position that he was very reluctant to leave it, even though ordered to by Munro, who recognised the possibility of this force being encircled. Even when ordered by Munro a second time to quit the hill and support him at Ednavaddy, McCance was so sure of his ground that he had the temerity to ask Munro to come to Windmill Hill to support him. It took an insistent third order to recall him.[11] Once McCance gave the command to leave Windmill Hill, the rebels scattered into small bands and ran through the town to Ednavaddy Hill.

Rev. James Townsend's detachment had been deployed in the centre of Ballynahinch during this same time. The unmistakable peril of this station and the temptations it engendered, had already obliged this young clergyman to bark at his troops that, "*the first man who would leave that he would run him through.*"[12] These men, who had also been recalled, joined the forces from Windmill Hill in their charge down Bridge Street (now Dromore Street) and into the demesne where they joined up with the main body.

The rebels had left Hugh McCulloch on Windmill Hill. He is sometimes referred to as a Bangor man, but this may be a mistake since Stephenson of the Downshires claims that McCulloch's brother was in his Hillsborough regiment.[13] One account says that he had been asleep, but this scarcely seems credible when one thinks of the roar of battle that must have gone on for some time.[14]

A few minutes after Nugent's soldiers took Hugh McCulloch; he was summarily hung by his neck from one of the sails of the windmill. His body was to hang there in full sight for many hours.

When the Windmill Hill detachment had come hurtling into the camp in Lord Moira's demesne that Tuesday evening, it cannot have surprised too many men in Munro's command. They had all seen and heard Stewart's troops, and messages had come about Nugent's great army burning a path across mid-Down. Thomson, with the benefit of his perspective of years later, wished that Munro had attacked Stewart when he had the chance. Now it was too late.

Thomson tells us in his account that the people all around Ballynahinch, now certain of the impending defeat of the rebels, and knowing that their own men were secure for the moment in the fast-nesses of Slieve Croob, had thoughts only for saving their homes, their liberty and their own lives:

> Beds and wearing apparel, barrels of meal, flitches of beef and bacon and casks of butter were deposited in meadows and cornfields, in the bottoms of ditches, in gardens, under rubbish, or in whatever places appeared least likely to excite suspicion.

Thomson also tells with some amusement of farm leases and sums of money being put under large stones in the middle of fields, and a hundred gold guineas being put out of sight, high in a tree in a magpie's nest.[15]

Any military commander faced with thousands of infantry soldiers concentrated on a strongly defensible hill, will choose any means to weaken their resolve, and possibly reduce their numbers before taking them on in open battle. Nugent had Barber's artillery with him, and did not hesitate to deploy his big guns. Barber began his bombardment of Ednavaddy Hill at six o'clock that evening. Colonel Stewart took a few pieces of artillery to some high ground, and Colonel Leslie took others to the top of Dromore Street. In a letter sent to Lake, and which appears to be a hastily written first draft of his official Report, Nugent had commented with military understatement, "*We had two Howitzers and 6 six-pounders with the two Detachments, which enabled us to annoy them very much from the different Parts of our Position.*"[16]

The cannonade continued until it became dark. Naturally the rebels on the hill returned fire as best they could. George Stephenson of the Iveagh Yeomanry, perhaps not as reliable as usual in the circumstances, wrote to Lord Downshire:

> We lay all night at our horses' heads till one this morning, when they began to fire on us, which was not returned till daylight. For some time the firing continued of cannon from hill to hill, their fire from the swivels whizzing in the air over our heads.[17]

The Royal Artillery gun captains had been firing iron roundshot into the trees of Montalto instead of grape. The former are inefficient in killing power on open ground, because the balls can only harm those few they hit. With their targets hidden in the woods, the solid cannonballs produced the same mayhem as they caused in naval battles. Large, heavy, and fast-flying wood splinters from the trees were intended to impale or decapitate a number of the rebels and to unnerve many more.

Nugent, as usual, was considering the bigger picture and from his own Report we know that the troop movements during that night were to secure the roads to Hillsborough and Downpatrick so as to, "*prevent Rebels making their Retreat by any other Route than to the Mountains in our Rere.*"[18]

There is no doubt that large numbers of Munro's forces deserted him during that evening and night. From the first day 'up' there had been some defections from the ranks. With so many under threat this was inevitable, but the numbers leaving Ednavaddy that Tuesday night were in many hundreds. The bombardment was one reason, but there were others. At the Tuesday evening council of war, many differing opinions were offered as the best strategy to adopt. Some felt that to best capitalise on the success at Saintfield the Ednavaddy force should march to Newry, occupy it and advance on Dublin. Others advocated a frontal attack on the royalist troops in Ballynahinch. Opinion on this latter tactic was further divided as to whether this should be a night or a dawn attack.

Munro certainly could have ordered a night attack on Nugent's forces before they were properly deployed. All witnesses except Nugent agree that in those wee small hours the crown forces were out of control. The soldiers may have been drunk and wild, intent on nothing less than the traditional rewards for troops everywhere, but it is open to argument whether this would have favoured a night assault, or would have made a dawn attack, as the soldiers were falling into stupor, more promising even than during their debauchery, when their blood was up.

Echoing Sir Ralph Abercromby's pronouncement on the behaviour of his soldiers three months before, an eyewitness in the small town of Ballynahinch wrote that he had been appalled to watch the King's troop entering the battered and deserted town in the early night of the 12th of June, "*It was plundered by them of everything valuable. They then set it on fire: 63 houses were burned; 69, including the houses of worship, were left standing; but all were pillaged.*"[19]

Eighteenth century warfare generally had a quite different code of ethics than is the case today. Opposing generals, officers and even the lower ranks observed a greater degree of chivalry than usually seen in modern warfare. But surprise has always been recognised as the fighting man's best ally. Ships sailed under false colours; expresses were sent out with misleading messages; and attacks were made at a time of best advantage. The number of dawn attacks in this war by both sides show that trying to catch your opponent at his weakest moment was regarded as a legitimate tactic.

However, there were many commanders who recognised that attacks made in the darkest hours of the night were always very confused affairs, even with trained and experienced troops. The risks would be even greater if the men making such an onslaught in the dark included raw, barely trained men who in the dark would neither see each other nor the necessary signals. The small experience Munro had in military matters is likely to have persuaded him to wait until first light before launching his assault.

Munro certainly had to cope with a number of pressures through that night and may have been forced into making a decision that was not his first choice. Dickson repeats what William Blacker, whom he describes as a hostile witness, said about this. Munro was:

> shrewd, brave and active and I have reason to believe that had his advice been followed on the night of the 12th there might have been a different story to tell in the morning...Munro's plan was to select three hundred stout pike men and steal upon Nugent's camp at the dead hour of night when the troops were asleep and tired...I have never been able to ascertain why a proposition so well concocted should have been neglected – some say the Popish portion of the rebels disliked going under the command of a Presbyterian.[20]

Charles Teeling, who had been paroled from his confinement, is more critical of Munro, blaming his over-confidence for the crucial decision to wait for the early morning:

> Too confident of his success, Monroe imprudently declined the advantage of a night attack, when the licentious and defenceless state of the enemy presented

an easy conquest...A despatch from his camp on the evening of the 12th, [stated] 'that victory was certain, and the British Army within his grasp.' [21]

There seems little doubt that some of the Defenders who had come to Ednavaddy with Magennis of Baleely, along with many of the South Down United Irishmen and a number of men from Killinchy, used the disagreements on Ednavaddy as their reason for leaving the field. They knew that Royal troops were springing the trap all around them. They well remembered the horrors of Saintfield, and some may have been carrying wounds that could provide both a reason and an excuse to desert.

They also had their worries about their loved ones, not too far away, and the possibility that their only retreats through Saintfield, Dromara and Katesbridge, or Castlewellan and Hilltown could soon close too. It would have been easy for anyone to dissemble and decamp in quick succession. Thomson saw many such men passing Spamount on their way towards Castlewellan, *During every hour of the night fugitives were seen passing our station. Some of these were slightly wounded.*[22]

Sir Richard Musgrave claimed in his early polemic history, that a party of two thousand Catholic Defenders left the rebel camp as a body that night,[23] but it must be remembered that Musgrave's work was never meant to be an objective history of the rebellion of 1798 and this claim must be treated with suspicion.

Many years later the County Antrim United Irishman, the weaver, James Hope, recorded his memories of '98 for R.R. Madden. Although mostly involved in Belfast activities before the breakout, and in Antrim after that, Hope was insistent that there was no such thing as a Catholic battalion at Ballynahinch. Any Catholics present fought side by side with the Dissenters. In the middle of that black night at Ednavaddy, he claimed, it was not so much the Catholics who left the field, but the whole of the Killinchy contingent, many of whom of course had experienced the horror of Saintfield. He claimed that they crept through Nugent's pickets and returned home, leaving the dreaded prospect of the next day to the men of the Ards and north Down.[24]

It is not known whether Dr. James Cord accompanied the Killinchy men back to the relative safety of the Strangford shore, but since he had brought them to Ballynahinch, it seems probable that he led them home. His execution a week later shows that this discretion certainly did not save him, nor did it let him fight another day.

The Rev. Samuel Edgar was very specific about the composition of the rebel forces. He noted that the bulk of the insurgents who faced Nugent's men on the Wednesday morning were men from the Ards, Bangor, Castlereagh, Donaghadee, Holywood, Killyleagh and, although it does not accord with James Hope, Killinchy. He also confirms that very few indeed from the Ballynahinch neighbourhood were involved in the battle.[25]

Teeling supports what Hope and Edgar say about the rebels of Ards and north Down, and reveals a self-confidence observed among these men:

> The forces immediately under the command of Monroe were drawn, almost exclusively, from the northern districts of Down, the population of which was considered more than sufficient to contend with all the royal troops that could be brought to bear on any point against them.

Teeling relates that he spent the night of 12th June with the Rev. Samuel Barber of Rathfriland, bedded down near there with the men of Munro's Central Division. Secure in their minds that the council of war had decided on the Newry option, the two men had prepared themselves for sleep in order ready themselves for action the following day. Early the next morning when they awoke, they were stunned to find that Munro was already defeated.

1. Humphrey Galbraith, (Downshire Papers, PRONI, D/607/F/235).

2. James McKey, Belfast to Lord Downshire, 11th and 12th June 1798, (Downshire Papers, PRONI, D/607/F/222 and D/607/F/232).

3. A.T.Q. Stewart, *The Summer Soldiers, The 1798 Rebellion in Antrim and Down,* Belfast, 1995, p. 213.

4. James McKey to the Marquis of Downshire, 12th June 1798, (Downshire Papers, D/607/F/232).

5. Maj. Gen. Nugent's Official Report of the Battle of Ballynahinch to Lt. Gen.

Lake, (Rebellion Papers, NAI, 620/38/137).

6. *Ibid.*

7. *Belfast Newsletter* 13th July 1798, quoted in Bill Wilsdon, *The Sites of the 1798 Rising in Antrim and Down*, Belfast, 1997, p. 161.

8. *Ibid.*

9. James Thomson (1786-1849) in *The Belfast Magazine*, 1825, Vol. I, No. I.

10. James Cochran of Lisdalgan, sworn before Rev. John Cleland at Saintfield House, 13th November 1798, (Lytton White Papers, PRONI, D/714/3/40).

11. W. G. Lyttle, *Betsy Gray, or the Hearts of Down*, Bangor, 1888, pp. 123-124, and Charles Dickson, *Revolt in the North, London*, 1960, p. 150. Aiken McClelland in a footnote in the latter says that McCance survived the action at Windmill Hill and the main conflict in Ballynahinch. He later moved to live with his son, Dr. William McCance of Donaghadee.

12. Hance Wilson of Ballygreny (sic), near Bangor, (Lowry Papers, PRONI, D/1494/2/16).

13. Lieutenant George Stephenson of the 3rd Lower Iveagh Yeomanry to the Marquis of Downshire, (Downshire Papers, PRONI, D/607/F/236).

14. W. G. Lyttle, p.124.

15. James Thomson (1786-1849) in *The Belfast Magazine*, 1825, Vol. I, No. I.

16. Maj. Gen. Nugent in a letter to Lake, wrongly datelined, Belfast, 12th June, 2 o'clock pm, 1798. (Rebellion Papers, NAI, 620/38/129).

17. Stephenson, (Downshire Papers, PRONI, D/607/F/236).

18. Maj. Gen. Nugent's Official Report to Lake, 13th June, (Rebellion Papers, NAI, 620/38/137).

19. Anonymous witness quoted by McComb in *Guide to Belfast*, Belfast 1861.

20. William Blacker, quoted by Dickson, p. 201.

21. Charles Hamilton Teeling, *Personal Narrative of the Irish Rebellion of 1798*, London, 1828, pp. 25 and 28.

22. James Thomson.

23. Sir Richard Musgrave, *Memoirs of the Different Rebellions in Ireland*, Dublin, 1801, p. 52.

24. James Hope, in R.R.Madden, *Antrim and Down in 1798*, Belfast, n.d., quoted in Dickson, p. 151.

25. Rev. Samuel Edgar, quoted in Stewart, *The Summer Soldiers*, pp. 186, 219.

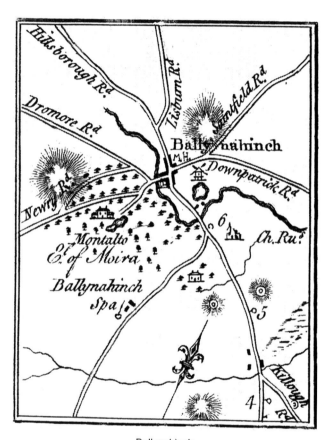

Ballynahinch

The Battle of Ballynahinch

At three o'clock on the morning of 13th June, Lieutenant-Colonel Stewart was given more men and artillery to go a little further out of the town of Ballynahinch to seek out an elevated position that would provide flanking fire on the rebels. He tried the high ground near the present Magheradroll Parish Church on Church Street, but soon led his men down that hill past the Mill and over the bridge on the Mill Brook. They then went up the present Crabtree Hill near the ruins of the old Magheradroll Church. As well as having a better vantage point Stewart and his men must have been glad to leave the blazing town and the clouds of acrid smoke still billowing from the torched houses.

The slowly rising sun began to show Stewart the first glints of the enemy's bayonets at the tops of their few stacks of pikes and muskets. Approving of this new position, Stewart soon set up a fusillade of grape shot over the lower slopes of Ednavaddy as an early reveille. What Thomson described as "*galling fire,*" was so ferocious that it unmanned many of those stationed there, even as they dashed the sleep from their eyes. The subsequent follow-up charge of Argyle Fencibles and three companies of Yeoman infantry drove in their outposts before they had properly organised them. Badly shaken, the rebels retreated to the top of Ednavaddy hill.

Stewart's troops now proved their own mettle, as large groups of the insurgents now turned and charged back at them. The loyal forces were later praised for withstanding repeated volleys of musket fire and standing steadfast against hordes of yelling pikemen.[1] All parties agree that there were three separate rebel counter attacks, all of which were repulsed.

At just the right moment the Monaghan Militia, under the command of Colonel Charles Leslie, supported by some dragoons and some field pieces were thrown into the fray in the town centre. They advanced quickly down Dromore Street to meet the rebels in a frontal assault. They forced their way through the front gates of Montalto and drove the rebels off the hill. The anonymous rebel quoted in an earlier chapter by McComb then found himself among those rebels who tried to make an advance up Dromore Street in a reorganised offensive:

> We were obliged to go up in the face of a party of the Monaghan Militia, who did not fail to salute us with a brisk fire. We ran up like bloodhounds, and the Monaghans fled into the town, where they kept up a kind of broken fire, which we returned, although only about twenty of us were armed. We obliged them to take shelter in the houses twice but a cannon which raked the street with grape shot compelled us to retire.[2]

By "armed" this man meant that only twenty of their number had firearms – mostly muskets. Nugent certainly noted the great numbers of pikes in their ranks. In his Report he emphasises the importance of his howitzer shells and the cannons firing their canister and grape shot. These weapons of destruction must have cut great swathes through the masses of the advancing pikemen. We know Nugent was impressed with these rebels, because he found space to commend the courage they displayed to carry off their dead and wounded in the heat of the action.

Thomson amplifies the bald language of the official report when he says:

> A number of the insurgents having posted themselves in the demesne behind
> a hedge adjoining the way which led to the hill poured on the party a volume of
> shot which instantly killed the Captain, and, I believe, obliged the rest to retire.

The Captain he was referring to was Henry Evatt, an executive officer with Leslie. Nugent made no mention of any retiring of troops, although he did comment, in his first letter to Lake after the battle:

> The rebels poured down with Impetuosity upon Col. Leslie's Detachment, and
> even jumped into the Road from the Earl of Moira's Demesne, to endeavour to
> take one of his guns, but they were repulsed with slaughter.

Once again Munro showed that he clearly had some idea of military tactics. At this moment he sent in the reserves he had been holding back. They went over the river, near the scene of slaughter two days earlier, and thence up the hill behind the Dromore Street houses to High Street. There they met up with their main body that had forced their way up Dromore Street. Their spirits raised by their now combined numbers, they pushed up the slight slope towards the Market House. This is the third such building to feature in the story of that week in Down. However, the building in Ballynahinch did not become a defensive citadel like those at Newtownards and Portaferry. This was to be a more fluid action than those earlier ones.

What Munro's men did not know as they approached the square, was that some of Nugent's musketry and field pieces had been deployed in the houses and doorways in the square for this very contingency. In a striking reversal of what had occurred in Saintfield on the Saturday, an ambush was awaiting the insurgents. Volleys of musket fire and canisters of grape flensed the first wave of the charging rebels. Charles Dickson, possibly relying on McComb's anonymous witness, asserts that the men from the Ards, especially a group from Ballyboley, near Carrowdore, were very prominent at this location. There must have been much grieving at Ballyboley during the following days, so heavy were the casualties here.

Infantry battles at this time often consisted of the two opposing forces making alternate charges at each other's defensive lines. The best musketeers in the world could load and fire their weapons three times in a minute. When one thinks that this meant firing a ball, turning the musket on to its butt, grabbing for a paper cartridge, biting the end off it, pushing the cartridge into the barrel, spitting a lead ball in after it, inserting a little piece of wadding to prevent the ball ignominiously rolling back out when the musket was levelled, ramming the lot down as far as it would go, remembering to remove the ramrod, then raising the weapon, aiming the next shot, all in twenty or so frantic seconds, this is a staggering achievement.[3] The average professional soldier was only able to work at about half this speed, or even slower when the enemy was firing back at him. Many of the Yeomen would undoubtedly have been even slower.

It is obvious that if the ranks of musket soldiers all fired at once, an approaching phalanx of pikemen would have anything up to a minute between volleys to charge unhindered towards the infantrymen. A fit young man could run nearly a quarter of a mile in that sort of time without having to resort to cover. If the attackers did have cover, they could still divide their charge into short bursts, even if the musketry was properly organised into alternating ranks of fire, one rank retiring to reload while the other advanced to fire. But Nugent had artillery.

It is often thought that artillery was used for battering down fortifications. This is true, but was only part of its great value in battle. Loaded with metal canisters of musket balls they could take a terrible toll on massed infantry. When the can burst as it left the gun's muzzle it sprayed fifty or sixty lead balls in a widening cone of death. Three hundred yards from the guns, the spread of shot from each was ninety feet across. For one infantryman the odds of being hit were slim at that range, but for packed ranks of soldiers advancing against cannon deployed with intersecting lines of fire, it was like walking into a driving hailstorm, but one of unforgiving metal. An extra refinement was that some canisters might have contained the evil mixture only recently devised by Major Shrapnel. It took steely discipline or a touch of madness to march or run forward against such a killing storm.

When inexperience or gut-curdling fear sabotaged the discipline, the first side to crack often turned and ran. If they then had the time and cover to reorganise, and the leadership to manage this, they could sometimes quickly turn the tables. This behaviour often produced the ebb and flow of action described by many observers of battles.

Accomplishing it also sorted out the good generals from the bad. Those who could best penetrate the smoke and confusion of battle to see exactly what was happening, and then deal with it, usually went on to become famous battlefield leaders - if they survived.

If a combination of experience, knowledge of tactics and some luck contrived to produce a well-placed ambush with a consequent devastating firestorm, the awful magnitude of the destruction could turn a battle in an instant. In their accounts of the battle at Ballynahinch, Dickson and McComb repeat Teeling's opinion that, at this point, an inability to understand British army bugle calls led the rebels to mistake the sound of retreat for an indication of the arrival of fresh troops. According to all of them this misapprehension then provoked an immediate retreat.

This story has such a romantic appeal that it is tempting to swallow it whole. Nevertheless, at a time when a third to a half of the British army was composed of Irishmen, there must have been many in the ranks of the rebels who would have known all the bugle calls, even when imperfectly heard. It is arguable that even those who did not know them would have been unsteadied much quicker by the hellish sight of their brothers and neighbours being unceremoniously blown to glory than by a confusion of bugle sounds.

Nugent himself described the story of the action in his Report sent to Lake later in the day as a very simple one, perhaps overly simplified:

> To favour Lt. Col. Stewart's attack I detached the Monaghan Militia with two Field Pieces, some Yeomanry Infantry and a few of the 22nd Light Dragoons, through the Town to enter Lord Moira's demesne, to attack the Rebels in front. At the same time I ordered a strong party of Cavalry to watch their motions on the right — By these movements together with a Cannonade in front and on their right Flank the Rebels began to retreat and it soon became general for they fled in all directions.

Through his telescope from the top of a hill a mile and a half away James Thomson saw much of the action very well. A few years later he stated that, on reflection, the action in Dromore Street was the most murderous part of the whole battle. He remarked that the rebels for a brief time in the turmoil had possession of one of the Royal Artillery cannons. Thomson was only twelve when he watched the battle, so it is perhaps unsurprising that he found the experience exciting, but he and his companions must have been appalled by the carnage they witnessed, and the, "*cheers, yells and shrieks of the combatants they heard.*"

In Market Square the rebels now had cannon and infantry to their right, their left and in front, and dragoons and cavalry to their left and amongst them. Their muskets were now useful only if they had bayonets, because they had run out of ammunition. The tide was about to turn.

Soon the hordes of insurgents were being pushed backwards. Yeoman Colonel Forde, of Seaforde, at this point recognised some of his own tenants among the throng of insurgents. As he watched some of them fall to the Yeomanry musket fire, the Colonel observed to a fellow-officer,

"*G-d d--n these stiff-necked Presbyterians, they won't run.*"[4] The gradual retirement soon did become a wholesale retreat, and suddenly, in an instant, a rout. One minute both sides were at each other's throats, and the next the rebels were in full flight, running down Dromore Street and headlong up Ballymacarn Hill. The battle was over. It was still only seven o'clock in the morning.

Nugent reckoned that there might have been as many as five thousand rebels at Ednavaddy on the twelfth of June, but considerably less than that the next morning. Thomson thought it was more than this; perhaps as many as seven thousand on the Tuesday, with between two and three thousand soldiers in Nugent's army. No one disputes that the large six-pounder guns of the Royal Artillery had been hugely effective in annoying the enemy, whereas, although the rebels fired the little three-pounder swivels a lot, the shot mostly flew over the heads of the King's Troops and did little damage. They were only really useful for raising the morale of the rebels.

As soon as Nugent was certain that the main fight was over, he directed Stewart to take possession of the top of Ednavaddy Hill. There the Lieutenant Colonel's men found the reason why the rebels appeared so short of arms and ammunition. Lying on the ground were scores of discarded weapons and a large amount of unspent cartridges and black powder that had been abandoned in the dawn confusion. They also captured the four green colours of the insurgents along with the eight swivels, the remaining provisions and the cars for carrying these. They also found that, "*a very considerable number of the Rebels were concealed in the Plantation near Lord Moira's House.*" The battle was over, but the killing was not. The men captured in Montalto were shot where they stood.

The 22nd Dragoons pursued those rebels who had fled south. As the latter ran headlong up the roads leading to the relative safety of Dromara, the Spa and the greater safety of the Dromara Mountains, they had no protection from the horsemen and their flashing sabres. Nugent later claimed that three hundred of the rebels had been killed in the confrontation in the town and a further two hundred afterwards. Although Lieutenant George Stephenson, usually a reliable witness, does give similar figures, these numbers seem a little exaggerated. Even if the global figures given for the total action are correct, the proportions are surely wrong. A fortnight later the Marquis Cornwallis, writing to the Duke of Portland, commented, with his unrivalled experience of battle, (and with his own underlining):

> The accounts that you see of the numbers of the enemy destroyed in every action, are, I conclude, greatly exaggerated; from my own knowledge of military affairs, I am sure that a very small proportion only could be killed in battle, and I am much afraid that any man in a brown coat who is found within several miles of the field of action, is butchered without discrimination. It shall be one of my first objects to soften the ferocity of our troops, which I am afraid, in the Irish corps at least, is not confined to the private soldiers.[5]

An account, written three years after the battle, states that the rebels lost 150 on the field of Ballynahinch, and the King's men lost forty.[6] Another source, given in McComb, but uncredited (probably deservedly so), claims that only 20 rebels died in the battle and 28 bodies were discovered in the surrounding country,[7] but these figures are unrealistically low to represent the victims of a pitched battle and a headlong cavalry pursuit.

In a classic cavalry action mercy was rarely shown to desperately fleeing men. Almost every time a dragoon swung his sabre he cut a running man to the ground and probably killed him. A galloping soldier did not pause to make certain of this, because he knew that with a well-honed sabre or a cavalry sword, a hit usually gave a fatal cut, or at least one that seriously wounded. Those men caught up by Nugent's horsemen either died instantly, or suffered the more awful slow submission to haemorrhage and septicaemia.

Nugent, meanwhile, was remembering the obligations of his rank. In the two hours before he began his march back to Belfast, he collected the butcher's bill and drafted his dispatches. He established that he had about fifteen wounded, and had lost only one officer, Captain Evatt, five men of the Monaghans, and several Yeoman infantry, about seventeen in all. Miraculously by the time he wrote his second and final draft, all of the deceased, with the exception of Captain Evatt and a Monaghan private, had been restored to health, or at least to the gory pallets of the wounded. George Stephenson's estimates are more in accord with Nugent's first version, "*Captain Evatt of the Monaghans was killed with eight or nine of his men, one of the Argyles and one of Mr. Forde's yeomen and about twenty-five wounded, but not badly.*"

Nugent graciously mentioned the good conduct and courage of his officers and troops to General Lake, and named in particular Colonel Stewart, Major-General Barber, Colonel Leslie, Lieutenant-Colonels Peacocke (his aide-du-camp), Kerr of the Monaghans, and Durham of the Fife Fencibles, Majors McKinnon of his general staff and Smith of the 22nd Dragoons, Captains Owen, Lindsay and Coulson and Lieutenants Tisdale and Shearman of the Royal Artillery.

He also expressed his gratitude to all the officers, non-commissioned officers and privates who had conducted themselves well throughout. It was perhaps nothing more than an oversight in writing out the final Report, but the comment, "*The Yeomanry behaved with extreme Steadiness and Bravery*", is included in the first draft, but is conspicuous by its absence in the final one.[8]

Henry Munro's strategy at Ballynahinch may have been to outflank the crown forces with a large detachment, who, going east from Ednavaddy, would cross the Mill Brook and circle round to attack Nugent's forces from the rear of Windmill Hill. It was his bad luck that Nugent's plan was to do almost the exact opposite with Stewart's men. This made the attack that Munro envisaged turn into desperate defence.

Some accounts describe Munro as the last man to leave the field of battle, but Stephenson insists that, "*Munro of Lisburne was the Rebel Commander and He ran away the first or second.*" Neither of these versions is of much use, because any writer's opinion of just when and how any general left the field probably depends upon which side his allegiance lay. Munro's departure and his exact movements for a day or two after the battle will probably never be known. However, three days later, on Sunday the 17th, Thomas Lane, who worked for Lord Downshire, wrote to his Lordship in London to tell him:

> Yesterday the Hillsborough boys, in searching for arms, heard of, and after a long tedious march found and secured General Munro who commanded the Rebel army, with his aide du camp, Neil, whom they brought in here.

Stephenson's professional rivalries with Lane in the management of Downshire's estate would never allow him to be upstaged by his colleague. He wrote to his patron the very same day giving the Marquis the same information, but making sure to get the names right. Munro's aide was not called Neil, but William Kean, formerly a clerk with the *Northern Star.* Some accounts say the searching troops found the two of them in a pig house. Another claims that they were, "*accidentally discovered and taken by three Orangemen.*" In this version the two men were lying in a potato field hiding under some litter between the rows of potato plants. Whichever version is correct the two men would more than likely never have been found if the searching soldiers had not been told of their whereabouts.

The persistent tradition is that they found themselves, after two days of frantic running and hiding, in the townland of Clontanagullion, three miles from Ballynahinch, on the way towards Dromara. There they asked a local farmer by the name of William Holmes to give them refuge. No reason has ever been given for his actions, but Mr. Holmes informed the authorities who was on his farm, and the two were arrested. Stephenson adds the sinister details that Mussenden and himself spent the whole of that day compiling the evidence against Munro. Stephenson assured the Marquis that, presumably after the proverbial fair trial, "*He will be hanged before night*"

There seems to be some confusion about the date of Munro's capture. Lane says the 16th of June. However, it appears that General

Nugent may have been gifted with clairvoyance, because he wrote to Brigadier-General Knox on Friday, 15th of June, telling him, "*We have taken Munro of Lisburn who commanded at Ballynahinch the other day, as well as many others of their leaders.*"[9] Kean later managed to escape, but Stephenson in another letter written on the Sunday says, "*Yesterday I saw the Rebel general, Munro, hanged at Lisburn, and his head is now fixed on the Market House there.*"[10]

Harry Munro walked the pages of history for only six days. He was chosen by acclamation at Creevy Rocks on Monday 11th, and executed on Saturday 16th of June 1798. During that short time, with the exceptions of his understandable flight and ignominious capture, he behaved with dignity, courage and charm.

It is remarkable that after the years of meetings, the Resolutions, the planning, the dealings with the French and the preparation that just as the call was coming for taking the field by the United Irishmen the forces of the two founding counties of Down and Antrim should be faced with the crucial necessity of each finding a supreme commander of the forces in the field. Simms's cooling ardour for the fight threw the County Antrim Committee into confusion until they were inspired to appoint Henry Joy McCracken. He seems to have been a man so eminently suited by courage, intelligence and "warmth in the cause" for the onerous job of Adjutant-General for his county that one is forced to wonder why his fellow-insurgents had not recognised it earlier.

Munro's acclamation at Creevy Rocks came after the insurrection had begun, and of course some days after the arrest of Steel Dickson, but the Lisburn man's credentials and the known descriptions of his character suggest that he too was the only fittest man for his county.

Both men were past callow youth, but still had the vigour required for the awesome tasks they had accepted. In fact the two men were almost of an age. The parallels can be recognised even in the arrangements for the executions of the two men and in the noble manner each displayed while facing it.

1. Nugent to Lake, (NAI, Rebellion Papers, 620/38/137).

2. Anonymous witness quoted by McComb in *Guide to Belfast*, Belfast 1861.

3. For anyone interested, time how long it takes to read the sentence describing the firing of a musket.

4. Robert M. Young, *Ulster in '98, Episodes and Anecdotes*, Belfast, 1893.

5. Marquis Cornwallis from Dublin Castle to the Duke of Portland, 28th June 1798, quoted in *The Decade of the United Irishmen, Contemporary Accounts, 1791 - 1801,* edited by John Killen, Belfast 1997.

6. J.B. Gordon, *History of the Rebellion in Ireland in the Year 1798*, Dublin, 1801.

7. Anonymous source quoted in W. McComb, *McComb's Guide to Belfast*, Belfast, 1861, p.125.

8. The story of the Battle of Ballynahinch in this chapter is a synthesis of the following original documents, Nugent's Reports to Lake, (NAI, Rebellion Papers, 620/38/129 & 137) and eye-witnesses George Stephenson of Hillsborough, (Downshire Papers, PRONI, D/607/F/236), and James Thomson (1786-1849) in *The Belfast Magazine*, 1825, Vol. I, No. I., and the more modern works by Charles Dickson, *Revolt in the North*, London, 1960, pp. 149-155, and A.T.Q. Stewart, *The Summer Soldiers*, Belfast, 1995, pp. 222 - 229.

9. Stephenson, (Downshire Papers, PRONI, D/607/F/246), Thomas Lane, Hillsborough, (Downshire Papers, PRONI, D/607/F/245), and Nugent to Brigadier-General Knox, quoted in Dickson, p. 156.

10. Stephenson, (Downshire Papers, PRONI, D/607/F/251).

Mopping-Up Operations

And Caesar's spirit, ranging for revenge,
Shall in these confines with a monarch's voice
Cry 'Havoc,' and let slip the dogs of war;
That this foul deed shall smell above the earth
With carrion men, groaning for burial.

William Shakespeare,
Julius Caesar, Act 3, Scene 2, Line 270.

Mark Anthony is not the only one to have recognised the soldier's need to purge his spirit of the terror and nausea of battle by giving release to his baser feelings. Orgies of almost inhuman behaviour have been recorded since the time of Alexander the Great. Any mass excitement can produce a subsequent hysteria, but the monster of war seems to demand it. Frenzy follows battles as inevitably as night follows day. Since Shakespeare's time victorious troops, their adrenalin flowing from fear and anger, have often shouted the words, "Cry 'Havoc'!" as a signal that the usual social constraints no longer apply. Their officers prudently avert their eyes. Soldiers left to occupy a town that has dared to resist them lose all fellow feeling for the citizens. The old folk now become objects of ridicule, the women objects of another sort.

Not every soldier behaves badly. Some will withdraw to an area of peace. Some will even try to prevent the worst excesses of others, if they dare. But many will be beyond control. If alcohol can be found, and soldiers will always sniff it out, then the process is exacerbated. In what may have been an early example of getting your retaliation in first, Nugent's men, as we have seen, were drunk and without discipline in Ballynahinch the evening *before* the battle. Many old soldiers would have guessed that their release from military discipline made it clear that the morrow would begin with a dawn attack, to be followed by a quick victory and finished with an early march back to base. If they were to enjoy the soldier's reward, then they should take it early.

Nugent's official account glossed over the undoubted debauchery and arson on the Tuesday night in Ballynahinch. He represented this undisciplined behaviour to General Lake (and to the newspapers who would later print his report) with the sentence, "*The Troops having been fired upon from the Houses in the Town of Ballynahinch, it was set fire to and a considerable part of it was consumed.*"[1] On the Wednesday, Ballynahinch, and the women left in it, perhaps felt fortunate that Nugent was anxious to march his forces back to Belfast just as soon as he could leave. Unfortunately for these residents, Nugent left a large detachment of the Monaghan Militia behind to act as its garrison.

As described earlier this Ulster regiment had badly tarnished its reputation about a year previously, when a serious mutiny resulted in four ringleaders being shot by a firing squad at Blaris Camp. Shortly after this a party of Monaghans had broken into the offices of the *Northern Star* and so badly damaged the printing equipment that the paper was never issued again. It is not known why this regiment was chosen for garrison duty; nor if they had been to the fore in the intemperate behaviour on the streets of Ballynahinch on the Tuesday evening, but they were not popular with the citizens of Ballynahinch. Just over a week later, these folk were probably glad to see that, "*The Sutherland Fencibles, 1000 men, landed yesterday and [are] encamped near Ballynahinch.*"[2]

The undisciplined behaviour of the yeomen and Nugent's regulars, with the possible exception of the Sutherlands, is in marked contrast with that of the rebels. From their homes until they were running headlong from the field at Ballynahinch, in general the rebels appear to have behaved slightly better than the crown forces. These men were essentially God-fearing, literate and honest farmers, tradesmen or labourers. They may have been going to war; they were not going to pillage.

Of course many things were taken from the great houses without permission. A few rebels, as they were setting out from Bangor, had been ordered to enter Captain Clealand's house at Rathgill. There James Robinson told how he and John Allen, "*burst open the corn room door and took out a Pistol,*"[3] and William Steele of nearby Balloo confessed that on the same occasion he, "*met Dr. Jackson and went with him into Mr. Jas. Clealand's house where he got some cartridges of powder and two or three old pistols.*" [4]

An advertisement was inserted later in the *Belfast Newsletter* on 26th June by James Clealand, describing the loss of a fowling piece with a gold touch-hole, a double-barrelled pistol and a small silver hilted sword with the twelve Apostles engraved on the blade. Clealand stated that if they were returned voluntarily, the possessor would receive the market value of the pieces, but if the thief were caught in possession he would be punished as a receiver of stolen goods.[5]

The culprits must have been confident their admissions of guilt would bring no punishment because they did return the more valuable weapons to Clealand. We do not know what happened to James Robinson, but on 1st August 1798, John Allen was charged at Newtownards with, "*endeavouring to execute treason and rebellion in Ireland.*" He was sentenced to serve in His Majesty's Regiments abroad.[6] Unfortunately for him this punishment was not in any sense a let-off. Service at that time in fever-filled locations such as the islands of the Caribbean was considered more deadly than ferocious battle.

However, it would seem that John Allen might have survived his military service. A pike length to the north of Archibald Wilson's gravestone in Bangor Abbey Churchyard there is a memorial to a John Allen of Ballygrot, who died in 1848 aged 82 years. Since this would have made him 32 years old in 1798, it is tempting indeed to claim that the stone marks the resting place of the old crony of Archibald Wilson and James Robinson.

Throughout the early days of the call-out a number of chronicled incidences where a loyalist gentleman thought he was robbed, but only later realised that he had merely been deprived of a horse or a weapon or two and that he had sustained no property damage.

Lord Londonderry discovered a signed receipt in Mount Stewart that he authenticated later. It was signed by Hugh Boyd, the Chairman of the foraging rebel committee that ordered the removal of much of Londonderry's possessions. This signature may have sealed the man's fate, because a Hugh Boyd, presumably the same man, was later to be executed at Newtownards.[7]

Humphrey Galbraith wrote from his refuge with the Belfast surgeon, Mr. Fuller, to his friend Edward Hull, who was waiting out the conflict, like many others, in Stranraer. He told Hull, self evidently at second-hand, of the activities of some Donaghadee and Groomsport men whom they both knew:

> They have David Campbell baking for them in Donaghadee and somebody else in Newtownards. They opened Lord Londonderry's Toll Chest and divided out the Toll meal. They drove his fat oxen in and shot and flayed them, so they are not amind to starve.[8]

Galbraith might have been more concerned had he known that the rebels had taken at least one bayonet from his home. The Donaghadee rebels had also taken flints, muskets and drums from Mr. Ker's house at Portavo, pistols from Catherwood's at Ballyvester and pistols from Hearth Tax collector Bernard Mulholland.[9]

Some of the area's big houses, such as Gordon's Florida Manor, near Killinchy, Savage's at Portaferry and Matthews's at Inishargie were all robbed of weapons and/or foodstuffs, but strangely, it seems of little else. It would appear that need was the spur rather than avarice.[10] James Arbuckle, who by chance (or possibly clairvoyance) was in Dublin when hostilities broke out, moaned from there to his Scottish M.P. friend, Patrick Heron:

> I am completely underhoused – D'Dee is in possession of the Rebels, and all my furniture, Books, Plate, Wines &C., &C. gone to the mischief.

Now, he tells his friend, he has probably lost his home, Ballywilliam House near Donaghadee, and will have nothing he can indisputably call his own. Nothing, that is, except his chaise, which is in Scotland, a cottage in Wales, property in Dublin, and:

between 50 & 60 Guineas in my pocket, some shirts & stockgs. & two black
coats,...thank H____n I have a Legacy of £500 in the Bank in Newcastle.[11]

In point of fact, Arbuckle, like many County Down gentlemen, was later to be astonished on his return home after the rebellion, to find that, although the Donaghadee rebels had conscripted one of the Ballywilliam House foot-boys, almost everything he owned remained untouched:

The rascals behaved well towards me; they never even entered my house.
They sent to borrow a spyglass and very handsomely returned it uninjured.[12]

Back on Movilla Hill in the early morning of Saturday the 9th of June the rebels waited for some hours while their numbers built. As always the traffic was not all one way. Galbraith was later able to tell his friend Hull about some well known gentlemen from Donaghadee who had run all the way back to that town. Nevin Logan simply hid; but John Nevin and Johnny Lemon did not stop until they had reached the sanctuary of the Copeland Islands, determined to have nothing more to do with the rebels.[13] Some ran even farther. Six men and a woman were apprehended in Whitehaven in Cumberland on the 16th of June. They had stolen a boat and crossed to England to escape the punishment of the rebels who were compelling them to join them. Some of the members of this party were probably quite young, because one told the Whitehaven magistrates that he had been a drummer boy, another said he was a fifer. All were sent to Cockermouth House of Correction.[14]

Those insurgents who had chosen to hide in the Slieve Croob Mountains during the fighting in Ballynahinch, found themselves in as much danger during those hazardous hours after the battle as those rebels who ran before the Dragoons down the Dromore Road. Just as Cornwallis was to declaim a few days later, anyone who appeared to be in flight, or anything other than an innocent farmer – or sometimes *even* an innocent farmer – was fair game for cavalry sabres.

If they had the time, the soldiers hanged the men they caught on the nearest tree. Anyone with an appearance of substance or education, or wearing any garments of green, was spared an ignominious and imme- diate execution on the grounds that they might have been rebel officers. Such suspects were manacled and returned to Blaris, to be saved for a fair trial and a public hanging.

This policy of arrest did not meet with universal approval. To the middle class loyalists, the numbers of rebels being made prisoners was beginning to be offensive. Stephenson, active throughout in the loyalist forces, leaves his master in no doubt about his opinion:

> We are tormented by the number of prisoners here. I wish from my heart they were all hanged for such a set of rascals I never heard of. Indeed I think it was wrong to make them prisoners. They should have been shot at once and then one would not have been plagued with them.[15]

Stephenson's lack of sympathy for all rebels becomes more and more apparent. Describing the actions of the Militia flushing the countryside for rebels, he coldly says:

> They also went to the house of one Rice, to take up a son of his that was at Ballynahinch, and they found him dying from being shot through the body. Of course they left him to his fate.[16]

The day following the Battle of Ballynahinch, James McKey heard that a fresh army of both horse and foot was to make ready to march from Belfast to Newtownards to punish any rebels that might be found in that town and neighbourhood. At last he was to get his wish and get into the fight. When this did not happen, he was devastated. He had been bursting to be involved from the beginning. But his stars were with him, because suddenly:

> Part of our troop, (I was of the number) was ordered to ride about the hills behind Castlereagh and the number of fellows that we saw returning, flying from Ballynahinch was beyond almost what you can conceive.

Telling about his adventures he complains and exults in the same breath to Downshire:

> In my life I never had so fatiguing a morning, galloping after well-ran fellows, all armed, but as their party was broke, they did not attempt to resist and we killed a number without any of our party receiving any damage. I am convinced thousands of these creatures were driven to join through fear. . . many of them declared it in their dying moment.[17]

The impressions McKey and Stephenson were giving in their letters to Downshire were probably not unlike any yeoman's. They give little appearance of humanity or regard for the persons of the rebels they caught and killed. They could not have been expected to. Just as with any soldiers throughout the ages, they had been conditioned to think of their enemy as less than human and undeserving of the usual considerations given to fellow citizens. After all had not these insurgents been striving, with great violence, to overthrow the state to which the army and the yeomen had sworn their loyalty? They would have reckoned that any insurgents they caught deserved their fate.

The professional soldiers, of course, were not idle. Major-General Nugent had sent memoranda to his senior officers immediately after the Battle of Ballynahinch. Lieutenant-Colonel John Joseph Atherton, who had taken over the command at Newtownards after Stapylton, wrote to Nugent a few days later, telling him how he had been getting on in the Ards area:

> I have had tolerable success today in apprehending the persons mentioned in the memorandum...We have burned Johnstone's house at Crawford's-Bourn-Mills, at Bangor, destroyed the furniture of Pat Agnew, James Francis and Gibbison, and Campbell's, not yet finished at Ballyholme; burned the house of Johnston at the Demesnes near Bangor; the houses of Jas. Richardson and John Scott at Ballymaconnell-Mills; burned the house of McConnell, miller, and James Martin, a Captain, and a friend of McCulloch's, hanged at Ballynahinch. Groomsport reserved. Cotton the same...We hope you will think we have done tolerably well. Tomorrow we go to Portaferry, or rather its neighbourhood.

Atherton was very critical of the well-affected loyalists who, when at the time of their home country's greatest need, were not very helpful, and in some cases, were not even to be found:

> Ought we not to punish the gentlemen of the country who have never assisted the well-disposed people, yeomanry, &c? For my own part a gentleman of any kind, but more particularly a magistrate, who deserts his post at such a period, ought to be - I will not say what. Mr. Echlin, of Echlinville [just south of Kircubbin]; Rev. [Francis] Hutcheson of Donaghadee; Mr. [James] Arbuckle, Collector of Donaghadee, an official man; Mr. Ker, Portavoe; Mr. Ward of Bangor is now, and only now, to be found.

List of inactive magistrates, or rather friends to the United Irishmen - Sir John Blackwood, John Crawford, of Crawford's-Bourn; John Kennedy, Cultra, &c. But among others, the Rev. H. Montgomery of Rosemount, who is no friend to Government, or its measures, and whom I strongly suspect. I have got his bailiff.[18]

Atherton was possibly being unkind to some of the named gentlemen of the district. One or two by chance were away from their usual residences when hostilities broke out. There certainly had been an unseemly exodus from the Ards, led, it must be said, by its senior loyalist, Lord Londonderry. Men like Blackwood and Arbuckle, however, were without doubt strong supporters of Government and had been very active in recruiting Yeomanry corps in Bangor and Donaghadee long before the outbreak of insurrection in the district.

Out of the flow of blood that enriched the earth of mid and north County Down in '98 there grew many stories, some of which have been handed down the generations. Often the story is still told over and over in a local area, hardly changed by thousands of repetitions, but sometimes just a wee bit embellished for the better telling.

One story in particular has spread far beyond the localities from which the central characters come, and from the scene of the action. Its origins may well be founded in truth, but over the years, the story has received so much nourishment from so many romantics and propagandists that whatever verifiable truth it once had has almost been obliterated by the imaginative detail added later.

The story is, of course, the tragic adventure of Betsy Gray and her companions. In essence it tells that she, her brother, George, and her lover, Willie Boal, went with the rebels to Ballynahinch where they eventually got caught up in the action. Recognising that all was lost on Dromore Street, the three ran away to the north-west to escape. There, in the townland of Ballycreen, they were caught by some yeomen and slaughtered.

There is no mention in the newspapers of the time of such an outrage, nor indeed of any of this trio. There is nothing in the copious court martial depositions, nor in any eyewitness accounts. But this is not surprising. Footsoldiers in the rebel ranks, even if female, would not have merited any particular attention. Betsy and her two male companions were certainly not leaders in any sense of the word. They would not have been wanted for trial, nor just to swell the numbers of prisoners. Especially in those bloody hours after the battle, the identities and lives of any fleeing insurgents would not have been worth a bent penny.

The summary hanging, or the sabre-slashing to death of a fleeing rebel might have provoked anger, but the killing of a young girl, with her sweetheart and brother beside her, created a martyr. If a deed like this occurred it would not have been forgotten by the people of the country, even those who may have had contrary political beliefs. We cannot know this for sure, but the appearance of Betsy Gray's story in print a few years later suggests that the tale was being told and re-told round the homes and hearths of Down for some time before anyone got round to committing it to print. The story took on a life of its own.

A curious story appeared in a book published almost a century after the event. A Mr. James O'Neill of Belfast related an anecdote told to him by his grandfather some years earlier. To anyone who knows the tale of Betsy Gray this account has a ring of familiarity. Some years after the Battle of Ballynahinch the grandfather had been approaching Crossgar Fair when his walking companion pointed to a roadside bog and said:

> I saw a bloody piece of work done there in '98. I saw a handsome young girl carrying a jug of buttermilk to the rebels. Three yeomen galloped after her as she fled on their approach to the bog for safety. They succeeded in reaching her, and cut her in pieces with their swords. Her cruel death had been witnessed by three pikemen on the hill above, who awaited the onslaught of the horsemen with their backs to a dry stone ditch. With the curved blade fixed at the side of their pike-heads they cut the horses' bridles, and soon had the yeomen sprawling on the ground at their mercy. They pled hard for their lives, but were told that there was, 'no quarter for cowards that would kill a helpless woman.'[19]

The name of this tragic young woman is not known. It is possible she was Betsy Gray; or it is equally possible that the tale of this anonymous woman as told by O'Neill's grandfather was amplified in the years following the rebellion, with names and other details being added. Of course, it is also possible that the whole story is a romantic confection of the sort that rivals those openly admitted tales of popular fiction sometimes called potboilers. What a historian would call the supportive evidence is copious, but of mixed provenance. Every antique rocking chair in the Ards is described as once belonging to Betsy Gray's mother, every unearthed bayonet is claimed to be Willie Boal's. Such claims indicate the continuing interest in the human tragedy of '98, but scarcely help to verify the stories.

For more than a decade after the rebellion there is not one known mention of anyone resembling the girl on the field of battle. The first known appearance in print of a character named Betsy Gray (or sometimes Bessie Grey) was in a volume of poetry written by Mary Balfour in 1810. All copies of this book seem now to be lost. We only know of its existence from the quotation of the actual poem in another book published fifty years afterwards.[20]

> The star of evening slowly rose,
> > Through shades of twilight gleaming,
> It shone to witness Erin's woes,
> > Her children's life-blood streaming;
> 'Twas then sweet star, thy pensive ray,
> > Fell on the cold, unconscious clay,
> That wraps the breast of Bessie Grey,
> > In softened lustre beaming.[21]

Charles Teeling, who had been imprisoned by Castlereagh in the autumn of 1796, was released shortly before the Battle of Ballynahinch. In 1828 he published his personal narrative of those times. In it he makes mention of Mary Balfour's poem, and tells the story of Betsy Gray in more detail.[22]

Teeling's book made the story more public than it had been, but the publication that really made her name nationally known was not to be published until 1888. In that year the weekly serialisations of the story of Betsy Gray, which had been appearing in the *North Down Herald and Bangor Gazette*, were published in book form. The author was Wesley Greenhill Lyttle, a journalist and popular novelist, who had developed the art of shaking up an entertaining cocktail of fact and fiction for the amusement of his readers.[23]

Lyttle took a large number of personal anecdotes, recollections and reminiscences of 1798, which he had collected. He then added in some detail from documentary sources he had read, and produced his story of the rebellion and the people involved in it. He never meant to write a definitive history of the days of June 1798, but, for many who knew no other source, that is how his book was perceived. Hardly a home in County Down was without its copy.

Betsy Gray and the Hearts of Down has never lost its popularity, being reprinted in 1968 and since. The 'facts' of the story may be blurred but its excitement and interest still appeals to many people. The bit-players in the novel such as Mat McClenaghan of Six Road Ends and James Dillon of Drumawhey are today better known to many than such historically documented characters as James Porter, Henry Munro and Major-General Nugent. Lyttle's account is full of historical inaccuracies, mixed up with some absolutely genuine information. For anyone who wants to absorb the flavour of those confused days of the summer of 1798, with small regard for total probity, Lyttle's book will certainly provide this, but for the serious student it is a confection which has to be taken with great care.

Since Teeling first wrote about her, Betsy Gray's home has been variously identified as Gransha (near Bangor), Killinchy and Tullyniskey (in the Parish of Garvaghy). All three possibilities have points for and against. The first two are more likely locations, if only because of the greater involvement of men from Killinchy, Ards and north Down, but each theory has its proponents. All versions agree that Betsy and her two companions were killed together, but how and where they met their ends is disputed. What is undisputed is that all three, but especially Betsy, have gone into popular folklore as epitomes of courage, youth and hope; the victims of meanness, treachery and brutality. Betsy, the young and beautiful girl, needlessly slaughtered, has become what one writer has called, 'Ulster's Joan of Arc.'[24] The reader who wishes to explore this question could do worse than start with Jack McCoy's book, *Ulster's Joan of Arc*, listed in the bibliography.

This slim volume, and W.G. Lyttle's historical novel, both end with an anonymous and totally sympathetic ballad, first written some years after the events it describes. It seems appropriate that we leave Betsy's story the same way:

BETSY GRAY - A BALLAD OF NINETY-EIGHT

Oh, many a noble lad and lass who joined the fight of ninety-eight,
To right the wrong of cruel years, did meet with sad and bloody fate,
On Ednavady's sloping heights, in June, upon the thirteenth day,
In thousands stood the Patriots bold to fight for home and victory.

But bravest of them all, I ween, who mustered there upon that day,
And drew the sword for fatherland, was lovely, winsome Betsy Gray.
From Granshaw, near to Bangor Town, with Willie Boal that day she came;
Her brother too, was by her side, inspired by patriotic flame.

And when the tide of battle raged and showers of bullets fell around,
Still in the thickest of the fight was noble-hearted Betsy found.
When adverse fate with victory crowned the loyal host upon that day,
George and Willie joined the flight, and with them lovely Betsy Gray.

Along the Lisburn Road they fled, pursuing Yeomen keeping watch;
Then Betsy drew her gleaming sword, and hid it in a farmhouse thatch.
She reached the vale of Ballycreen, her friends some distance were behind,
And quickly did she look around, a quiet hiding-place to find.

But ere 'twas found she heard a cry, alas, too well she knew the sound;
Her brother, and her sweetheart true, had by the Yeoman band been found.
Then from the grassy vale she sprang, this beauteous, noble, fearless maid,
And back she ran with bounding step, that she might seek to give her aid.

Ah! What sight then met her gaze; her Willie weltering in his gore,
And George, her brother, by his side, pleading for life in accents sore.
A Yeoman raised his sword to strike, as Betsy to the rescue ran;
"Oh, spare my brother's life!" she cried, "Oh, spare him if you be a man."

She raised her white and rounded arm as if to ward the dreaded stroke.
Vain was her prayer, the weapon fell and smote her hand off as she spoke.
Another of the murderous crew, a man who came from Anahilt,
Laughed at the brutal deed, and cried, "More rebel blood must yet be spilt!"

He drew a pistol from his belt and shot poor Betsy through the eye.
She sank upon the heathery mound and died without a sob or sigh.
That night the murdered three were found by Matthew Armstrong, then a lad;
Who quickly running to his home, related there his tidings sad.

No tombstone marks that humble grave, no tree nor shrub is planted there,
And never spade disturbs the spot where sleep the brave and rests the fair.
Shame on the cruel, ruthless band who hunted down to death their prey!
And palsy strike the murderous hand that slew the lovely Betsy Gray![25]

****

On the same day that General Nugent had been approaching Saintfield from Belfast, Colonel Stewart marching from Downpatrick and the rebels relaxing in the sun on Ednavaddy Hill, some men were meeting behind closed doors in the Military Barrack on Millisle Road, Donaghadee. William Brown, who appears to have been a loyalist, later stood before James Clealand and stated under oath what he had seen and heard. Because of the date and time, it seems that the men named in Brown's deposition had been left in charge of Donaghadee and its important port, while their comrades went to face General Nugent and the other Crown forces. The role of these men was hugely important, not to say effective. The town of Donaghadee in itself was no more than a typical small town of the Ards, but its port and Packet Station had assumed national importance during the century. For the duration of hostilities and beyond the authorities were unable to enter the port. Because the Packet Company immediately moved its Irish terminal to Carrickfergus, this did not affect matters in Antrim too much, but it was of great nuisance value for communications and transport between Britain and County Down. Brown deposed that:

on Tuesday the 12th of June last, about 12 o'clock in the day, he was at the
Barrack in Donaghadee, and thinking that a Committee [of United Irishmen]
was sitting in a Room in the Barrack, and wishing to know who they were…
Deponent looked through the Keyhole into the Room, and saw Wm. Blair
of Donaghadee, Carman, and John Johnston of Donaghadee, Grocer, and
Deponent verily believes they were part of the Committee assembled in the
Barrack for the purpose of Carrying on the War, and supporting the Rebels, and

Deponent says that Hamilton McIlea had a Sword and Pistol and ordered out the Deponent, and that Saml. Boal had the command of a party of Men and was armed with a Blunderbuss.[26]

He may not have been present when William Brown was peeping through the Barracks window, but weaver Bernard Crosby seems to have been the man in charge of the rebels in the port right through the rebellion. Another weaver, James Dillon of Loughriscouse [the same one as Lyttle's hero?], a farmer called William Ferris, William Carson from Killaughey and Hugh McKelvey, a servant of the Rector, all testified at Crosby's Newtownards court martial on 7th July 1798 that they had seen him at the Barracks, or drilling men in the street, or at the Rectory Green, always with a sword in his hand. No one testified on Crosby's behalf and he was convicted and hanged.[27]

Below is a list of suspected rebels from Donaghadee that was found after the rebellion on a scrap of paper. There is no indication why it was written, or by whom, but it is by no means a complete list. It does contain the interesting name of Samuel McCance, Henry Munro's First Lieutenant at Windmill Hill, and has him living in Ballyvester, near Donaghadee. Being named in this fashion did not harm McCance much. He survived the round of punishments and died peacefully in the home of his son, Dr. William McCance, in Ballyvester, in 1841.The citation of his name on the above list, when we know that throughout the action at Ballynahinch he was with Munro, suggests that the list may have been drawn up in the weeks after the battle, when the flames of rebellion were not yet quenched and all scores had not yet been settled. It cannot, however, have been very long after the battle, because the list includes the name of William Morrison, who was convicted and hanged during those high-summer weeks.[28]

List of suspected rebels in Donaghadee

Wm Morrison	Ser[van]t. to Mr Adams
Hunter	Brewer to Mr Tomb
Ham[ilton] McIlay	Brewery Lane
Jas Fullerton	Baker
Jn. Duke	Herdstown

Robt. Wilson   Ballyvester

Saml. McCance   "   29

From Scotland, Edward Hull would have known little of the details of the rebel rule in his home town, but he clearly was aware of its effectiveness. He was able to pass on news that had been brought over by the packet boats, Portpatrick being only three or four hours away from Carrickfergus. Other swift craft might have been able to better this passage from the Down coast, if they could dodge the rebels. Hull displays an understandable interest in Donaghadee, and talks about a camp on Scrabo. This was probably the one formed by the insurgents before they marched to Ballynahinch, and the news had been slow in reaching Hull in Scotland:

> The principal part of the D'Dee Republican troops are in that camp. They, however, begin to be frightened as some of them have attempted to escape to this country but have been taken up. I sincerely hope in the course of a few days Rebellion will be completely settled in the County of Down, but strong garrisons will be required for some time. …The person who commands the rebel army on Scrabo calls himself General Granard. They have few arms and hardly any ammunition, but they direct their fire principally against the officers of the King's Troops. Their pike are not of much use after they are thrown into disorder by the artillery. Lord Ranelagh of the *Doris* covers both sides of the Lough of Belfast. He is arming all the Revenue vessels and Barges along the coast from the *Doris* to prevent attacks from Donaghadee on the Packets or other vessels conveying the troops to Ireland. I have just had the honour to receive a letter from His Lordship informing me that he is just dispatching armed boats to cut all the vessels out of the harbour at Bangor and that he has retaken Mr. John Brown of Belfast (late Sovereign), who, with his family, had been taken prisoner from on board a brig by the Donaghadee insurgents.[30]

The capture of John Brown and his family had occurred on Tuesday 12th of June in Donaghadee Sound, between the town and Copeland Island. In his time Brown was Sovereign (or mayor) of Belfast for four terms, Worshipful Master of the Orange Lodge of Freemasons, High Sheriff of Antrim, a Major in the Belfast Volunteers, an ardent loyalist and reputedly the wealthiest man in Belfast.[31]

In the face of the threat of a French invasion, this formidable man had raised four Yeomanry companies in the city. So great was his contempt for the liberal ideas espoused by the Belfast radicals that in the summer of 1796 he had published at great personal expence, "*1500 sixpenny copies of Bishop Watson's Apology for the Bible in order to contend with the cheap editions of Paine's Age of Reason that are industriously circulated through the country.*"[32]

He had been in Cheltenham at the outbreak of the rebellion, and, unlike so many of his more timid friends, he had spared no effort to get back to his home. The lack of wind that was preventing the dispatch of reinforcements to Nugent turned the journey of Brown's *Linen Hall* from Carlisle into a five-day odyssey. He would not have known it, but his destination of Donaghadee had been under rebel rule the whole time his ship was on the Irish Sea.

The town's mariners, having faster sailers in the calms than Ranelagh's *Doris*, had been stopping all boats in the Sound looking for arms and powder. Brown's fame, and his friendship with Donaghadee's Customs Collector, James Arbuckle of Ballywilliam, had possibly made his a familiar face to these seamen, or else other passengers may have betrayed his identity. Whatever the reason, he was certainly recognised by the Donaghadee rebels, and taken ashore there. Brown was told that he was going to Munro's camp at Ednavaddy the next morning for court martial and that he and his family would be housed for the night with a Mrs. Smith at the Head Inn.

The next morning's news changed everyone's plans. Both Brown and the rebels discovered that General Nugent had defeated the insurgents at Ballynahinch. Brown later wrote that, "*The news arrived at Donaghadee, and also that the troops were marching in there about 10 o'clock, when every man fled and my two sentinels also.*"

The resourcefulness and determination then shown by Brown, not to mention a certain lack of false modesty, demonstrates why he had become such a wealthy businessman and Sovereign:

> I then procured a small boat with a pair of oars, and with Mrs. Brown and an old man rowed to Belfast Lough, where the *Doris* Frigate [of] Lord Ranelagh, lay, and after being twice pursued by boats from the shore we, in about 4 hours, got safe aboard the Frigate and his Lordship, who had the evening heard of our misfortune, very politely gave us his boat to land us at Carrickfergus and that evening I got here [to Belfast].[33]

The fact that he was once again seeking the position of Sovereign of Belfast at the time, and indeed was elected to that office on the 25th of June, might have contributed to his urgency and determination to return to Belfast.[34] *The Newsletter*, with more than a hint of news management, reported that:

> John Brown Esq., late Sovereign of Belfast, and his family, arrived here yesterday from Carlisle. This Gentleman, with that truly patriotic spirit, has come forward, at this critical period, to join his Yeomanry Corps.[35]

If the rebels of Donaghadee had been able to recognise the value of well-known prisoners and the potential propaganda benefits of high profile trials, they had learned well from the properly constituted authorities. All over the county, and of course beyond, clergymen, physicians and other prominent citizens who had been taken up were having their trials arranged. Some notorious leaders were quickly and summarily tried, convicted and hanged. Others had to wait for their show trials.

1. Major-General Nugent to Lieutenant-General Lake, (Rebellion Papers, NAI, 620/38/129 & 137).

2. Geo. Stephenson, Hillsborough, to Downshire, 22nd June 1798, (Downshire Papers, PRONI, D/607/F/265).

3. James Robinson, (Lytton White Papers, PRONI, D/714/3/6).

4. William N. Steele of Ballow, (Lytton White Papers, PRONI, D/714/3/28).

5. James Clealand, *Belfast Newsletter*, 26th June 1798.

6. Court Martial of John Allen, 1st August 1798, (Rebellion Papers, NAI, 620/2/15/17).

7. Eleanor Bennett and Mary McCollum in an unsigned note, July 1798, (Lytton White Papers, PRONI, D/714/3/31).

8. Galbraith to Hull, (Downshire Papers, PRONI, D/607/F/235). *Belfast*

Newsletter, Tuesday, 24th July 1798.

9. John Catherwood to David Ker, 12th June 1798, written in full in *County Down Spectator,* 18th December 1911.

10. Court Martial of Archibald Warwick, John Sibbett and John McKnight, (Rebellion Papers, NAI, 620/2/15/32, 620/2/15/15 and 620/2/15/23).

11. James Arbuckle, Donaghadee to Patrick Heron, 12th June 1798, (Transcripts of Heron Papers, PRONI, T/3162/1/5). The original letter is in the Scottish Record Office in the Heron of Kirroughtrie MSS GD 307/16/17.

12. Arbuckle to Heron, 11th July 1798, (Heron of Kirroughtrie MSS, Scottish Record Office, GD 307/16/17).

13. Galbraith to Hull, (Downshire Papers, PRONI, D/607/F/235).

14. *Belfast Newsletter*, Tuesday, 3rd July 1798.

15. Geo. Stephenson to Downshire, 27/8 June 1798, (Downshire Papers, PRONI, D/607/F/283).

16. Geo. Stephenson to Downshire, 4th July 1798, (Downshire Papers, PRONI, D/607/F/299).

17. James McKey, Belfast to Downshire, 14th June 1798, (Downshire Papers, D/607/F/244).

18. Lt. Col. J.J.Atherton to Maj. Gen. G. Nugent, 20th June 1798, quoted in W.J. Fitzpatrick, *The Sham Squire, and the Informers of 1798; with Jottings about Ireland a Century Ago*, Dublin, 1855, pp. 347-348.

19. Robert M. Young, *Ulster in '98, Episodes and Anecdotes,* Belfast, 1893, p. 74.

20. William McComb, *Guide to Belfast*, Belfast, 1860.

21. Mary Balfour's poem quoted in full in Jack McCoy, *Ulster's Joan of Arc,* Bangor, 1989.

22. Charles Hamilton Teeling, *Personal Narrative of the Irish Rebellion of 1798*, London, 1828.

23. Kenneth Robinson, Introduction to Jack McCoy, *Ulster's Joan of Arc*, Bangor, 1989.

24. Jack McCoy, Bangor, 1989.

25. *Ibid.* and W.G. Lyttle, *Betsy Gray or Hearts of Down: A Tale of Ninety-Eight*, Bangor, 1888, reprinted Newcastle, 1968.

26. William Brown, Donaghadee, Deposition sworn on 3rd August 1798, (Lytton White Papers, PRONI, D/714/03/26).

27 Court Martial of Bernard Crosby, (Rebellion Papers, NAI, 620/2/15/30).

28. Charles Dickson, *Revolt in the North,* London 1960, p. 150.

29. List of suspected rebels in the Donaghadee area in 1798, (McCance Papers, PRONI, D/272/35B). This unsigned, undated piece of paper somehow fell into the possession of the McCance family, where presumably it was kept as a trophy.

30. Edward Hull, from Portpatrick in Scotland to Lord Downshire in London, 14th June 1798, Downshire Papers, PRONI, D/607/F/243).

31. A.T.Q. Stewart, *A Deeper Silence, The Hidden Roots of the United Irish Movement,* by Faber & Faber, London 1993.

32. James Arbuckle from Donaghadee to Downshire in Dublin, 18th September 1796, (Downshire Papers, PRONI, D/607/D/180).

33. Shannon S. Millin, *Sidelights on Belfast History,* Belfast and London, 1932, quoted in A.T.Q. Stewart, *The Summer Soldiers,* Belfast, 1995, pp. 198-199.

34. *Belfast Newsletter,* 26th June 1798.

35. *Ibid.* 15th June 1798.

TRIALS AND EXECUTIONS I

Lay then the axe to the root, and teach governments humanity.
It is their sanguinary punishments which corrupt mankind.

Thomas Paine,
The Rights of Man, 1791.

The 'black-mouthed' ministers

It came as no surprise to anyone that there were many trials and a number of executions after the rebellion. An inordinate number of these were of men from the Ards. A disproportionate number of those convicted in the courts were Presbyterian clergymen. The stories of the hanging of the three of these men who lived and preached the Gospel in the Ards Peninsula serve as models of this admonitory policy. It should be stressed that men of the cloth were not worse treated than others in these terrible days and not all Dissenting clergymen were embroiled in the rebellion activities. But their status in an almost universally Presbyterian Ards made their treatment an example that could not be ignored. The three executions were meant as a message to the populace in order to ensure their future good behaviour. Hindsight would suggest that for many who were 'out' in June 1798 what they had seen and felt for those few days had already been enough of a disheartening experience. More than ever many looked for inspiration and guidance to the shepherd of their flock. For these, the show trials and executions served as a reminder to keep their heads down and to ensure that for the next few years at least any resentment they felt against authority should be left to simmer unseen.

The stories of the three executed clergymen can be told with some authority, because their particulars are better preserved than most. The reason why so much documentary detail about these men survives is unknown, but it was perhaps because after each was hanged, it was not just family and neighbours who wanted to treasure their memories, but whole congregations and a larger community.

The oldest of the three, and by far the best known, was the Rev. James Porter of Greyabbey, who was 45 years old in 1798. Porter was known as one of the handsomest men of his time. Throughout the Ards Peninsula and beyond he was famous for his magnetic personality, his pastoral excellence, his scorn for sycophancy, his radical opinions and his unconcealed reformist sympathies.

For the duration of the action in June 1798 and a couple of weeks afterwards, not much is known of his activities. He was well aware that his pre-rebellion writings had marked him in the eyes of the establishment as a danger to them, so he hid himself in a nearby house in Ballydoonan. He was discovered, possibly by an informant, and summarily arrested. He was then held in the Market House of Newtownards. This building had been temporarily converted into a prison, and Porter shared it with many others who had preceded him. He was confined there for a short time in total ignorance, wholly unconscious of any charges which might be made against him -- until Friday morning the 29th of June, when he was casually handed a piece of paper. It was a note from the military commander in Newtownards, and read:

Newtownards, June 29 1798

The Rev. Jas. Porter of Greyabbey, confined on a charge of High Treason, of Rebellion and of Sedition and of divers treasonable, rebellious and seditious practices contrary to the Peace of our Sovereign, George the Third and his Kingdom of Ireland.

Signed J.J. Atherton,
Lieut. Col. L. L. D.
[Lancashire Light Dragoons][1]

When Porter asked what the note meant, the young officer turned on his heel and left him, telling him only that he must prepare for trial. His sons kept the piece of paper. James Porter Jnr., who in later years became one of the most eminent jurists in the United States, commented on it, "*Perhaps no man was ever tried on charges so vaguely and informally prepared.*"

As soon as he could, Porter wrote a letter to General Nugent begging to know what offence he was charged with. He protested his innocence and said he could disprove any allegation if he could summon witnesses. No notice was taken of this. His court martial was convened for the very next day.

On the bench sat Colonel Atherton, two Captains and four subalterns. This would have been daunting enough to Porter, but when he saw that Lord Londonderry was there too, he must have been completely dismayed.

Years earlier, after the fashion of so many of his Presbyterian contemporaries, Porter had completed his studies in Scotland. He had then accepted a call to Greyabbey in 1787. He had come from a poor family in Tammany [sometimes Tamna] Wood, near Ballindrait in County Donegal, leaving his family after an unhappy dispute. When he arrived in Greyabbey, he was already married to Anne Knox of Eden Hill, near Dromore.

Such were his qualities and personality that Porter charmed all who met him. In his sons' account of his life they quote the Rev. James Hall, an Episcopal Minister in New Orleans, who knew their father well before he went, like them, to America. He had once told them he had never seen any man of such fascinating manners and conversation.[2]

A former pupil of Porter's wrote thirty years later that he had never in his life met as good a man, and that his school of sciences and natural philosophy at Greyabbey was unequalled. He was certain that Porter did not bear arms in the insurrection, and that he had been convicted on very uncertain evidence and the poison of a, "*vile informer.*"[3]

During the later 1780s and early 1790s Porter evidently found the company of the local gentry as congenial as they found his captivating. The Porters were soon constant dinner companions of the

Londonderrys at Mount Stewart. Perhaps it was Alexander Stewart's origins in Ballylawn in Donegal, not far from Porter's childhood home in Ballindrait that made the initial connection.

During the 1790s the couple became very close to the Londonderrys and were introduced at Mount Stewart to, among others, Ireland's Viceroy, Lord Camden and Lord Rawdon of Montalto, Earl of Moira. At a time when the distinctions of rank were more strictly observed than they now are, it must have seemed strange to some that an impecunious pastor and his wife were socialising with many of Ireland's most prominent citizens. But James Porter Jun. was adamant that it was Londonderry alone who was to turn against his father:

> To my father's intimacy in that family may be traced all his misfortunes. He was soon excluded from the house, persecuted by the Earl with a cold and malignant vindictiveness which times seemed rather to augment than diminish, and finally, as I shall show, by the influence of this noble man, basely murdered.

Porter Jnr. insisted that the causes that led to the estrangement between His Lordship and Porter Snr. were of a very delicate nature. Lady Londonderry had always shown Porter great attention and respect. There was no suggestion or thought of any impropriety from anyone, "*save him who knew her best, and ought to have valued her most.*" Many contemporaries agreed that Lord Londonderry had a cold nature and a jealous temper; he may well have viewed the relationship in a suspicious light. According to Porter's sons at least, his doubts grew in his soul like a cancer until the day when he realised he could exact a final retribution for the wrongs he felt Porter had done him.

During these years Porter first of all lost the Marquis's friendship, then his respect and in return gained his bitter hatred. It must be said that Porter had done nothing to help his own cause. More than a year before the rebellion it would not have pleased Londonderry when he discovered that Porter was the author of the humorous but scurrilous essays in the *Northern Star* about Lord Mountmumble, Billy Bluff, Noodledrum and Squire Firebrand. These disrespectful caricatures were identified by all as Londonderry himself, a local farmer called William Lowry, the Rev. John Cleland and Hugh Montgomery of Greyabbey.[4]

In February 1797, on the very day that the government had decreed a fast day for celebrating deliverance from their foreign foe on the dispersal of the French fleet off Bantry Bay two months earlier, Porter had preached a sermon in Greyabbey. This had immediately been published in Belfast to almost universal public acclaim. To the loyalist landowners and placemen his writings only fanned the growing flames of a personal resentment. He was thenceforth known and denounced by them as an advocate of the peoples' rights, if not a sworn United Irishman. By association, his fellow clerics were also tainted. James Arbuckle, the ultra-conservative Customs Collector, and a staunch Episcopalian, declaimed:

> A Presbyterian parson, Porter of Greyabbey, has published a sermon for which, provided the proof of publication should not fail, I should think he might be handsomely trounced. These fellows [Presbyterian Ministers] ought to be deprived of the Regium Donum. They all, save two or three, in the whole Province, are avowed incendiaries.[5]

About eight months later Humphrey Galbraith followed his superior's opinions about Porter and the Dissenting clergy:

> the devil is not yet out of the hearts of the croppies, for Porter, the Presbyterian Minister of Greyabbey, and young McCullough of Bangor and young White of Ballyree and others had a meeting in Paddy Agnew's in Bangor on last Sunday night after dark. They are all notorious high United men and could be about no good. God preserve honest and honourable men from their wicked machinations.[6]

When Porter saw Lord Londonderry on the bench at his court martial he would have been all too aware that his former friend and patron was now an implacable and deadly enemy. Anne Porter maintained that from the moment of her husband's arrest she was certain the hatred of Lord Londonderry would cost him his life. On the other hand, Castlereagh's official biographer claimed that Porter was one of three 'black-mouthed' ministers who had planned to divide the Mount Stewart estates between them in the event of the rebellion proving successful.[7]

We cannot say that the Londonderrys were wrong about Porter's objectives, only that he does seem to have been an active United man in the months leading up to the rebellion. He certainly held the views that parliament was in need of urgent reform and that Catholic Emancipation was long overdue. But in 1798 there were many witnesses to say that when the country was 'up', Porter was not. In this he was not unique. Many ardent supporters of the principles of the United Irishmen harboured sufficient misgivings at the non-appearance of the French and the mass arrests of the leaders that they chose to sit it out in June 1798.

Porter's family always contended that he was entirely innocent of any, "*act of treason, unless taking the oath of United Irishmen amounted to such.*" They believed that an accidental meeting on a Greyabbey street was the only overt cause of their father's destruction:

> An express, forwarded by the commanding officer from Newtownards to Portaferry, was obliged to pass through Greyabbey, and was stopped by a party [of] insurgents. Our house was in the neighbourhood. It so happened that not one of the persons who had so stopped the messenger could read or write. They brought him to my father and called on him to read the letter found on the bearer. He did so – and this was the head and front of his offending.

His court martial heard this expressed as, "*that at the head of a body of rebels he had stopped a King's Messenger.*" Captain Charles Matthews of Inishargie House, now being celebrated as the loyalist hero of Portaferry, told the court that he had sent his servant, George McChesney, at six o'clock in the morning to Colonel Stapylton at Newtownards requesting reinforcements. McChesney confirmed that he had given the note to Captain Fowler at Newtown and, as he was riding back towards Portaferry, he was stopped by a small party of rebels at Kilnatierney Bridge just north of Greyabbey.

A weaver and dyer from Greyabbey called Robert Millar, agreed that Porter was in charge of this party and that he had taken McChesney's papers and read them. Millar then, in answer to a direct question, said that Porter had also been seen trying to persuade men in Greyabbey on Pike Sunday to join the rebellion, adding that this was at the request of *the other leader of the rebel forces, the Rev. Montgomery.*

The italics are this writer's and are used to indicate amazement. This

Rev. Montgomery has already appeared in this narrative, and will again very soon, but certainly not very overtly as a rebel. Lt. Col. Atherton had voiced his suspicions about this cleric to General Nugent, but Montgomery's personification as Squire Firebrand in Porter's Billy Bluff writings, suggests that Millar's identification of such an unlikely alliance is totally erroneous. In the extremely improbable event that the charge contains any truth, then it is certainly food for thought.

Porter was not permitted by the legal procedures of the day to speak in his own defence. He was not allowed to call his wife to the stand. He asked for time to produce witnesses who could totally refute the charges. This was refused and a few minutes later he was told he had been pronounced guilty. He was also informed that he was to be executed in two days time.

Porter was distraught for his wife and her seven children who were to be orphaned, and because the verdict had shown that Londonderry had no heart and his fellow judges no spines. Before leaving the court, Porter, with great dignity, stated, "*I freely forgive all my enemies; may God in his infinite mercy forgive them also.*"

Mrs. Porter suppressed her anguish and took herself and all the children to Mount Stewart there to beg Lady Londonderry to intercede, just as that well-connected lady had tried in vain to do two years before for William Orr. The Marchioness was moved to give her a letter to take to General Nugent. However, just as Mrs. Porter was taking her leave, his Lordship entered the room, read his wife's letter and insisted that she add a postscript to it.

When Mrs. Porter went to see General Nugent, he turned her away from his door, but Mrs. Porter retained the letter which was kept by her family. It is produced below in full for readers to make their own judgments about the sincerity of Lady Londonderry and the determination of her husband. Lady Londonderry's letter reads:

Mount Stewart, June 30th 1798

The wife of Mr. Porter, the dissenting minister of Greyabbey, solicits me in a state of absolute despair to address you on behalf of her husband, who is accused of being a leader of Rebellion. She asserts that he never was engaged in the transaction at any time, and that his being found amongst them was accidental. How this might be I cannot presume to say, I only know that Mr. Porter is a man of sense and acquirements whose interest it could hardly be to overturn the government under which he was protected. Perhaps, however, you are better informed, but the great humanity of your character, which is considered to be equal to your fairness, spirit and ability exposes you to importunity and perhaps to impertinence, which I would rather risk at this moment than await an opportunity of giving a mind like yours occasion to make enquiry. I hope, therefore, to be sanguine in asking, at the urgent request of this most wretched woman, whether the sentence may be engaged to transportation or any penalty but life, a life important to the wife and seven children.

I have the honour to be, Sir,

Your much obliged and very humble servant,

D. S. L.

D. L. has just come in. L. does not allow me to interfere in Mr. Porter's case. I cannot, therefore, and beg not to be mentioned. I only send the letter to gratify the humour.

Mrs. Porter was never able to forget the treatment she had received from her landlord and former friend. James Porter Jnr. said that until the day she died his mother often said that:

Nothing in her life ever filled her with so much horror as his Lordship's smile as he handed her the letter with the postscript added to it, and told her she might now make what use of it she chose.

Two days later Porter was hanged near to his own Meeting House in Greyabbey, "*in the prime of life and vigour of manhood, the victim of public tyranny and personal revenge*"[8] Years later James Porter Jnr. added a personal note to the manuscript, worded with the command of language one would expect from a man who by then had become the Attorney-General for the State of Louisiana:

Not only in sight of the Meeting House – but with a refinement of cruelty such as fiends only could have imagined – commanding on the other side a near view of his cottage, where his wife and children were waiting in a horrible state of agony for the lifeless body of a husband and father. Whether Lord Londonderry or Atherton suggested this…torment on a dying man we do not know. I will not attribute it to either for fear of depriving the other of credit.

JP

The Porters' "humble dwelling" was half a mile from Greyabbey on the road towards Carrowdore. It was on a small piece of land rented from Porter's Squire Firebrand, the above-mentioned Rev. Hugh Montgomery of Rosemount. From this hill one can still clearly see Greyabbey village and the hill on which Londonderry ordered the gallows to be erected. After accompanying her husband on his final journey from the cells under Newtownards Market House to Greyabbey, Mrs. Porter made her farewells, kissed him a last time and went straightaway to her children, leaving him to the mercies of the Lancashire Light Dragoons.

In those days an execution invariably drew large and noisy crowds. It is a mark of the regard of the people of Greyabbey for their minister that this awful spectacle was shunned. Only a few soldiers were present to witness Porter struggling for life on that crossbar.[9]

Viscount Castlereagh's biographer tells us that, thanks to the great compassion of Lord Londonderry, Porter's head was not severed.[10] Mrs. Porter later took her husband's unmutilated body to be buried in Greyabbey churchyard. There it remains, buried under a simple horizontal stone. Six weeks after the execution, the Presbytery of Bangor at Newtownards recorded their grief at losing one of their leading lights, with a cruel irony that seems to have escaped them, "*It is reported that Mr. Porter of G'Abbey departed this life the 2nd of July last. Next Meeting at Belfast 1st Tues. Nov.*"[11]

Porter's headstone can still be seen near the east wall of Grey Abbey. It is inscribed:

Sacred to the memory of

Rev. James Porter,
Dissenting Minister of Grayabbey,

who departed this life

July 2nd 1798 aged 45 years.

After his conviction Porter had spent his last two days in the Newtownards cells with a number of other prisoners. We can imagine that he would have had conversations with his fellow-prisoners. One man whom Porter had probably known before these eventful days was a young probationer named Robert Gowdy. He was also a Dissenting clergyman, from the neighbouring church at Dunover. It is often said that Gowdy cannot have been a minister because there is no trace of him in the records of the Presbyterian Church. As in the case of James Townsend (explained in an earlier chapter) the record of Gowdy's ordination was probably lost along with the others for the years between 1793 and 1797. He was certainly referred to quite often as the Reverend Robert Gowdy.

On the 2nd of July, at almost the same moment that Porter was being hanged in Greyabbey, another party of soldiers was taking this young man to his execution in Newtownards Town Square. He had been found guilty a few days before Porter and sentenced to be hanged on the same day as his clerical colleague.

The accusations against Gowdy certainly adorn him with an unlikely ubiquity. Gowdy had been charged with being in touch with Henry Munro at Creevy Rocks and with carrying messages to Andrew Orr at Cunningburn near Mount Stewart, not to mention the usual string of general charges of treason and rebellion. Henry Boyd, whose credibility was called into question by his estimate that there had been up to 60,000 men in Munro's army, swore he had seen Gowdy in command of men at Ballynahinch.

More damning were the testimonies of James Kearns, a farmer from Greyabbey and William Bowman of Ballygrangee. They told the court that the Rev. Robert Gowdy of Dunover was the man who had chosen Inishargie for the rebel camp and that he had taken possession of Captain Matthews's house there. They also accused him of collecting 20 or 30 men from Dunover to join the Greyabbey men and of appearing to have a command. Interestingly, Bowman felt it necessary to tell the court that Gowdy did not wear a green cockade in his hat, but it is impossible to know how significant this was.[12]

On the day Porter was tried, Robert Armstrong, a cotton manufacturer of Falls, near Collin Mountain to the west of Belfast, told the Newtownards Magistrate, Captain James Clealand, that he had visited Gowdy in his Newtownards cell earlier that day. Whilst there he had received a message from a Yeoman that the Rev. Mr. Hugh Montgomery would see him on the road to Greyabbey as soon as he left the Market House.

Armstrong's visit to Gowdy being over, he had caught up with Montgomery's chaise to discover what his business was. Probably through ignorance that Porter had already been sentenced to death, Montgomery told Armstrong that Porter had pleaded guilty and that if Armstrong saw Porter that night he should tell him to prepare for the worst. Montgomery apologised for bringing Armstrong so far out of his way, but that he could not wait for him in Newtownards because, "*he was so watched by that fellow Cleland.*" This dogged clergyman had been following him all day, watching everything that he did. Montgomery claimed that he had tried to speak to Colonel Atherton, but Cleland, by his sinister presence, had so far prevented him doing so. It would seem that Montgomery was being, 'all things to all men' around these difficult days.

According to Armstrong's deposition to Clealand, Montgomery then told him that the Dragoon officers were men of humanity, but described John Cleland, who was the Public Accuser, as, "*a Bloodthirsty Hellhound and the only Man of Blood among them.*"[13] Clealand the magistrate did not record what he thought of this description of his brother, Cleland the minister.

It would appear that Armstrong went back to see Gowdy again shortly after his conversation with Montgomery. There, in a short space of time, Gowdy heard what Montgomery had said he would do and that he had not done it. Immediately prior to his execution Gowdy composed a letter to Hugh Montgomery, explaining to him exactly what he thought of him and his behaviour. He obliged Armstrong to deliver this letter to Hugh Montgomery as soon as he could. Armstrong took the precaution of returning to James Cleland with a copy of the letter that he had already delivered.

The letter quoted below leaves one in no doubt that Gowdy was not impressed by Armstrong's message from Montgomery. In his own mind, and facing his Maker, he knew Montgomery for the calibre of man he was:

Sir,   Newtownards, 2nd July 1798

You have betrayed me, and you have betrayed the people, and had the people succeeded, you would have betrayed your King. You are known and acknowledged by all our Barony to be a Bloody Judas.

Black & dissembling as your heart is you will one day meet a fate more awefull than me, whom you have consigned to Death. I now leave you forever to ruminate over your Bloody Principles and Politicks.

[Signed] Robt. Gowdy

To the Revd. Hugh Montgomery.[14]

There exists a letter from a man called Hugh McComb to John Catherwood Esq. of Ballyvester, which connects Porter and Gowdy with rebel activities. McComb was an ardent loyalist who almost certainly resided in the Dunover area, and knew Gowdy. It is generally believed that this letter was found in Porter's pocket when he was arrested. McComb emphasises in the letter that the flame of rebellion burned for an inordinately long time in the Ards when he tells Catherwood what he thinks ought to be done to such villains:

In consequence of the length of time that the Rebellion has been raging in the neighbourhood of Dunover we think it would terrify them if Mr Gowdie were punished at home, more than if it were done in N.T. Ards as I told you they are the most dangerous knot of rebels . . . Have all the witnesses told that if they do not discover all they know that their property will be destroyed and their persons punished.[15]

McComb then gives Catherwood a long list of men of Donaghadee Parish whom he knows to have remained loyal, and who were home during the insurrection, and suggests that they be deposed for information.

The Rev. Hugh Montgomery's thoughts about Robert Gowdy after receiving his letter that day are unknown to us, but a visit to Grey Abbey graveyard can tell us something about the man and the place his family felt he merited in society. A few yards from Porter's grave, on the north wall of the nave of this beautiful old ruin are a number of stone tablets. One of them has the Montgomery and Ward coats of arms intermingled. The inscription on it reads:

> Hugh Montgomery, Clerk in Holy Orders, born June 24th, 1754, died March 30 1815. The Honble. Georgina Charlotte Emilia Hannah [Ward], his wife, young-est daughter of Bernard, 1st Viscount Bangor, born July 6 1762, died November 16 1843. Both lie buried in this abbey. This tablet is dedicated to their memory by their son, Colonel Francis Octavius Montgomery, A.D. 1879.

The whereabouts of Robert Gowdy's remains is unknown.

Another young licentiate from the Ards Peninsula to face the courts martial was, "*a young man of much promise, learning and eloquence … imposing in his appearance – with the carriage of a soldier and the ardor of a patriot.*"[16] The story of the Rev. Archibald Warwick of Kircubbin is widely known, but unfortunately it is sometimes wildly exaggerated. When W.G.Lyttle introduced him into his hugely popular novel, *Betsy Gray and the Hearts of Down*, almost a century later, he gave Warwick the same romantic aura that he gave all the principal heroic figures he included in his novel. Unfortunately historians cannot indulge in such a luxury.

Two men from Kircubbin who may have been brothers, James and William Baillie, and the town's publican, Tom McGee, told the court that Warwick had been very active in recruiting for the rebel army on Sunday morning, the 10th of June. To encourage this, Warwick had sent horsemen to neighbouring townlands they named such as Inishargie, Ballymullan and Greyabbey. This frantic activity was hap-pening about the same time that Captain Matthews was defending Portaferry Market House. None of the recorded evidence mentions any of this band going into Portaferry, so we shall have to assume that they only met up with those men when they were on their later march to Inishargie.

William Deal, a weaver, and Pat McGrath a tailor, both from Irish

Quarter, supported this story, adding that the party went then to Broom Hill, five miles away. The party had dispersed when a rider galloped up with the story that a troop of the 22nd Dragoons Light Horse was on its way.

The excise officer William Harvey, who had been caught up by rebels and taken to Inishargie Camp, swore that on the way there he saw Warwick in Greyabbey on the Monday with a case of pistols in his pocket. The next day Harvey saw him again, "*stood in front of the armed men that evening with drawn pistol putting them in ranks.*" He also saw him reprimanding John Dalzell, "*for leading his men onwards too hastily,*" and that he would have them all slaughtered because of this haste.[17]

By the following day Warwick appears to have discovered discretion. James Macartin, a farmer of Ballybogilbo, witnessed that the young pastor had been going around Inishargie camp advising the people there to take advantage of General Nugent's Proclamation promising clemency to all. A copy of this document had arrived at the camp that morning and had caused some debate. Macartin's testimony lets us know that the rebels at Inishargie had commandeered Matthews's home as well as his estate for their headquarters. He states that Warwick was at the head of the stairs discussing plans of action with men he believed were committee members.

A series of witnesses told similar stories to the court. Unless there was a massive conspiracy, we can only conclude that Warwick was seriously implicated, incredibly naive or terminally unpopular. The court chose the first interpretation and he was sentenced to hang.[18] For some reason, the execution of the punishment was stayed, or as the gallows humour of the day had it, "suspended", until 15th October 1798. On that day Warwick was hanged, his head severed and his remains taken by his Loughriscouse family for burial in Movilla Cemetery. Thus the part of the rebellion located in the Ards can be said to have started and finished on Movilla Hill.

The circumstances of Porter, Gowdy and Warwick, as far as they are known, and the evidence from their trials, indicates in all three men something of that cross-grained impatience with the establishment often seen in Ulster people. The certainty of redemption they appear to have shared also gave these men great fortitude with which to face the terrors of the hangman's noose.

When one compares their death sentences resulting from suspect and sometimes-slim evidence with what happened to other arrested Ulster clergymen, one is conscious of an unpleasant smell still detectable after two centuries. The actions in the Ards Peninsula during those heady June days were relatively unimportant compared with what was happening in Saintfield, Ballynahinch and in County Antrim. That three Dissenting ministers, all living within a three-mile radius, should be executed for an involvement scarcely demonstrated as beyond reasonable doubt, raised great disquiet at the time. The high regard these men clearly enjoyed among their own congregations and beyond, contrasts chillingly with the brevity of the conservative *Belfast Newsletter* reports of their executions. In each case there is only a bald statement that they were executed, perhaps with the rider, "*head not severed.*" In the very same edition of the paper there is yet another harsh contrast. Beside the summary notice informing readers about Porter and Gowdy is a long and detailed report of the court martial of John Storey, an otherwise unknown Belfast printer.[19]

Over the two centuries since then, the degree of involvement in the rebellion of these three ministers has been portrayed as anything from negligible to total. For some, their very accusations demonstrate their guilt, while for others the neckcloth and Geneva Bands they wore prove their innocence. For some, the court-martial witnesses are seen as courageous and loyal subjects of the King. Others brand them as informers and touts without honour. The witnesses perjured themselves for more favourable treatment, or they were intimidated; the courts were corrupt, or perhaps the accused were incorrigible, black-hearted villains. Tightly closed minds cannot admit any light.

Other men of the cloth were implicated, suspected, charged, tried and convicted in the months after Ballynahinch. The Newtownards minister, William Sinclair, "*after a long and rigorous confinement, was forced into exile.*" He went, like so many, to America. Once there, according to Charles Teeling, Sinclair was able to enjoy, in contrast to his treatment in his native land, "*the honors which a free government was proud to confer on talent and worth.*"[20]

The Presbyterian minister from Rathfriland, the Rev. Samuel Barber, although he had been very instrumental in securing Castlereagh's election victory in 1790,[21] was senior both in years and in the ranks of the United Irishmen. He had been taken up in the summer of 1797 and had been confined in Downpatrick Gaol for a time. Just before the battle at Ballynahinch he had confided to Charles Teeling:

> The freedom of Ireland depends on the useful energies of her sons. I am not fitted for the active duties of the field, but I will aid you with my counsel, and second you with my arm; and what a man of sixty years can do, I pledge myself to perform.[22]

Teeling himself, having been taken up again after the battles, wrote to Lord Castlereagh, stating that he had not taken part in the rebellion (He later wrote that he had) and that he thought he deserved to be released. In view of Castlereagh's long friendship with Teeling's father and his gentle treatment of the son on his arrest before the rebellion, his annotation on Teeling's request displays the cold aloofness for which the Londonderrys were famous:

> If Mr. Teeling has not a Commission as Captain, or a superior Commission, if he has not been a County, or Provincial Delegate or a Member of an Executive Committee and has not corresponded with the Enemy he will be admitted to His Majesty's Pardon.[23]

In the same two letters in which he tells Lord Downshire about Munro, Stephenson writes about the Rev. Thomas Ledlie Birch being arrested by Hugh McKee and James Fulton, with a party of the 24th Light Dragoons, in the early hours of the morning of the 17th of June and taken to Lisburn.

In one letter Stephenson comments on the reasons for Birch's arrest, "*He was admonishing the Rebels to pursue their cause in the camp at Saintfield on Sunday last,*" and in the other gives his forecast of what is soon to happen, "*Birch of Saintfield is to be tried this day and it is thought he will be hanged.*"[24] Three days later Stephenson was writing to the Marquis that Birch was, "*still not hanged.*" In fact the court martial of Birch lasted for three long days. Although the charge was a straightforward one of "Treason and Rebellion", several thousand words were transcribed into the record of the trial before it was finished. Witnesses came before the President of the Court, Major Boswell of the 64th Regiment, with evidence of Birch's presence at Creevy Rocks, and depositions were taken from men who had heard him preach there. Some witnesses went further and had Birch advising and commanding at different times. Birch swore that he was elsewhere at the time alleged and was able to produce witnesses to corroborate this.

But the question remains as to why the trial lasted so long while other suspected rebels, some of them quite prominent, were being given summary hearings, and sometimes not even that, before being swiftly executed. The verdict, when it finally came, surprised almost everybody. Birch was sentenced, not to hanging, but to transportation to America. Many reasons have been put forward for this and people can take their choice as to whether one in particular, or a combination of a number of them, was the instrument which saved his life.

Birch was the minister of Saintfield Presbyterian Church, which was part of the General Synod of Ulster. But many of the United Irishmen were Synod ministers, including James Porter of Greyabbey, Samuel Barber of Rathfriland, Arthur McMahon of Holywood and the three young probationers from the Ards, James Townsend, John Miles and David Bailie Warden. These radical pastors were in a minority among their fellows; most Presbyterian clergymen abjured politics and overt radicalism.

On the one hand, Birch had been a vocal supporter of the American colonists in their struggle for independence, even corresponding with George Washington and naming his Manse outside Saintfield, Liberty Hill. In January 1792 he had formed the first Society of United Irishmen in County Down and he was, by 1798, a sworn enemy of the landlord of Saintfield, Nicholas Price and his acolyte, the Rev. John Cleland.

On the other hand, Birch was a prominent member of the Freemasons. He was also still well thought of by the Stewarts of the Ards, Lords Londonderry and Castlereagh. His brother, Dr. George Birch, was a prominent physician in Newtownards, a Captain in its Yeomanry and a friend of Lord Castlereagh. He had wealthy relatives, through his wife's connections, who remembered his sterling support in some bitter election campaigns.

As his trial ground towards its prolonged conclusion, Birch asked to address the court. Considering that the court still had not given its verdict, and that he still protested his total innocence, the plea that Birch made on this occasion is astonishing:

> Gentlemen, I may have done wrong, but I was in error. I love my king and country and shall ever pray for their happiness. I have the most perfect confidence in the justice and humanity of this court, and most cheerfully resign my honour and life to its disposal, and sensible that I cannot be any longer happy or useful in this country, I shall, when ordered by General Goldie or any other person authorised to order me, quit his Majesty's Dominions, never to return without subjecting myself to such punishment as is inflicted on persons returning from transportation without leave, and retire to America or some other country not at war with his Majesty.[25]

George Birch had already told his brother that such an offer would give the court the chance to commute his sentence, but the announcement was received with incredulity and anger. Thomas Lane was able to give Lord Downshire a flavour of this anger and a forecast of how it might be assuaged:

> There was strong murmurings among the yeomen, helped not a little by the soldiery, yesterday evening at Lisburn, occasioned by their not hanging Blubbering Birch, who has petitioned to transport himself to America for life. If a strong guard is not kept over him, the parties will, in my opinion, be very apt to take the law into their own hands.

Some yeomen were only prevented from lynching Birch the next day by the resolute stand of a platoon of dragoons. Two days later he was taken to join prisoners such as Steel Dickson, Warden and Sinclair on board the prison tender in Belfast Lough. Two months after that, he was on his way on board the *Harmony* of New Bedford to start a new life in the United States.

As he sailed to join the thousands of Ulster Presbyterians who had voluntarily gone before him, Birch must sometimes have reflected how his treatment and honour compared with those of former friends and colleagues such as the generals, Henry Joy McCracken and Harry

Munro, and the Ards ministers, Archibald Warwick of Kircubbin, Robert Gowdy of Dunover and James Porter of Greyabbey.[26]

Sir Richard Musgrave, in his list of, "*Dissenting ministers in the counties of Down and Antrim implicated in the rebellion 1798*",[27] beside the seven names given for Antrim noted that two were ordered to leave the kingdom, one was "partly guilty", one was acquitted and three were never tried. In marked contrast, he lists eleven County Down ministers, two of whom, Porter and Warwick, were hanged. Men such as Thomas Ledlie Birch of Saintfield, William Sinclair and James Simpson of Newtownards and David Bailie Warden of Killinchy, were transported to America, where some of them made great contributions to their new homeland.

William Steel Dickson of Portaferry, William Stavely of Knockbracken and Samuel Barber of Rathfriland were imprisoned for two years in Fort George in Scotland, William Adair of Ballygraffan, James Hull of Bangor and Arthur McMahon of Holywood were "proclaimed", a sentence which seems effectively to have been not much more serious than being publicly named and forbidden to be seen in their old haunts. Robert Gowdy of Dunover, although he was executed for treason, does not even rate a mention in Musgrave's list. Nor do James Townsend of Greyabbey and John Miles of Moneyrea. These last two, and William Adair, were later required to immigrate to America, and Arthur McMahon escaped to France.[28]

It is a measure of the difficulties of assembling information that Musgrave missed a few names. Five years after the rebellion he had still not discovered that Gowdy had been one of the three clergymen hanged in the north, that Miles was extremely active throughout the 'hurry' in County Down, and that Townsend was arguably the most senior officer of the county's insurgents between the arrest of Steel Dickson and the elevation of Henry Munro. Indeed, at his court martial, Munro had actually named James Townsend as the man who persuaded him to act as Adjutant-General.[29]

In those later weeks of July, General Nugent, through the columns of the *Belfast Newsletter*, offered a reward of Fifty Guineas for the apprehension of a number of known rebels who were somewhere in hiding. If the carrot of reward was not attractive enough he wielded the big stick too. Harbouring any of the men named was to be regarded as a capital offence. No mercy would be shown to those guilty. It should be no surprise that the men listed below were soon given a proud epithet. With a fine disregard of financial exactitude these men became famous as the "Fifty Pounders." On Nugent's never-completed list, some are ministers of religion and some are not:

The Rev. Mr. Adair	near Cumber
John Beattie	Knockbracken
Andrew Bryson	Newtownards
_____ Davidson	Col. near Ballynahinch
Richard Frazer	Ravarra
James Hamilton	Moneyrea
Rev. James Hull	[Ballyvarnet, Bangor]
Dr. [James] Jackson	Newtownards
Nevin Kearns	Magheriscouse
Hugh Loughlin	Ballygraffan
[Samuel] McCance	in or near Ballynahinch
John McCandless	Cardymoor
Thomas Matthews	near Saintfield
William Minnis	Lisdoonan
Thomas Rainey	_____
Dr. _____ Shields	in or near Cumber
_____ Sibbet Snr.	Killinchy
David Thompson	Saintfield
Joseph Thompson	Ballyrush
_____ Torney	Killinchy
Rev. James Townsend	Greyabbey
Rev. Archibald Warwick	Kircubbin
James Wightman	Bryansburn[30]

A measure of how much some of these rebels were wanted by the authorities is found in the edition of the *Belfast Newsletter* of 7th September. The names of those underlined above, with the addition of the Rev. William Warnock and the Rev. Arthur McMahon, were published with the ultimatum that if they did not turn themselves in, all their properties would be forfeited to the crown.

All of the above were sought, not just because of their involvement, but because loyalist informers, perjurers and those rebels who were turning King's evidence in exchange for clemency, had promised to testify against them. Many known insurgents were wanted, but with no likelihood of their being convicted. These men were encouraged to flee the country. The Rev. Steel Dickson, the Rev. William Stavely, the Rev. John Miles, Dr. William Phillips, surgeon of Bangor, John Cowan of Carnew, the Rev. Bernard Magennis, a Roman Catholic Priest of Cabra and Francis Falloon, the Donaghadee Innkeeper who had threatened William Orr's denouncer were never punished. They all made the difficult choice of continuing to live in their communities, secure that there existed no evidence that would convict them. Some of their neighbours would have revered them for their courage; others would just as sincerely have despised them for their duplicity.

The military and the magistrates worked strenuously to compile dossiers of evidence against all the senior figures in custody, especially the already identified Adjutants-General. Because of his fame, or notoriety, Steel Dickson presented a special challenge. The Crown Solicitor in Belfast, Mr. John Pollock, "*an attorney, not higher than the second class,*" as Dickson described him, came to see the imprisoned minister at a late hour one evening. According to Dickson, Pollock was drunk, and using offensive and blasphemous language. After asking for, "*the scoundrel Dickson,*" Pollock swore he would, "*hang the traitor next day.*"[31]

On subsequent days Dickson was taken to Pollock and the Rev. John Cleland where Pollock regularly promised to hang him. Pollock, on one occasion, said, "*You are d—d confident. By —, I have information against you, sufficient to hang twenty men.*"

The two men then had a bitter contest where Pollock tried to trick the clergyman, and Dickson, using his considerable brain and a bit of sophistry, tried not to be caught out. By now he was being held in a cell in the Artillery Barrack in Belfast. The brunt of the evidence against him came from the notes and letters Nicholas Mageean had been feeding Cleland, Price and Lord Londonderry and thence, inevitably to Castlereagh, by now Pelham's successor as the Chief Secretary to the Lord Lieutenant. In a letter to Castlereagh, General Goldie shows that he was as anxious to convict as any:

> I beg pardon for troubling you but Mr. McGeen, from the neighbourhood of Saintfield has just now been with me to say that he has come to the Resolution

of appearing against the principal Rebels, agt. whom he formerly gave information to Parlt. . . . Doctor Dickson in particular he seems certain of being able to
convict.[32]

Nicholas Mageean was certain of Dickson's guilt, and few would
have known better. He had told Cleland and Price that Dickson was:

the most active & persevering of the Rebel Traitors in promoting the System of
United Irishmen & the Rebellion that ensued, he would, in case no other person
offered, come forward & give his Evidence against him.[33]

When he was challenged to produce incontrovertible proof of
Dickson's guilt, Mageean took fright and claimed that he could not
because his corroborative witnesses were all United Irishmen and were
all fled.

Every possible exertion was now made to convict Dickson. He himself claimed to be astounded that they could not come up with some
device, even though he persisted in asserting his innocence. He was
moved yet again, this time to the prison ship in the Pool of Garmoyle,
where, Dickson relates that, "*had it not been for the lively, rational,
and entertaining conversation of a Mr. David B. Warden,*" his hours
there would have passed very heavily. On the 26th of March 1799,
the Reverend Doctor was moved to Fort George where, held with a
number of Dublin United Irishmen, such as Thomas Addis Emmet
and Arthur O'Connor, and other northern prisoners like Robert
Simms, William Tennent and Samuel Neilson, Dickson was to stay
for, "*3 years, 7 months and 7 days,*" until his release in 1802.

At the end of that year Dickson received a call from the congregation
of Keady in County Armagh, where he ministered for thirteen years
until he retired due to ill health. For the last years of his life he was
supported by a number of former United Irishmen, who could not forget the contribution he would never publicly acknowledge. Just after
Christmas in 1824, Dickson died. He was buried in a pauper's grave
in Clifton Street graveyard, unmarked until the following inscription
was erected over it in 1909:

William Steel Dickson patriot, preacher, historian.

Born at Carnmoney, 1744

Died at Belfast, 27th Dec. 1824.

"Do cum onora na hEireann."[34]

1. James Porter Junior, (having edited his brother Alexander's manuscript), published 1844, (Porter Manuscripts, PRONI, D/3579/2). The great majority of the information for this account of the Rev. James Porter's life and death has come from this source. Other detail comes from Porter's court martial, 30th June 1798, (Rebellion Papers, NAI, 620/2/15/54).

2. One cannot escape the thought that this clergyman may really have been called the Rev. James *Hull*, which would beg a few questions, but for the moment this can only be a question and not an answer.

3. Charles H. Teeling, *Personal Narrative of the Irish Rebellion of 1798*, London, 1828, pp. 35-36.

4. Dr. Trevor McCavery, *Reformers, Reactionaries and Revolutionaries: Opinion in North Down and the Ards in the 1790s*, published in *Ulster Local Studies*, Vol. 18, No. 2, *The Turbulent Decade*, Belfast 1997, p. 77, and Francis Joseph Bigger, *Four Shots from Down*, republished Ballynahinch, 1982, p. 52.

5. James Arbuckle to Downshire, 15th March 1797, (Downshire Papers, PRONI, D/607/E/192).

6. Humphrey Galbraith, Donaghadee to Downshire, 1st November 1797, (Downshire Papers, PRONI, D/607/E/365).

7. H. Montgomery Hyde, *The Rise of Castlereagh*, London, 1933, p. 31. It is tempting, but dangerous, to ponder about whether the other two suspected Presbyterian clergymen were Robert Gowdy and Archibald Warwick.

8. Charles H. Teeling, p. 37.

9. James Porter Junior, (Porter Manuscripts, PRONI, D/3579/2).

10. H. Montgomery Hyde, *The Rise of Castlereagh*, London, 1933.

11. Minutes of a meeting of the Presbytery of Bangor at Newtownards on Tuesday 17th August 1798, (PRONI, D/1759/1D/15).

12. James Kearns and William Bowman at Rev. Robert Gowdy's court martial, 27th

June 1798, (Rebellion Papers, NAI, 620/2/15/28).

13. Robert Armstrong, a deposition given to James Clealand at Newtownards, July 2nd 1798, (Lytton White Papers, PRONI, D/714/3/11A).

14. Robert Gowdy letter submitted by Robt. Armstrong to Captain James Clealand, 2nd July 1798 at Newtownards, (Lytton White Papers, PRONI, D/714/3/11B).

15. Hugh McComb to John Catherwood, (Porter MSS, PRONI, D/3579/1).

16. Charles Hamilton Teeling, *Sequel to Personal Narrative of the Irish Rebellion of 1798*, London, 1828, p. 41.

17. Patrick C Power, *The Courts Martial of 1798-99*, Dublin, 1997.

18. Court Martial of Rev. Archibald Warwick, 15th August 1798, (Rebellion Papers, NAI, 620/2/15/32).

19. *Belfast Newsletter*, 3rd July 1798 and 16th October 1798.

20. Teeling, p. 39.

21. *Dictionary of National Biography.*

22. Teeling, p. 202.

23. Teeling to Lord Castlereagh at the Castle, 13th August [1798], (Rebellion Papers, NAI, 620/52/222).

24. George Stephenson, (Downshire Papers, PRONI, D/607/F/246 and D/607/F/251).

25. Aiken McClelland, 'Thomas Ledlie Birch, United Irishman', *Proceedings of the Belfast Natural History and Philosophical Society,* 2nd Series, vol. 7 (1963), pp. 24-35, quoted in A.T.Q. Stewart, *The Summer Soldiers*, Belfast, 1995.

26. Dickson, pp. 143-144, Stewart, pp. 250-251, Stephenson and Lane, (Downshire Papers, PRONI, D/607/F/259 and D/607/F/272).

27. Sir Richard Musgrave, *Memoirs of the Different Rebellions in Ireland*, Dublin, 1801, p. 50.

28. Charles Dickson, *Revolt in the North*, Dublin and London 1960, Appendix XXIV, pp. 241-242. Dickson names eleven County Antrim Dissenting clergymen who were accused of involvement in the insurrection. Unlike in the Ards peninsula, none were hanged.

29. Court Martial of Henry Munro, 16th June 1798, (Rebellion Papers, NAI, 620/2/15/9/2).

30. Major-General Nugent's Pronouncement, 18th July 1798, published in *Belfast Newsletter*, 20th July and 27th July 1798.

31. Rev. Dr W Steel Dickson, *A Narrative of the Confinement and Exile of William Steel Dickson*, D.D. pp. 57-116.

32. Gen. Goldie to Castlereagh, 31st January 1799, (Rebellion Papers, NAI, 620/46/027).

33. Rev. John Cleland, N'Ards to R. Marshall, Phoenix Park, 14 July 1800, (Lytton White Papers, PRONI, D/714/5/3).

34. Charles Dickson, pp. 184-189, and the Rev. Dr W Steel Dickson, *A Narrative of the Confinement and Exile of William Steel Dickson, D.D.* pp. 57-116.

TRIALS AND EXECUTIONS II

"I'll be the judge, and I'll be the jury" said cunning old Fury:
I'll try the whole cause, and condemn you to death.

Lewis Carroll (1832-1898),
Alice in Wonderland, Ch. 3

As the blood lust of the military and yeomen began to cool those loyalists who had been frightened, horrified or just plain angered by the insurrection began calling for a more considered, but definite conclusion to it. They needed assurance that it would not happen again. There were immediate public calls for some visible signs of lawful retribution, supported by more private and baser feelings of vengeance. There were already numerous rebel prisoners held in the cells in Belfast, Newtownards, Downpatrick and Lisburn, and warrants could be issued for those who were still at liberty. It was a matter of urgency that proper trials be arranged and suitable punishments ordered.

George Stephenson in Hillsborough reminded his patron Lord Downshire of his Lordship's differences with the Stewarts and how these could hamper the business of chastising the rebels, especially those who came from Stewart's homeland of the Ards. He suggested that the authorities should stamp out any sparks of insurrection that still glowed in the county by choosing some local leaders from the great Ards and using them as examples:

We have got strong and positive evidence against several of the leaders or
Captains in this diabolical business from the neighbourhood of Newtownards

and Bangor, and provided Lord Londonderry does not make any improper inter-
ference, some of his tenants will be hanged, and they may thank him and his
son's opposition to your Lordship for it.[1]

The pursuit of leading insurgents was by no means confined to clergymen. Over one hundred men were tried at court martials in Newtownards and Downpatrick during the three months after the Battle of Ballynahinch. Virtually all were convicted, and only a very few sentences were commuted. Their punishments ranged in scale from being fined, through suffering varying numbers of lashes, to serving in the army overseas, sometimes for a period of a few years but more often for life. Of course the most extreme punishment was execution by hanging.[2] The *Belfast Newsletter* each week published brief accounts of a number of rebels' convictions and punishments. Some of these are:

July 3rd 1798:
Thomas McKnight, found guilty, sentenced to be hanged at Bangor on 3rd inst.[3]

July 6th 1798:
Hugh Grimes, a leader among the rebels at Creevy Rocks on 11th and 12th of June, hanged.

Lambert Brice of Dundonald, sentenced to hanging for being a leader at Ballynahinch on Tuesday 12th June, and stealing from Kennedy McCreery in Dundonald five and a half guineas and his watch.

James Wallace and John Gribben transported for life for robbing Mr. Kennedy of Cultra Manor; and James Trimble for above theft with Lambert Brice, transported for life.[4]

17th July 1798:

James Dunlop, Thomas McKnight and Robert Robinson, all of Bangor, were executed there on Tuesday last [10th July].

Bernard Crosby and William Morrison, both of Donaghadee, have been executed there a few days ago.

> William Heron, Rev. Wm. Sinclaire and Rev. James Simpson, all of Newtownards, to be transported for life. John Quinn, Dr. Wilson and James McKittrick, all of Newtownards, to be transported for 14 years.

This same newspaper names some rebels who were sentenced to be lashed. Adam Mullan of Cardy was to suffer an almost certainly fatal 500 lashes; Andrew Orr of Cunningburn [This is probably the same man to whom Robert Gowdy was accused of passing messages from Henry Munro] was sentenced to 500 lashes too. Given the choice of the cat or serving abroad in the army or navy for life, Orr chose the latter. This would not have been much of a choice. Life expectancy for a soldier serving in the tropics was a year or two at best, whereas two to three hundred lashes shredded the flesh, and over that number was generally fatal.[5]

Some of the rebels were not even granted the dignity of being named in the local newspapers:

> 10th July 1798:
>
> A court martial continues to sit at Newtownards. Three men were found guilty last week (besides those formerly mentioned), one of whom was executed in that town, one in Donaghadee, and one at Bangor.[6]

We can only guess at the identities of these three miscreants. Other anonymous victims were mentioned in the *Newsletter*, the death of one of them raising an eyebrow of doubt:

> 31st July 1798:
>
> Two men were executed last week at Newtownards and six transported.
>
> Last week, a person who was in confinement in the Market House at Newtownards fell from the upper window, and was killed on the spot.[7]

Although robbed of some attractive prey, the courts martial proceeded with the chase. All of the leaders convicted in the early days of the courts martial were hanged. It was only after the appointment of the much wiser Marquis Cornwallis as Lord Lieutenant, that sentences of death were commuted to transportation and compulsory military service.[8]

In the 31st of July edition of the *Newsletter* the fate of one of the "Fifty Pounders" is reported:

> Monday se'nnight Richard Frazer was brought before a Court Martial held in the Exchange Rooms for trial[9]

Frazer pleaded guilty to charges of treason and rebellion, and was sentenced to death. Later, in October, on the same day as Warwick's hanging was reported, the Newsletter also carried the following short pieces:

> John Cuthbert was on Thursday last executed at Scrobbie [Scrabo?] Hill and his head placed upon a spike.

> Same day a person of the name of Clark was also executed at Comber and his head placed on a spike.

As early as the 29th of June the editor of the *Belfast Newsletter* wrote some wry comments about the insurrection in the north. As a footnote to a long column of court martial reports, there is a postscript that has appeared innumerable times since:

> It is now a common saying among the folk in the Ardes, county of Down, with that shrewdness for which our northerns are remarkable – that no body will ever prevail on them to go *to catch cannon-balls on the points of pikes and pitchforks again*.[10]

The newspaper also carried some information showing where the authorities reckoned the seeds of United Irishism flourished best, and how they intended to prevent it in future:

> By the new Spirit License Act it is enacted, 'that no person whatsoever shall be capable of receiving a license who does not previously take an oath that he or she is not of the Society called United Irishmen.'[11]

Oaths were regarded very seriously in the society of those days. One or two of the accused at the Assizes made this clear to the bench. William McClookey and Daniel McCaughey, both from near

Ballynahinch, told Downpatrick Court that they had sworn to his Majesty on three previous occasions, twice, "*in the steps of masonry*," and once by an oath of allegiance. Quite what these men meant to gain, if anything, is unclear. What is clear is that separately, but together, they were sentenced to be transported to Botany Bay.[12]

It is difficult to escape the conclusion that a prisoners' chances at these trials depended, not upon the balance of evidence presented at trial, but upon a number of factors, sometimes perhaps not even including their actual guilt. For anyone who thought that the courts might be harder on the prisoners who carried with them an air of menace or a bestial quality, one of the first published histories of the rebellion, written in 1801, has an instructive paragraph:

> The display of humanity by a Rebel, was, in general, in trials by Court Martial, by no means regarded as a circumstance in favor of the accused: strange as it may seem in times of cool reflection, it was very frequently urged as a proof of guilt. Whoever could be proved to have saved a loyalist from assassination, his house from burning, or his property from plunder, was considered as having influence among the rebels, consequently a Rebel Commander. This has been seen by some supposed to have arisen from a policy in Government to discourage all ideas of humanity in rebels, that in case of another insurrection, they might be so sanguinary as to render themselves and their cause as odious as possible, and consequently, unsupported.[13]

As one would expect in the aftermath of such a traumatic event, the months following the rebellion and its subsequent court hearings produced some rough justice. Not only were some of the courts' verdicts dubious, but some citizens suffered from the heat engendered by the passions raised therein. Cottages were torched, animals were maimed and people were killed as punishment or retaliation.

This account deals with the insurrection as it affected County Down, but one execution in Belfast would have had as strong an impact on all the people of Down as that of any of those in their own county. Like that of Henry Munro in Lisburn, this hanging took place no more than a few hundred yards from the River Lagan boundary with County Down.

On the 17th of July, Henry Joy McCracken, Adjutant-General of the Antrim rebels, and the senior Ulster figure in the militant wing of the United Irishmen at the time, was taken from his place of trial at the Exchange to a temporary gallows at Cornmarket. Martha McTier knew her brother, Dr. William Drennan, would want to hear the details of the last moments of his old friend's life. Drennan had known and loved Henry Joy for many years, but was now resident in Dublin. Martha wrote to him that at the very last moment McCracken, "*was offered a pardon at the gallows if he would inform on R S*", but that he had declined. Martha and William would both have known R S to be Robert Simms, a man Castlereagh and others were very anxious to destroy.

Mrs. McTier added that McCracken's dear old father at the foot of the gallows desired him to, "*do all he could to save his life with honour.*" She knew that her brother would appreciate that this appeal, worded as it was, encapsulated the father's vain hopes of a reconciliation between his love for his son and his moral principles. Henry Joy was thus left with only one decent course of action. "'*Farewell then,' said the son, embracing him, and was immediately turned off.*"[14]

McCracken's hanging may have had the widest impact in the north of Ireland, but before Cornwallis called a halt to the blood-letting, a total of nearly forty rebels had been hanged in counties Antrim and Down. This of course does not include the four soldiers from the Monaghan Militia nor those escaping from Ballynahinch who were simply strung up on convenient branches.

Belfast prisoners were being held on the *Postlethwaite* prison ship in the Lough, in the Artillery Barrack or in the Donegall Arms, then still serving as the Prevost prison. This last-named gaol, because of its unusual location, did not employ the usual methods of confinement. The Rev. Steel Dickson described his confinement there:

> Four others and I were thrust into a room, about sixteen feet by ten broad, without table, chair, or any other furniture, whatever; and, as our only window was unsecured, by iron bar or bolts, a chalked line was drawn across the floor, about six feet from it, and intimation given to us, not to set a foot over said line, under pain of instant punishment.[15]

The Dragoons of the 22nd Regiment had their own subtle ways of letting these prisoners know their feelings about them. One of these prisoners recalled, "*On more occasions than one, some of them got into the Prevost, made their way to the door of our apartment, and threw in dead fingers, thumbs, &c. &c. with loose gestures, and words, awfully expressive.*"

The following is a list of men from County Down, almost all of them from the Barony of the Ards, who were hanged for their part in the rebellion:

John Clarke (Rich'd Miers)	Newtownards
John Kerr, or Carr	Newtownards
William McCormick	Newtownards
Bernard Crosby	Donaghadee
William Morrison	Donaghadee
John Cuthbert	Ballyboley
Hugh Boyd	Ballycastle (near Mount Stewart)
Samuel Dunlop	Ballymoney (near Carrowdore)
Rev. James Porter	Greyabbey
Rev. Robert Gowdy	Dunover
Rev. Archibald Warwick	Kircubbin
Lambert Brice	Dundonald
James Dunlop	Bangor
Archibald Wilson	Conlig
Robert Robinson	Ballygrainey
Thomas McKnight	Gransha
Dr. James Cord (or Choorde)	Killinchy
James McCann	.Carragullin (near Killinchy)
Thomas Coulter	Lecale
Henry Byers	Saintfield
John Skelly	Creevytenant (near Ballynahinch)
Hugh Grimes (Graham?)	Creevytenant
Thomas Maxwell	Lisburn
Henry Munro	Lisburn
Richard Vincent	Lisburn
William Armstrong	Lisburn
G. Crabbe	Lisburn
William Magill	Loughbrickland[16]

Although Lisburn technically is in County Antrim, Munro and the others from Lisburn are included in this list because it was for their participation in the County Down part of the rebellion that these men were executed.

In order to make an example of Munro, his hometown of Lisburn was chosen as the best place for his court martial and execution. The officer in charge of the Down leader's military escort was present at both. Later he gave Munro the respect soldiers considered due to an enemy officer but not always given. He said Munro, "*conducted himself with great propriety before the court, but made no defence, indeed he seemed to disdain doing anything of the kind.*"

As soon as he was convicted, Munro asked to be granted a few moments to allow him to receive his last Sacrament. This was allowed and he went for a few minutes into the home of the Rev. Snowden Cupples. Munro's anonymous escort officer has left us a detailed description of the scene on that Saturday when Munro was brought out to the side of the Market House in Lisburn's town square at four o'clock in the afternoon. A gallows had been erected very near the spot where later burghers were to raise an equestrian statue to another warrior son, Captain James Nicholson of Indian Mutiny fame.

In the fashion of the day, Munro's gallows was not of the cantilevered construction one usually envisages. It would have been more like a crossbar supported on one side by a tripod and on the other by one of the windowsills of the Market House. Munro's religious faith and the courage for which he had become noted, sustained him through those awful moments:

> It is impossible to imagine anyone more cool and firm without anything of bravado. There was a barrel standing on the spot on top of which he placed his shop books which he caused to be brought and settled his account with several persons as if he had been in his own shop.

His business affairs settled, Munro said a few short prayers, sprang like the athlete he was from the platform on to the ladder placed to enable him to climb to the noose. Once steadied there, he declared he was ready to meet his Maker. The hangman had arranged with Munro to signal the moment by dropping his handkerchief. No sooner than the rope was securely round his neck than the prisoner dashed the cloth to the ground, saying, "*Tell my country that I deserved better of her.*"

The hangman was unable to turn Munro off the ladder and the occasion was briefly in danger of transforming into farce or perhaps omen. The sympathetic officer was quick to act:

To aid him was mercy to the culprit, and indeed under this feeling I beckoned to my orderly-sergeant, Thomas Porter of the Seagoes, to put his hand as I did mine and Munroe swung into eternity although a light man, apparently without a struggle.

This must have been much remarked on by the onlookers. The "long drop" most people think of was designed to snap the neck and cause instantaneous unconsciousness and rapid death. But in 1798 hangings were still being conducted with what later became known as the "slow drop", which caused death through asphyxiation. This method was popular with the crowds who clamoured at public hangings, because the victim could sometimes give the baying mob many minutes of entertainment as he struggled for life. Munro seems to have denied the watchers in Lisburn that shameful thrill. Two hours later he was unable to deny them the sight of his head being severed from his body and then being put on a spike on the wall of the Market House.[17] The time elapsed between Munro's being taken up and his corpse being taken down was a few short hours.

Many of the leaders of the United Irishmen were convicted on the evidence of reluctant men who had been forced into carrying a pike during this treacherous time. In a short period of distrust, hatred and revenge that evoked memories of the reign of terror in revolutionary France, many old scores were settled. Not all the evidence came from those who insisted they had been forced to go to Newtownards, Saintfield or Ballynahinch. Some of the men who were of most help to the authorities had been 'turned' a long time before.

As we have already seen, there were a few such informers active in the north, but some stand out for both the quality and the quantity of their intelligence. Newell and Murdoch shot across 1797 like comets, bringing intelligence and charges of great impact, but not for any sustained time, and they do not appear to have been active in the year of rebellion at all. Newell later claimed that their information was mostly false and was only given to Barber in an effort to confuse him, but this was just Newell's attempt to dissemble. Two other informers were John Hughes, a bookseller from Belfast, and Nicholas Mageean, the Catholic smallholder from Lessans, near Saintfield. Hughes, a Protestant, reported directly to Colonel Lucius Barber, in charge of military intelligence in the north, while Mageean usually gave his information to the Rev. John Cleland of Newtownards.

Both of these informers had been members of the United Irishmen for some years and had risen to fairly senior positions. After the rebellion they were put into the Prevost prison in the Donegall Arms with the rebels in an attempt to discover evidence from their own mouths that might convict them. Mageean tried to ingratiate himself with Dickson by confessing apprehension about his fate and warning him to be careful because he had bitter enemies.

Hughes adopted the manner of a deranged man and was able to fool Steel Dickson for some time after his arrest. He visited him in his cell and prayed with him. Dickson later wrote that he was, "*quite delighted with the wonderful comfort which devotional exercises seemed to give him.*"[18] Dickson later recorded that his companions did not share his own naivety, and when Hughes was removed a few days later, "*consigned to infamy*"; he had learned nothing of note.

The regular information these two men, and others, were supplying before, during and after the rebellion, not only secured the convictions of many rebels, but ensured that the military and the establishment knew what the rebels were about to do, sometimes before some of the rebels did. Just before Christmas of 1798, General Nugent was able to inform Marquis Cornwallis:

> Mr. Mageean was a Provincial Member for Ulster and a tenant of Mr. Price's. He entered into the Societies of United Irishmen to be of service to government and gave the information of the rising in Antrim on the 7th of June last, which enabled us to counteract the proceedings of the rebels.[19]

Mageean, of course, was passing on information about his own county as well as telling Nugent about Antrim. Cleland received an anonymous message a few days before the outbreak of the rebellion. Although this message actually names Mageean, it is generally believed that he himself was the author:

> On Thursday the 31st of May the Cols. of the Co. Down met at Saintfield...They generally determined to act. This resolve was carried to Doctor Dickson by N. Mageean. After this the Revd. Dr. Dickson sent N. Mageean to Belfast with a letter to John Hughes and Robert Lyons declaring the resolves of the meeting.[20]

Mageean had no qualms about behaving in this fashion. Any fears he had were of his fellow men, not of the Almighty. Two years after the rebellion was over, Nicholas Mageean's brother, who always called himself John Magin, wrote to Lord Castlereagh at Mount Stewart about his brother and the way he had been treated subsequent to the rebellion:

> When he first entered on the business his motives were pure; he neither expected fee or reward; his conscience told him he should not associate with murderers and cut-throats. He was the means under Providence of saving the live of many important members of Society. He conceived it to be duty he owed to his God to disclose their horrid schemes & machinations as soon as he became acquainted with them and all he askd. in return was the concealment of his name which I understand was pledged to him in the most solemn manner.[21]

After the action, as Mageean's true role began to be realised, he suffered at the hands of his neighbours. The Rev. John Cleland felt obliged to pass on news of this treatment to John Magin in one of his many letters to him:

> I am very sorry to acquaint you that an attack was made last week on your Brother in your Father's house by 4 of Mr. Price's Yeomen in the Night time. The[y] were I hear in Liquor but broke the Door & Windows…Two of these Rascals are Strain of Ballyagherty, Sloan of Killynure, the two others I forget their names.

Cleland was once again pointing out to Magin that he now thinks the time for Nicholas's evidence has passed. After nearly four pages of rambling argument in close, small handwriting, he concludes:

> To say any more on this Subject to a person of your Superior & highly cultivated Understanding & Experience in the world is needless…
>
> Yours &c.
>
> John Cleland
>
> N. T. Ards, Febry. 28th 1799.[22]

The long drawn out exchange of letters between Cleland and Magin is an indication of how much Nicholas Mageean's evidence was worth. Cleland and, of course, his masters, needed Mageean to testify, but baulked at the price it would cost. Other difficulties were that the days were rushing by and their secrecy was threatened by every one of them. Magin at one point met the Marquis of Downshire in London. Magin later explained to Cleland that he had been appalled to find that his Lordship was of the opinion that his brother's motives were purely mercenary. Then a few paragraphs later he ends his letter to Cleland with the advice:

> Should it be convenient for you to send the Balance between us you can enclose the Bill for me to John Bruce Esq. @ Navy Office, London,[23]

The sum Magin was referring to was £2,000, to be obtained from Major-General Nugent and Crown Solicitor John Pollock. This, according to him, was necessary for the removal of Nicholas, his father and the rest of the family from Lessans to England or Scotland.[24]

The urgency of the negotiations was because of the widespread belief towards the end of 1798 and into the New Year, that a second insurrection was imminent. In the same letter in which Nugent was informing Cornwallis about Mageean's role, he warned about:

> the intention of the disaffected to rise in rebellion in the course of Christmas. Illegal meetings have been also held and timber has been cut down in many parts, . . . and some assassinations have taken place very lately of persons who have given evidence against rebels before Courts Martial.[25]

It is obvious that Nugent is concerned about these matters, but is not so troubled that he will risk his superior's wrath by, *"resorting to the system of terror,"* to subdue any disaffection. Nugent continues to regret the death of Captain Evatt at Ballynahinch because the Monaghan Militia has not shown great discipline since the loss of their fine Adjutant. Nugent voices his worries about General Thomas Goldie too. It was not Goldie's well known vice of card-playing which concerned him, it was that, in Nugent's opinion, Goldie was not up the job if a new insurrection should occur.

However, the feared rebellion at Christmas 1798 never happened.

Nicholas Mageean never came to court. He had reported the proceedings of every United Irish meeting he had attended between 14th of April 1797 and 31st of May 1798. Even Castlereagh had accredited him with enabling Nugent to crush the northern revolt. Mageean had asked to be put in protective custody before the action in his home town of Saintfield, and had remained there for some time afterwards.

After his return from a brief exile in England, Mageean bought a good farm of land at Greenhill, near Banbridge. He is known to have been working the farm in 1810, but after that nothing is known of him. Stories exist that he descended into drunkenness, and either died in gaol or was killed by a rebel with a long memory. Mageean's tragedy is not that rebel sympathisers despised him in the after-days, but that the loyalists, the very people he always claimed he was trying to save, abandoned him.

John Magin, a more perceptive man than his brother, had expressed his cynicism to Castlereagh:

> Gratitude he might naturally expect from whose heads he warded the assassin's blow, but whether he has experienced it to the extent he deserved they themselves can judge.[26]

1. Geo. Stephenson to Lord Downshire, Hanover Sq. 4th July 1798, (Downshire Papers, PRONI, D/607/F/299).

2. Thomas Bartlett, *Repressing the Rebellion in county Down*, Pp. 187-210 from *1798, Rebellion in County Down*, Eds., Myrtle Hill, Brian Turner, Kenneth Dawson, Newtownards, 1998.

3. *Belfast Newsletter*, 3rd July 1798.

4. *Ibid.*, 6th July 1798.

5. *Ibid.*, 17th July 1798.

6. *Ibid.*, 10th July 1798.

7. *Ibid.*, 31st July 1798.

8. Patrick C. Power, *The Courts Martial of 1798-99*, Dublin, 1998, p. 162.

9. *Ibid.* 31st July 1798.

10. *Ibid.* 29th June 1798.

11. *Ibid.* 16th October 1798.

12. Court Martials of William McClookey and Daniel McCaughey, 31st July 1798, (Rebellion Papers, NAI, 620/2/15/16).

13. J.B. Gordon, *History of the Rebellion in Ireland in the Year 1798*, Dublin, 1801, p.228.

14. Mrs. Martha McTier to her brother, Dr. William Drennan, p.m. 18th October 1798, (Drennan Papers, PRONI, D/531/723).

15. Dickson, The Rev. Dr. William Steel, *A Narrative of the Confinement and Exile of William Steel Dickson, D.D.*, Dublin, 1812.

16. Charles Dickson, pp. 233-234. This list includes all those executed in Antrim, the Monaghan Militia shot at Blaris and Thomas Russell, who was hanged at Downpatrick, but not until 1803. The gravestones of many, but not all, of the people on the list have been located. A good source for those interested in visiting these is, Bill Wilsdon, *The Sites of the 1798 Rising in Antrim and Down,* Belfast, 1997.

17. The story of Munro's trial and execution is mainly a synthesis of Dickson, pp. 199-201, and Stewart, p. 250.

18. Dickson, The Rev. Dr. William Steel, A Narrative of the Confinement and Exile of William Steel Dickson, D.D., Dublin, 1812.

19. Maj. Gen. Nugent in Armagh, to Marquis Cornwallis, 21st December '98, (Rebellion Papers, NAI, 620/41/98).

20. Anonymous letter to John Cleland, June 2nd, 1798, (Lytton White Papers, PRONI, D/714/2/23).

21. John Magin, Surgeon on board His Majesty's Ship Princess Royal, Plymouth, 30th June 1800, to Lord Castlereagh, MountStewart, (Lytton White Papers, PRONI, D/714/5/2).

22. Rev. John Cleland, Newtownards to John Magin, 28th Feb. 1799, (Rebellion Papers, NAI, 620/46/044).

23. John Magin, London to Rev. John Cleland, Newtownards, June, 1800, (Lytton White Papers, PRONI, D/714/5/1).

24. Rev. John Cleland, to Nicholas Price at Saintfield, no date, but probably February 1799, (Rebellion Papers, NAI, 620/51/181).

25. Maj. Gen. Nugent to Marquis Cornwallis, 21st December 1798, (Rebellion

Papers, NAI, 620/41/98).

26. John Magin to Castlereagh, June 30th 1800, (Lytton White Papers, PRONI, D/714/5/2).

The Aftermath
of
The Rebellion

The conduct of a losing party never appears right:
at least it never can possess the only infallible criterion
of wisdom to vulgar judgements – success.

Edmund Burke,
Letter to a Member of the
National Assembly, 1791.

Two days after the Battle of Ballynahinch, the *Belfast Newsletter* carried this despondent editorial:

There is every reason to conclude, that the Insurgents in the county of Down, vexed with disappointment, and terrified by the consequences of their late conduct, will not again be able to collect in any considerable numbers.In foreign wars humanity and valour generally go hand in hand; the glory of being merciful seems to be as much fought for, as the renown of being victorious. But in civil contest how different is the scene? Personal resentments, private malice, party attachments, pride of opinion, lust of power; in short all the passions that blend and dishonour human nature, conspire to enrage the hearts of the contending parties, and to render them more fierce and savage than the monsters of the wilderness.[1]

The *Newsletter* has no further comment on the rebellion, except to say that the stock markets do not seem to have been adversely affected by the insurrection. However, there is the clear implication that the resentment, malice and dishonour cited by the editor will dissolve now that the rebellion has been put down. As we know from the trials and punishments, this was not the case, but such was the relief and euphoria in the country that many citizens expressed their convictions that the worst was over.

James McKey, fresh from his exertions in hunting down the fleeing insurgents in the Ards, sent his hopeful opinions to the Marquis of Downshire:

> We will have a much more settled country in a short time than ever your Lordship thought. . . For some years past there was something brooding in the minds of the Republicans, and now that it is broke out and that they could not succeed, they will become loyal subjects.[2]

Although he was also a Yeomanry officer, George Stephenson did not share McKey's elation. He recognised that the rebels may have been defeated but they were not yet beaten. He confided his views about the rebels to Downshire a few days later, "*I am much afraid that all is not yet over. They must be watched very closely or they will rise again.*"[3] Robert Ross, the M.P. for Newry, often added comments to Stephenson's letters on their way to Downshire. On one of these dated the 17th July he noted his concurrence, "*We now think the Rebellion is nearly at an end, but I fear we shall have some trouble when the nights lengthen.*"[4]

In a letter of his own just a few days later Ross makes a wonderful prediction, which fortunately was never able to embarrass him by its inaccuracy, "*The Rebellion is over, or at least adjourned for a century and a half, by which time Popery will be extinct, if not all religion.*"[5]

What Ross did not know when he penned this from Dublin was the exact situation on the ground. Thomas Lane had a much better grasp of these matters. The day before Ross's letter, Lane had told the Marquis he had just received a letter from someone with strong rebel sympathies, telling him that if he did not cause everything stolen by the soldiery, Yeomanry and Orangemen from Lord Moira's tenantry to be returned, he would suffer for it.

Clearly there were men in the area who were still angry and confident enough to threaten the agent of one of the richest and most powerful men in Ireland. Lane recognises the reasons for this anger, but is hurt that it should be directed at him. He recognizes the depredations of the soldiers – but shamelessly blames the rebels for them:

> No man has done more to check, or reprobates in a higher degree the licentious proceedings that has followed that battle, but the horrid acts of the Rebels created such a paroxysm of revenge that even General Nugent could not restrain the Monaghan Militia from despoiling Montalto.[6]

It is often imagined that the great majority of the men of Down and Antrim either rose in rebellion in that month of June, or joined the Yeomanry to oppose it. The editor of the *Belfast Newsletter* was convinced that the countryside told him different:

> The circumstance of the lands in the county of Down and Antrim, being this year highly cultivated, and covered with grain to an unusual extent, is a proof that the decent part of our farmers never expected or wished for the vile proceedings that have lately taken place...It would appear that the farmers of County Down, are at length convinced that the late disturbances were leading fast to their ruin as much as to their landlords – the robbery of the poor and rich being the object of the leaders, and the chief "order of the day."[7]

It was mostly the superb summer season that had provided the prolific state of the countryside that June. In addition the sudden and late onset of the call-out had allowed much early-season work to be done in the fields by the end of May. But the main establishment news organ of the day was perhaps reading too much into the potentially rich harvest when it suggested that this was due to the great majority of the population being loyal and wanting nothing to do with protest. There were some local reactions to the insurrection in Belfast, County Antrim and County Down published in the *Newsletter* but it would seem that, as is almost always the case in such times of trial, the silent majority, loyalist or republican, had kept their heads down during the excitement and, after the dust had settled and had done their best to get on with their lives.

On Wednesday, the 27th of June, a fortnight after Ballynahinch, 980 inhabitants of the adjoining parishes of Killinchy, Kilmud and Tullynakill met together in the Rev. David Bailie Warden's Dissenting Church in Killinchy. This venue was very deliberately chosen. There they affirmed their loyalty to the King and Constitution and proclaimed their unanimous disdain for the men of Killinchy who had rebelled against him. They particularly stressed the loss of honour this showed for the rebels, some of whom, days before the breakout of the insurrection, were volunteer yeomen. They required their Chairman, David Gordon Esq. of Florida Manor, significantly the landlord of many of the company, to ask for the establishment of a new corps of Yeomanry in the district to ensure their continued safety. They concluded by resolving that Gordon should present their warmest thanks to Major-General Nugent, the Hon. Colonel Stapylton and the officers of the York Fencibles for their:

> Just discrimination in the inflicting of punishment in these parishes, by which humane and soldier-like conduct we have escaped being involved at large in the horrors of military vengeance, incident to a district of country late in a state of Rebellion.[8]

Some of the Dissenters of Portaferry published a similar disclaimer. This disavowal did not mention Dr. Dickson, their Pastor, but made it crystal-clear that his opinions were not theirs. Similar petitions and advertisements of disavowal appeared in a number of the June, July and August editions of the *Newsletter* for Belfast and country parishes.

Those charged with making the Kingdom of Ireland governable again, many of whom today would be called hard-liners, received a setback on 20th June, when Charles, 1st Marquis Cornwallis, took up his appointment as Governor-General of Ireland and Commander-in-Chief of the forces. As we have already seen, he quickly let it be known that he did not believe in overly repressive measures.

He had been asked to accept the position as early as 31st March, but only arrived a week after the overt trouble in the north was quelled. Within a few days he was writing to his old friend, Major-General Ross, about his low opinion of the job he has finally accepted, but that he is determined to make a success of it, "*The life of a Lord-Lieutenant of Ireland comes up to my idea of perfect misery, but if I can accomplish the great object of consolidating the British Empire, I shall be sufficiently repaid.*"[9]

The bitterness of Ireland and its people was a shock to the hugely experienced Cornwallis. He encountered it in every level of society and recognised that it constituted one of the major difficulties to a successful and permanent solution. He was surprised to find that the Anglican nobility and gentry were as narrow-minded as many of their Catholic and Presbyterian tenants:

> The conversation of the principal persons of the country all tend to encourage this system of blood, and the conversation even at my table, where you will suppose I do all I can to prevent it, always turns on hanging, shooting, burning, &c., &c., and if a priest has been put to death the greatest joy is expressed by the whole company. So much for Ireland and my wretched situation.

Displaying the knowledge gained some years earlier across the Atlantic during and after the American War of Independence, Cornwallis made some very perceptive comments to Ross:

> The Yeomanry are in the style of the Loyalists in America, only much more numerous and powerful, and a thousand times more ferocious. These men have saved the country, but they now take the lead in rapine and murder.[10]

It was not Cornwallis's plan to suppress any lingering feelings of rebellion with an iron fist. On the contrary, he realised that the blood-letting had to stop. He had expressed his intentions to the Duke of Portland almost immediately he took up his appointment:

> I shall immediately authorize the General Officers in the different districts which have been the seat of warfare, to offer (with certain exceptions) to the deluded wretches . . . the permission of returning quietly to their homes, on their delivering up their arms and taking the oath of allegiance.[11]

Unsurprisingly this policy did not meet with universal popularity among the loyal citizens of Ireland. By August letters of complaint and disagreement were flying. One member of the Irish Parliament expressed his disgust as follows:

> We are busy in the House of Commons in trying whether men have been guilty of High Treason who have been already hanged for the same. What do the people on the other side of the water really think of our method of extinguishing rebellion, killing about 25000 of the followers and then pardoning between 70 and 80 of the leaders?[12]

At this point we begin to see the promotion of the Ascendancy argument that the objectives of insurgency had always been directed more against them than for the redress of any wrongs. These men now insisted that the rebel foot-soldiers in turn had been deluded and then betrayed by the duplicity of the educated, middle-class leaders of the Directory of the United Irishmen. Discussing the Report of the Secret Committee about the United Irish leadership with Lord Downshire, Richard Annesley claimed that:

> McNevin, Arthur O'Connor, Emmet and Neilson were all of the Directory and have on oath declared these facts: that Reform or Catholic Emancipation were never the objects, nor were they considered of importance by the people, but merely used to spur up their passions; a better condition and abolishing of tithes, were their objects and was held out to them, but the establishing a Republic and destroying the Established Church was the object of the Directory.[13]

A Petition was sent to Lord Castlereagh from Downpatrick Gaol. Somewhat surprisingly it is a printed document, and was clearly meant for wide circulation. It is not dated, but was almost certainly sent to Castlereagh by men who had known his Lordship for most of his life. Many of these were Ardsmen. For a number of paragraphs the spokesman for the prisoners castigates Castlereagh for having turned both his coat on his principles and his back on his erstwhile friends. The paper concludes with a declaration of what these prisoners stand for and, with a delicious irony directed at Castlereagh, a contempt for those who oppose them either from the corrupt citadel of Dublin Castle or from one of its outlying redoubts:

> For our part, in or out of Prison, bound or free, we pledge ourselves, as you have done, never to forsake the cause of Catholic Emancipation, and Parliamentary Reform, knowing that if we be Felons, 19 out of 20 of our Fellow Citizens are likewise so…
>
> [Signed] A FELONIOUS FREEHOLDER
> (for himself and upwards of 100 fellow Prisoners)[14]

That the prisoners in Belfast were conscious of their political prisoner status is clear from a Petition they sent to the Lord Lieutenant on the 31st of January 1799. They had been imprisoned with neither charge nor trial, then released by General Goldie, and later, on request, had voluntarily resubmitted themselves to prison again. They were complaining that it was offensive to read about themselves described in Parliament and in the public press by Edmund Alexander McNaghten M.P. as, "*some of the most desperate and abandoned traitors that ever infested this country.*" They continued, "*We challenge Mr. McNaghten to substantiate any charge that will justify those vile and malevolent Epithets.*" Two of the 16 who put their names to this were William Tennent and Robert Simms. Nine County Down men also signed. Many of them were men this story has already met. The nine were:

> Rev. John Miles of Moneyrea, Francis Falloon of Donaghadee, Dr. William Phillips of Bangor, Joseph Tannahill of Spa Wells, Robert Hunter of Belfast, John Cowan of Craignew (or Rathfriland), John Magennis of Balleely, James Wallace of Banbridge and Alexander Finlay of Knockbracken.[15]

Another letter sent to Dublin Castle was to have great repercussions for the United Irish leaders, both north and south. It is not dated, but must have been sent in July 1799. Almost 80 prisoners held at Newgate, Kilmainham and the Bridewell Prisons undertook to give all information about the Society, short of implicating anyone by name, in return for permission, "*to emigrate to such country as should be agreed upon between them and the government*" and to remain there for ever without punishment. The signatures to this letter included those of famous United Irish leaders such as O'Connor, Emmet, Neilson and McNevin.

The Belfast prisoners, on hearing about this, submitted a similar paper of their own. The relentless Crown Solicitor, John Pollock, who composed a letter in his own words for the prisoners to sign, perfunctorily dismissed this. Those in the Prevost prison signed willingly enough, but when Colonel Barber brought it to the Artillery Barrack, some of the prisoners there hesitated.

Steel Dickson, with his usual obstinacy, refused, in writing, to Colonel Barber, "*I would not sign any paper, either implying that I was guilty of crimes that I had not committed, or admitting any thing, as a crime, which I had done as a duty.*"

Pollock was already incensed by Dickson, and the latter's refusal to sign provoked Pollock to throw the whole paper into a fire. He tried a second time with the same result. Dickson reasoned that if the government really meant to grant the indulgence, the lack of his signature was immaterial. His fellow-prisoners disagreed and took great offence at him. Dickson claims in his own Narrative that he was later vindicated when many of those in Dublin who had signed were, "*transported to the Continent of Europe...to work, or beg, their way, through foreign lands, till the grave, or some hospitable country, should yield them rest and shelter.*"[16]

Just over 400 rebels were sentenced to transportation, almost half of them from the north. Of the whole of the northern command of the Society of United Irishmen, seventy per cent of those hanged were from County Down; over sixty per cent of these were from the Barony of the Ards. In other words over forty per cent of those executed for their parts in the northern theatre of the rebellion came from that country round Comber, Newtownards, Bangor, Donaghadee and the Ards Peninsula. It is probable that a similar proportion would have been killed in the actions and the immediate follow-up. The exact numbers will never be known for certain, but the military figures of battle casualties, supplemented by estimates of the numbers killed in post-battle flight, indicate somewhere between five hundred and one thousand Ardsmen having been killed between Friday 8th June and the beginning of July 1798.

The population of Ards Barony in 1798 was about 25,000 souls. This means that roughly two or three per cent of the Barony's population, most of them young men, were killed in little over a week. When one considers the deliberate burning of the towns of Ballynahinch and Saintfield and the many cottages in between, there may actually have been as many houses destroyed as people. This was a devastating blow to this society, and undoubtedly wrought great hardship, and not only to those of a green hue.

After the rebellion, loyalists all over Ireland who had suffered damage to or loss of property sought and received compensation from the government. The people of County Down received the third highest amount, after Wexford and Mayo, for damage. This amounted to

£12,129 .. 0 .. 8d, almost 10% of the total amount for the entire island, for an area with a population of about 3% of the whole of Ireland.[17] By mid-July the rebellion in Antrim, Down and Wexford was, to all intents, over. General Lake and the government forces captured the Wexford stronghold of Vinegar Hill on the 21st of June. Five weeks later, on the 1st of August, and a very long way from Ireland, Horatio Nelson defeated l'Amiral de Brueys and the French fleet at the battle of the Nile. Reflecting on this denial of his ambitions to conquer the east through Egypt, Napoleon Bonaparte was to say in his prison on St. Helena many years later, that he had been wrong to disagree with Hoche. The wisdom of France invading England through Ireland's rear door had not come to him until too late.

On the 22nd of August, or Cinquième Fructidor, as the Directoire de la France designated it, General Humbert landed 1,100 men in regiments of infantry, artillery and chasseurs from his division of frigates in Killala Bay in County Mayo. His army was soon augmented by thousands of Connaught rebels. But Humbert had arrived too late. After capturing Ballina and Castlebar, and terrifying everyone who thought the real insurrection was soon to follow, he surrendered to General Lake at Ballinamuck on the 8th of September.[18] The fighting on land was over.

Two months later, yet another French fleet sailed from Brest with three thousand soldiers of La Grande Armée, and was soon seen off the west coast of Ireland near Killala Bay. The four frigates and a brig were captured off Donegal by the ships of the Royal Navy. On Wednesday the 31st of October 1798, Lord Ranelagh in the *Doris*, the man who had kept the North Channel open for shipping between Scotland and the north of Ireland through the summer months, towed the French ship, *La Hoche* into Lough Swilly, escorted by His Majesty's ships, *Robust* and *Ethalion*. Under guard on board the *Doris* were Theobald Wolfe Tone and a number of other United Irishmen who had come with him from France. All of the captured men were sent to Dublin for trial.[19]

On the 20th of June that year Tone had reflected on his life and what he had accomplished. With an obvious regret he wrote the following entry in his Journal:

Today is my birthday. I am thirty-five years of age; more than half the career of my life is finished, and how little I have been able to do…I had hopes, two years ago, that, at the period I write this, my debt to my country would have been discharged, and the fate of Ireland settled for good or evil. Today it is more uncertain than ever.[20]

Two years earlier he had similarly confided to his Journal that, at thirty-three, Alexander the Great had conquered the world, and more recently General James Wolfe had saved Canada. He moans that his lack of success was not because of a lack of ambition:

It is not my fault if I am not as great a man as Alexander or Wolfe. I have as good dispositions for glory as either of them, but I labor under two small obstacles at least – want of talents and want of opportunities; neither of which, I confess, I can help. If I succeed here [France] I may make some noise in the world yet…the liberty and independence of my country first.[21]

Tone's court martial unwittingly gave him the chance to make some noise for posterity. The court predictably did not take long to sentence him to death by hanging. But Tone had a horror of the gallows. He insisted he was a French officer, a Chef de Brigade, and asked if he could be shot as a soldier. This was considered to be too much of a hero's death, and the request was denied. There is an opinion that Tone knew that any man with a serious neck injury would never be hanged until it healed. Others contend that he was simply trying to cheat the hangman. What is certain is that he took his small penknife, allowed in his cell for sharpening his quills, and stabbed himself in the throat. His throat injury turned septic, and he died as horrible a death as any of the executed rebels.

All over Ireland actions were being taken in an effort to return to some sort of normality. As soon as he decently could, Edward Hull, the Secretary of the Donaghadee Packet Company, anxious to reinstate the service between Donaghadee and Portpatrick, resumed his copious correspondence. The Packet Company board was afraid that a punishment of the town could have disastrous effects on their lucrative business. Hull wrote frequent letters to General Nugent, Lord Downshire and Francis Freeling, the Secretary to the General Post Office. His efforts, and those of others, were finally rewarded. On

13th November 1798, Hull exultantly reported to the Chairman of the Company, Lord Downshire, "*The first Mail to Donaghadee arrived a few days ago.*"[22]

In the course of his pleading and explaining, Hull mentions that the Agent for the Packet Company has been held on suspicion of rebel sympathies. His case is an exemplar of many similar cases. The Agent, James Lemon, was the wealthiest businessman in Donaghadee at the time, and what happened to him is an object lesson in the importance of perception. Whatever a person's real sympathies, it makes subsequent living easier if one was seen to have been allied with the side that comes out the winners in any conflict. Lemon had been a Churchwarden in Donaghadee Parish Church, but had converted to Presbyterianism. He was often at odds with establishment figures such as James Arbuckle and Daniel Delacherois. (His argument about tithes with Arbuckle's assistant, William Getty, was quoted in Chapter 4.) The insurrection had given the loyal gentlemen of Donaghadee and district the opportunity to give Lemon what they thought he deserved. As soon as the rebellion was over he was put in confinement on remand for two months.

Unable to find any substantial evidence against Lemon, the authorities were forced to release him. Arbuckle had then called a Board Meeting of the Packet Company and engineered a motion to remove Lemon from his Agency. The excuse was that there was no use for an Agent in Donaghadee while the Packets were using Carrickfergus, and the grounds for dismissal were that during the emergency he had refused to join the Yeomanry.

Lemon's family knew a curious story of 1798 that, had it been generally known, may have had some bearing on the attitudes of his fellow citizens. One night in the middle of May, Lemon had been rudely awoken. A gentleman and his valet who had lathered their horses all the way from Dublin were in a great hurry to get to Scotland. Lemon had arranged for a boat for them, and entertained his visitors for some hours until it was ready to sail. On taking his leave, the gentleman discovered from Lemon that neither he nor his wife, Elizabeth Johnston of Ballykilbeg, had any family crests.

Some days later a parchment arrived with all the details of both families inked on it in colour. It had been presented by the grateful Duke of Leinster as some return for the Lemons' kindnesses during the Duke's distressful flight from the taint attached to him following the arrest and shooting of his brother, Lord Edward Fitzgerald.

Lemon, on his release from confinement, and knowing how the land lay, appealed directly to Downshire. He insisted that malice against him was the only reason for his troubles and that he was willing to swear on oath that he had never been a member of the United Irishmen. Lemon was never convicted, and we do not know if Downshire stood by him.

If he harboured any grudges against Arbuckle, Delacherois or Hull he never allowed it to interfere with his business interests. Although deprived of his Packet Boat Agency, he continued to thrive as a ship owner, and, according to his family, Seneschal, or manager, of the proprietorial estates in Donaghadee. He either built, or restored, Lemon's Wharf in the town as a safe shelter for his vessels, and served as an elder of the Presbyterian Church in Donaghadee for fifty years. He later became a wealthy Ships' Chandler in Belfast and died in 1851 aged 93, doubtless still getting some satisfaction from having outlived most of the other protagonists in his time of difficulty in 1798.[23]

There is a memorial to him still on the wall of Donaghadee Parish Graveyard. It looks down on the gravestones of a few of his contemporaries. Identified from the gravestone inscriptions, but generally unperceived by posterity, there are buried there other men of action from the days of 1798. With a mathematical incongruity the eleven men actually identified comprise seven named as active rebels, and five as potential yeomen. The numerical confusion is because in 1796 James Arbuckle had named Nevin Taylor as being a possible recruit for his Donaghadee yeomen, and at the trials held in Newtownards immediately after the rebellion Taylor was named in depositions as an active insurgent. One wonders just how many other coats were turned during all the confusion.

Some other rebels memorialized in this churchyard are David Campbell, who had been spotted cooking for them, William Brown, William Carson and James Fullerton, all of whom were named as rebels. William Morrison, who was publicly hanged in Donaghadee, lies buried in Donaghadee Churchyard. His fellow-victim, Bernard Crosby, was buried in an unknown grave.

Elsewhere in Ireland, Michael Dwyer and the Byrnes were to continue their guerilla warfare in the mountain fastnesses of County Wicklow, until they surrendered shortly after Emmet's abortive rising. They were then transported to the penal colonies in New South Wales on the *Tellicherry* in 1805.[24]

Robert Emmet, that great idealist, inspired orator, and hopeless organiser, had started and finished his rebellion in Dublin in the late evening of the 23rd of July 1803. Choosing such a time to commence his rebellion may not have been his best plan, because a number of drunken and bitter louts, fired up with patriotic fervour, stopped the coach of Lord Kilwarden, Chief Justice of Ireland, and piked him and his nephew to death. So widespread was the horror this engendered that the Castle was immediately able to suspend the Habeus Corpus Act, implement the Martial Law Act and try, convict and execute fifteen prisoners, including Emmet. The rebellion that bears his name was a total failure, but the speech from the dock delivered by Emmet was to be his legacy to those Irishmen who believed that they still had not achieved their freedom and continued to be inspired by his words.

Thomas Russell, who had done so much to bring about the 1798 rebellion in the north, had been a political prisoner in Fort George between 1796 and 1802. He was accused of being actively concerned in the northern events of 1803. On the 19th of October of that year at Downpatrick Courthouse he was convicted of treason. Shortly afterwards, along with James Drake and James Corry, he was taken out of a doorway in the upper storey of the Down Gaol and hanged. Both Emmet and Russell, by all accounts, were exceptional men, and yet they lost their lives over an ill-considered attempt at insurrection. That shrewd observer, Mrs. McTier, told her brother a day or two later that Russell had gone to his end with dignity, a gentle assistance to the hangman and secure in his Protestant faith. She concluded, "*Few, few, have I known like him.*"[25]

In Downpatrick Church of Ireland Cathedral Graveyard is his tombstone, put there by Henry Joy McCracken's sister, Mary Anne. It states, with stark simplicity:

THE GRAVE OF RUSSELL, 1803

By the 12th of November 1798, the Duke of Portland was sending secret and confidential documents containing the heads of a Treaty of Union from Whitehall to Marquis Cornwallis for him to circulate privately among his influential friends for their comments. After almost two more years of hard bargaining and political horse-trading, much of it done by Lord Castlereagh, the Act of Union was given the royal assent on the 1st of August 1800.

Lords Castlereagh and Cornwallis, the Chief Secretary and the Commander-in-Chief of the army in Ireland, found common cause and matching integrity in 1801, when George III refused to grant the promised Catholic Emancipation to Ireland. In protest against what they saw as a great wrong, both men resigned their positions. Cornwallis later served for a second period as Governor-General of India in 1805 before taking a well-earned retirement. In 1802 Castlereagh was persuaded to re-enter state affairs as President of the East India Board of Control, after which he pursued a glittering career in British politics and European statesmanship for twenty more years.

A decade later, in 1812, while Napoleon Bonaparte was trying unsuccessfully to extend his empire into Russia, the United States of America's Minister to France, Joel Barlow, decided to make personal representations to the Emperor. Just as it later was for many soldiers of the Grand Armée, the Russian winter was too much for Barlow, and he died on his journey. The significance of this to the present story is that his junior immediately assumed his position as Consul-General and demanded that the French foreign ministry recognise him as the U.S. government's sole representative.[26] This man was David Bailie Warden, the former minister from Ballycastle near Greyabbey, who had made a new life in the United States.

Immediately after the rebellion, and possibly because of his well-known participation in the events of June 1798, and his strongly expressed views, the Bangor Presbytery, "*from motives of prudence*," had refused Warden a licence to preach. Warden had then published a very critical attack on the Presbytery's hypocrisy and pragmatism, alleging that they had unanimously supported "*republican morality*" and a few months later, from motives of expediency, they had, "*met as a military inquisition.*" He had then left the church and left his dear Ireland too. In his new country he obtained a degree as a Doctor of Medicine, and then had switched career paths and made a successful career in the world of diplomacy.

It is sometimes said that by 1814 he was so highly regarded that he was sent as a United States representative to the Congress of Vienna.[27] If the ex-consul was present at the Congress it can only have been as an interested, but unofficial observer.

His precipitate demand for all of the papers at Barlow's legation and his assumption of the position of Minister, or Consul-General to France immediately upon the news of the death of Barlow had infuriated many in the American Government. They immediately appointed Senator William H Crawford their official Minister. Shortly after Crawford arrived in Paris he had sacked Warden, largely for his presumption.[28] Warden is often portrayed as a prickly natured fellow, and by one as a, "*testy ambitious Irishman*". Although he continued to live in Paris for the rest of his life, his government never employed him again.

The National Trust in Mount Stewart House outside Greyabbey preserves the chairs used by the delegates at this council of Europe. Although he would already have realized that his own diplomatic career was over, it is very likely that Warden would have taken the opportunity to reintroduce himself to Britain's senior negotiator, the Foreign Secretary, Lord Castlereagh. They perhaps even sat for a while on the above-mentioned chairs. If they did meet, both men must have spent a little time conversing about their lives a quarter of a century earlier when Warden was the young son of a Stewart tenant, living on the other side of the estate wall from Castlereagh's childhood playground of the Mount Stewart demesne.

The business discussed at Vienna was of crucial importance to the division of Europe, so history does not record if such a tête-à-tête ever took place. But the two men must surely have found a few minutes to talk about their memories of the momentous impact that hot summer of 1798 had had on both their lives. What an interesting read any notes of that exchange would be.

Castlereagh became the 2nd Marquis of Londonderry in 1821. The following year, in a fit of depression, he committed suicide. Warden, who had given so much precedence in the activities of the men of the Ards in 1798 to William Fox, and thought by many to have led the men of the Ards, died in Paris in 1845.

The life of James Townsend, the more probable leader of the Ardsmen in their attack on Newtownards and the march to Creevy Rocks, took a serious downturn after the rebellion. He did manage to escape the manhunt for him, taking ship to America. According to an anonymous letter sent to the *Belfast Newsletter* Townsend had ended up in Savannah, Georgia seven dissolute years later, having spent his own money, and that of two orphan children who had somehow been put into his guardianship.

The censorious *Newsletter* correspondent continued that Townsend by then had become so ashamed of his "*dissipated and wicked life*" that he had shot himself.[29] This short letter must have been an interesting topic for discussion both for his former comrades-in-arms and other old contemporaries back in the Ards. Perhaps his apparent fall from grace served to detract from his stature in the eyes of old foes and old friends. Any loss of his good name would soon have served to diminish in folk history his prominent role in the rebel activities during that summer of 1798.

The two most energetic defence advocates at the trials of a number of rebels were John Philpot Curran and William Sampson. In the years after the Act of Union Curran eventually became Master of the Rolls and a Privy Counsellor, whilst Sampson was convicted of involvement in the rebellion, and sent to America, where he eventually became one of the most eminent lawyers in New York.[30]

Some of the principal figures on the loyalist side during the rebellion later played on larger stages than those in June 1798. Many achieved high positions and a certain amount of glory in the further reaches of the empire. Gerard Lake was made a Viscount, and served His Majesty as Commander-in-Chief in India from 1800 until 1803, immediately preceding Arthur Wellesley, Earl of Wellington. In 1801 George Nugent was appointed Lieutenant-Governor of Jamaica, and later, still following Lake, he too became Commander-in-Chief of the

British Army in India in 1811. By one of those vagaries of history, he in turn was succeeded in that position by Francis Rawdon-Hastings, 1st Marquis of Hastings and 2nd Earl of Moira, although there seems to be no record of Moira complaining to his predecessor about the damage done to his estate at Montalto by Nugent's troops in '98. During Moira's nine year term as C-in-C, India, he was responsible for the British purchase of Singapore in 1819.

Thomas Pelham, later the 2nd Earl of Chichester, became Home Secretary between 1801 and 1803, and Postmaster-General from 1807 until his death in 1826. Sir Ralph Abercromby proved that his concern about poor military morale and misconduct was not confined to the situation in Ireland in 1798. He is credited with restoring discipline and efficiency to the whole of the British army. Three years after his resignation in Ireland, he defeated the French at Alexandria, only to die of his wounds shortly after the battle.

Major-General Robert Ross, friend and correspondent of Cornwallis, had a career of distinction in the Peninsular War, and commanded British forces in North America in the War of 1812, where he achieved lasting fame. On 24th August 1814 he led an army of about 4000 men to victory over a much larger American force at Bladensburg. He then led his victorious troops the twelve miles to Washington and occupied it where he ordered the burning down of the White House, Congress and all public buildings. Ross was unable to capitalise on this great defeat of the colonists' forces because three weeks later he was fatally wounded at the Battle of Baltimore. Ross's intelligent policy of sparing the private houses of Washington's citizens moved Lord Liverpool to write to Lord Castlereagh the following month regretting that more troops had not been placed under Ross. The General was so highly thought of in the succeeding months that monuments were erected to his memory, one a tablet in St. Paul's Cathedral and the other an obelisk beside the Rostrevor-Warrenpoint road where his family estates were.[31]

James Clealand was able to leave his Yeomanry duties behind him after the emergency abated, and devote his energies to improving his estate at Rathgael House between Conlig and Bangor. His brother, the Rev. John Cleland, through his assiduous management of Lord

Londonderry's affairs, managed to increase his own fortune to a point where in 1805 he was able to marry well, and build himself a new mansion at Stormont near Dundonald for his remaining time on earth.[32] His widow and his son, Samuel Jackson Cleland, rebuilt the house as Stormont Castle. This man also left posterity a huge edifice near Dundonald Moat, rivalling the impact on the landscape made by the Moat itself, beside which it stands as a mausoleum for his remains and a memorial to his family. Cleland's assistant, Billy Strean, saw his own fortune dissipated by a contest over a will.

Because of the civil unrest and the danger of encouraging large crowds, the Maze Races had been suspended for a few years. In July 1800, the Marquis of Downshire decided to risk their restitution. Accordingly he sent out many invitations, even including some for the Londonderrys and the Castlereaghs. Unfortunately Downshire seems to have succumbed to the strain of his responsibilities. Knowing that the Act of Union, which he did not want, was imminent, he verbally attacked his guests in the grandstand at the race meeting and said, "*the most insulting things before them against all that promoted the Union,*" and, unforgivably given his position, that, "*70 thousand troops which England sent over for our protection during the Rebellion were to ram the Union down the throats of the Irish nation.*"[33]

Downshire's earnest opposition to the Act of Union provoked him into even rasher action a few months later. He circulated a petition against the measure round his own militia regiment. This was a grave breach of military discipline, and the establishment, now tired of his discordance, decided to make an example of him. In double-quick time he was shorn of his command of the Down Militia, his governorship of County Down, and struck off the Privy Council. Downshire, once one of the most influential men in Ireland, was now confined to the relative tedium of his Hillsborough estates after his lifetime of power brokering. Hardly surprisingly, he went into a decline, and soon died of "*gout in the stomach.*"[34]

As in all of history, the last two centuries in Ireland has seen both continuity and change. The Ards Peninsula and County Down still survive. The official name of the country that contains them is the United Kingdom of Great Britain and Northern Ireland. The monarchy continues too, but no longer with its status of Divine Right. In Ireland, Home Rule, the Easter Rising and the Civil War came and went, resulting in a twentieth century Republic of Ireland, but one containing only twenty-six of the island's thirty-two counties. There are many who will never be satisfied until the remaining six counties become part of the Republic, and of course there are also many who just as passionately desire them to remain British. These disagreements are for another story.

Both modern-day loyalists and republicans still hold their opposing views about the United Irishmen's political aspirations and their relevance to today. However there would be a broad measure of agreement that if the men of ninety-eight were mistaken in attempting to change their world, then it was mostly in their timing.

Hindsight suggests that the men of the Ards should have taken the field in 1797. By the spring of 1798 their organization was compromised by informers, their leadership was decimated, and for many the fervour of the previous few years had diminished. Like many other disaffected peoples who felt driven to take the field against their government the United Irishmen were unable to choose their own timing. Propelled by events outside their control they suddenly moved when they had no real prospect of success. It has been demonstrated all through history that most political change, large or small, is achieved by discussion, persuasion and negotiation. This truth was as well known in 1798 as at any time, but exasperation and frustration often conspire to undermine more thoughtful and deliberate methods.

Revolution comes about by overwhelming the status quo, taking popular opinion along with the activists and, mostly of course, by succeeding. Without success any insurrection against the authorities is merely a rebellion. It may catch posterity's popular imagination because of its rarity and excitement, but if it does not inspire subsequent success, a rebellion on its own can only be regarded as a failure, no matter how stirring the events of the day were.

However, it must be recognized that over the two centuries following the rebellion the Catholic subjects in Ireland were eventually emancipated, Parliament was gradually reformed, social inequalities were ameliorated and tithes were abolished. Although the 1798

Rebellion must be seen as having been defeated, almost everything that the United Irishmen had objected to was changed. Today it cannot be denied that most of what the men of the Ards and other United Irishmen fought for, if not all, has been achieved

1. *Belfast Newsletter,* Friday, 15th June 1798.

2. James McKey, Belfast to Downshire in London, 14th June 1798, (Downshire Papers, PRONI, D/607/F/244).

3. Geo. Stephenson to Lord Downshire, 4th July 1798, (Downshire Papers, PRONI, D/607/F/299).

4. Robert Ross, note in letter of Geo. Stephenson, Hillsborough to Lord Downshire, 15th July 1798, (Downshire Papers, PRONI, D/607/F/323).

5. Robert Ross to Lord Downshire, 20th July 1798, (Downshire Papers, PRONI, D/607/F/330).

6. Thomas Lane, Hillsborough to Downshire, 19th June 1798, (Downshire Papers, PRONI, D/607/F/255).

7. *Belfast Newsletter*, 326th June 1798.

8. *Ibid.*, 3rd July 1798, Advertisement and news report.

9. Marquis Cornwallis, Dublin Castle, to Major-General Ross, 1st July 1798, quoted in John Killen, ed., *The Decade of the United Irishmen, Contemporary Accounts, 1791 - 1801*, Belfast, 1997, p. 144.

10. Marquis Cornwallis, Dublin Castle, to Major-General Ross, 24th July 1798, quoted in John Killen, ed., p. 149.

11. Marquis Cornwallis to the Duke of Portland, 28th June 1798, quoted in John Killen, ed., p. 143.

12. Robert Johnston to Downshire in London, 18th August 1798, (Downshire Papers, PRONI, D/607/F/351).

13. Richard Annesley to Lord Downshire at Hanover Square, 22nd August 1798, (Downshire Papers, PRONI, D/607/F/358).

14. Petition to Right Hon. Lord Viscount Castlereagh, Knight of the Shire for the County of Down, (Rebellion Papers, NAI, 620/53/34).

15. Prisoners' Petition to the Lord Lieutenant on being maligned, 31 January 1799. (McCance Papers, PRONI, D/272/23).

16. State Prisoners in Dublin Prisons, (McCance Papers, PRONI, D/272/21), and Steel Dickson, *A Narrative of the Confinement and Exile of William Steel Dickson D.D.*, Dublin, 1812, pp. 84-86.

17. Patrick C. Power, *The Courts Martial of 1798-99*, Dublin, 1998, p.154.

18. General Humbert to the Executive Directory of France, 28th of August 1798, quoted in *Belfast Newsletter*, 20th October 1798.

19. *Belfast Newsletter*, 6th November 1798.

20. Theobald Wolfe Tone, in his Journals, June 1798, quoted in John Killen (ed.), *The Decade of the United Irishmen*, Belfast, 1997, p. 137.

21. Tone, in his Journals, June 1796, *Ibid.* p. 73.

22. Edward Hull, Donaghadee, to Castlereagh, Nugent, Downshire and Freeling, August to November 1798, (Downshire Papers, PRONI, D/607/F/369, 370, 424, 441, 478, 483, 488, 512 and 533).

23. Edward Hull to Lord Downshire, 28th August 1798, (Downshire Papers, PRONI, D/607/F/369), James Lemon, Donaghadee to Downshire, 8th November 1798, (Downshire Papers, PRONI, D/607/F/525) and J.W. Lemon, An unpublished history of the Lemon family, (Lemon Papers, PRONI, D/3093/5/7).

24. Kieran Sheedy, *The Tellicherry Five*, Dublin, 1997, pp. 56-61.

25. Mrs. Martha McTier, Cabin Hill, Belfast, to Mrs. S. Drennan, 25th October 1803, (Drennan Letters, PRONI, Chart's book, p. 331).

26. *"Who's in Charge?"*, a paper by Peter P. Hill, Emeritus Professor at George Washington University, *The Society for Historians of American Foreign Relations* at the Contemporary History Institute at Ohio University. 16 July 2002.

27. *Dictionary of American Biography*, Vol. 19, pp. 443-444, A.T.Q. Stewart, The Summer Soldiers, Belfast, 1995, pp. 261-262, and Charles Dickson, *Revolt in the North,* London and Dublin, 1960, pp. 201-201.

28. *Maryland Historical Society Library,* Description of the Collection of Warden Papers, Pages 2 – 3. Warden Papers, 1797-1851, http: www.mdhs, org/library/Mss/ms000871.html

29. *Belfast Newsletter,* Friday, 19th March 1805.

30. *Webster's Biographical Dictionary*, Springfield, Massachusetts, 1943.

31. *Webster's Biographical Dictionary*, Springfield, Massachusetts, 1943, and *Dictionary of National Biography*, London, 1921.

32. Peter Carr, *The most unpretending of places: a history of Dundonald, County Down,*

Dundonald, 1987 (pp. 110-112).

33. Bishop Percy to his wife, December 18th 1800, (Percy MSS, British Museum, Add. 32,335, quoted in H. Montgomery Hyde, *The Rise of Castlereagh*, London, 1933.

34. H. Montgomery Hyde, pp. 329, 330, 406.

BIBLIOGRAPHY

SECONDARY SOURCES

Bardon, Jonathan, *A History of Ulster*, Belfast, 1992.

Barker, Juliet, *The Brontes* , London, 1994.

Barkley, John M., *A Short History of the Presbyterian Church in Ireland*, Belfast, 1959.

Benn, George, *A History of the Town of Belfast from the Earliest Times to the Close of the Eighteenth Century*, London, 1877.

Biggar, Francis Joseph, *Four Shots from Down*, republished, Ballynahinch, 1982.

Braidwood, J., *Ulster and Elizabethan English in Ulster Dialects,* Belfast, 1964.

Brims, John, *Scottish Radicalism and the United Irishmen* in Dickson, David, Dáire Keogh, and Kevin Whelan, (Eds.), *The United Irishmen, Republicanism, Radicalism and Rebellion*, Dublin, 1993.

Crawford, W.H., and Brian Trainor (Eds.), *Aspects of Irish Social History, 1750-1800,* Belfast, 1969.

Curtin, Nancy J., *The United Irish Organisation in Ulster: 1795-1798*, in Dickson, David, Dáire Keogh and Kevin Whelan, (Eds.), *The United Irishmen, Republicanism, Radicalism and Rebellion,* Dublin, 1993.

De La Tocnaye, Jacques Louis de Bougrenet, Chevalier, *A Frenchman's Walk Through Ireland, 1796-1797*, Cork, 1798 and Belfast, 1984.

Dickson, Charles, *Revolt in the North, Antrim and Down in 1798*, Dublin and London, 1960.

Dickson, The Rev. Dr. William Steel, *A Narrative of the Confinement and Exile of William Steel Dickson, D.D.*, Dublin, 1812.

Elliot. Marianne, *Partners in Revolution: The United Irishmen and France*, London and New Haven, 1982.

Fitzpatrick, W.J., *The Sham Squire, and the Informers of 1798, with Jottings about Ireland a Century Ago*, Dublin, 1855.

Ford, Henry Jones, *The Scotch-Irish in America,* Princeton, 1915.

Gordon, J.B., *History of the Rebellion in Ireland in the Year 1798*, Dublin, 1801.

Hanna, Ronnie, *Land of the Free, Ulster and the American Revolution*, Lurgan, 1992.

Harris, Walter, *The Antient and Present State of County Down*, Dublin, 1744.

Hill. G., *The Montgomery Manuscripts*, Belfast, 1869.

Hill, Myrtle, Turner, Brian and Dawson, Kenneth, Eds., *1798 Rebellion in County Down*, Newtownards, 1998.

Hyde, H. Montgomery, *The Rise of Castlereagh*, London, 1933.

Jacob, Rosamund, *The Rise of the United Irishmen, 1791-1794*, London, 1937.

Kee, Robert, *Ireland, A history*, London, 1980.

Killen, John, Ed., *The Decade of the United Irishmen, Contemporary Accounts, 1791-1801*, Belfast, 1997.

Latimer, W.T., *A History of the Irish Presbyterians*, Belfast and Edinburgh, 1893.

Lecky, W.E.H., *A History of Ireland in the Eighteenth Century*, London, 1892-1896.

Lyttle, Wesley Greenhill, *Betsy Gray, or Hearts of Down*, republished Newcastle, 1968.

McCavery, Trevor, *Newtown: A History of Newtownards*, Belfast, 1994.

McCavery, Trevor, *Reformers, Reactionaries and Revolutionaries: Opinion in North Down and the Ards in the 1790s*, Ulster Local Studies, Vol. 18, No. 2, Belfast, 1997.

McComb, W., *McComb's Guide to Belfast*, Belfast, 1861.

McCoy, Jack, *Ulster's Joan of Arc*, Bangor, 1989.

R. B. McDowell, *Ireland in the Age of Imperialism and Revolution, 1760 -1801*, Oxford, 1979,

McSkimmin, Samuel, *Annals of Ulster, or Ireland Fifty Years Ago*, Belfast, 1850.

Madden, R.R., *Antrim and Down in 1798*, Glasgow, N.D.

Marshall, W.F., *Ulster Sails West*, N.P., 1943.

Maxwell, W.H., *History of the Irish Rebellion in 1798*, London, 1868.

Miller, David W., Ed., *Peep o' Day Boys and Defenders: Selected Documents on the County Armagh Disturbances*, Belfast, 1990.

Millin, Shannon S. *Sidelights on Belfast History*, Belfast and London, 1932.

Musgrave, Sir Richard, *Memoirs of the Different Rebellions in Ireland*, Dublin, 1801.

Newell, Edward John, *The Apostacy of Newell*, London, 1798.

Pakenham, Thomas, *The Year of Liberty*, London, 1969.

Power, Patrick C., *The Courts Martial of 1798-99* , Dublin, 1998.

Pynnar, William, *Calendar of the Carew Manuscripts*, London, 1867.

Robinson, Philip, *The Plantation of Ulster*, Dublin and Belfast, 1984.

Roosevelt, Theodore, *Stories of the Great West*, New York, 1888.

Sheedy, Kieron, *The Tellicherry Five*, Dublin, 1997.

Stevenson, John, *Two Centuries in County Down*, Belfast, 1920.

Stewart, A.T.Q., *A Deeper Silence, The Hidden Roots of the United Irish Movement*, London, 1993.

Stewart, A.T.Q., *The Summer Soldiers, The 1798 Rebellion in Antrim and Down*, Belfast, 1995.

Taylor and Skinner, *Maps of the Roads of Ireland - Surveyed in 1777*, London and Dublin, 1778.

Teeling, Charles Hamilton, *History of the Irish Rebellion of 1798, a Personal Narrative*, Glasgow and London, 1876.

Teeling, Charles Hamilton, *Sequel to the History of the Irish Rebellion of 1798, a Personal Narrative*, Glasgow and London, 1876.

Tone, Theobald Wolfe, *An Argument on Behalf of the Catholics of Ireland*, Belfast, 1791.

Tone, Theobald Wolfe, *An Autobiography of Theobald Wolfe Tone, 1763-1798*, O'Brien, R. Barry, ed., London, 1893.

Webster's Biographical Dictionary, Springfield, Mass., 1943.

Wilsdon, Bill, *The Sites of the 1798 Rising in Antrim and Down*, Belfast, 1997.

Young, Robert M., *Historical Notices of Old Belfast and its Vicinity*, Belfast, 1896.

Young, Robert M., *Ulster in '98, Episodes and Anecdotes*, Belfast, 1893.

Zimmermann, Georges Denis, *Songs of the Irish Rebellion: Political Street Ballads and Rebel Songs, 1780-1900*, Dublin, 1967.

PRIMARY SOURCES

Public Record Office of Northern Ireland (PRONI)

Anonymous Letter, (T/3042)

Donaghadee Resolutions Papers, (T/3465)

Downshire Papers, (D/607)

Drennan Letters, (D/591)

Groves MSS,(T/808)

Hamer letter (copy), PRONI,(T/2286)

Lemon Papers, (D/3093)

Londonderry Papers, (D/3030)

Lowry Papers, (D/1494)

Lytton White Papers, (D/714)

McCance Papers, (D/272)

Pelham Papers, (T/765/5)

Porter Papers, D/3579

Rebellion letters, (T/3048)

National Archives of Ireland (NAI)

Rebellion Papers, including Courts Martial Proceedings (620)

Linenhall Library

Belfast Newsletter

Northern Star

East Sussex Record Office (ESRO)

Sheffield Papers, reproduced with the permission of the County Archivist of East Sussex, copyright reserved.

Public Record Office, Home Office (PRO HO)

Portland Letters, PRO, London, HO 100/69)

Archiepiscopal Library at Lambeth, London

William Pynnar, Calendar of the Carew MSS, preserved in the 1867-73 section.

Maryland Historical Society Library

Warden Papers, 1797 – 1851, Biographical Sketch, @ http://www.mdhs.org/library/Mss/ms00087.html

ARTICLES AND MAGAZINES

The Belfast Magazine, 1825, Vol. I, No. I. An Eye-witness by "Iota", (James Thomson).

Proceedings of the Belfast Natural History and Philosophical Society, 2nd Series, vol. 7 (1963).

Index

Dear Reader

I hope you have enjoyed this publication from Ballyhay Books.
It is one of a growing number of local interest books published
under this imprint including Hugh Robinson's *Back Across the
Fields of Yesterday* and *The Book of 1000 Beautiful Things and Other
Favourites;* Viv Gotto's *Footprints in the Sea;* John O'Sullivan's
Belfast City Hospital, a Photographic History and Aideen D'Arcy's
Lie Over Da.

To see details of these books as well as the beautifully illustrated
books of our sister imprint, Cottage Publications, why not visit
our website at **www.cottage-publications.com** or contact us at:–

Laurel Cottage
15 Ballyhay Rd
Donaghadee
Co. Down
N. Ireland
BT21 0NG

Tel: +44 (0)28 9188 8033

Timothy S Johnston

BALLYHAY BOOKS